Rules and Guidance for Pharmaceutical Manufacturers and Distributors 2007

Compiled by the Inspection and Standards Division of the Medicines and Healthcare products Regulatory Agency

London • Chicago **Pharmaceutical Press**

Published by the Pharmaceutical Press
An imprint of RPS Publishing

1 Lambeth High Street, London SE1 7JN, UK
100 South Atkinson Road, Suite 200, Grayslake, IL 60030-7820, USA

© Crown Copyright 2007

Medicines and Healthcare products Regulatory Agency
Market Towers 1 Nine Elms Lane
London SW8 5NQ
Information on re-use of crown copyright information can be found on the MHRA
website: www.mhra.gov.uk

Designed and published by the Pharmaceutical Press 2007
(PₕP) is a trade mark of RPS Publishing

RPS Publishing is the publishing organisation of the Royal Pharmaceutical Society of
Great Britain

First edition published in 1971 as the *Guide to Good Pharmaceutical Manufacturing
Practice*, second edition in 1977, third edition 1983, fourth edition as the *Rules and
Guidance for Pharmaceutical Manufacturers* in 1993, fifth edition as the *Rules and
Guidance for Pharmaceutical Manufacturers and Distributors* in 1997, sixth edition in
2002.

Previously published by The Stationery Office (TSO), 2002.

Typeset by Techbooks, New Delhi, India
Printed in Great Britain by Cambridge University Press, Cambridge

ISBN 978 0 85369 719 0

Contents

Preface to the 2007 edition

Since the 2002 edition of Rules and Guidance for Pharmaceutical Manufacturers and Distributors (the "Orange Guide") there have been many changes and additions to the detailed European Community guidelines on Good Manufacturing Practice (GMP). In addition, there is a new Directive dealing specifically with GMP and the Community code relating to medicinal products for human use (Council Directive 2001/83/EC) has itself been the subject of substantial revision, via amending Directive 2004/27/EC, and these changes have been transposed into UK domestic legislation.

GMP Directive

The principles and guidelines of GMP are adopted by the European Commission under powers conferred by Council Directive 2001/83/EC. The objective of GMP is to ensure that products are consistently produced and controlled to particular quality standards.

Commission Directive 2003/94/EC (the "GMP Directive") sets out new requirements relating to the implementation of good manufacturing practice for medicinal products for human use (including Investigational Medicinal Products). The GMP Directive broadens the definition of good manufacturing practice set out in Directive 91/356/EEC and repealed the previous Directive in its entirety.

Changes to the Community Code

The amendments made by Directive 2004/27/EC in relation to manufacturing, wholesale dealing, supervision and sanctions are contained in Articles 1(32) to (39) and (55) to (60), (77) and (78). These provisions were implemented in the United Kingdom (along with some other miscellaneous "tidying-up" changes) by making regulations amending the relevant provisions of the Medicines Act 1968. The new arrangements came into force on 30 October 2005. The headline changes are as follows:

- New Community requirements[1] on pharmaceutical companies to adhere to the principles of GMP in the manufacturing processes of active substances used as starting materials. This includes any repackaging or re-labelling activities carried out by a distributor or broker.
- New duty on QPs extending the need for full batch analysis and testing[2] (or re-testing) in a Member State to product imported from third countries (i.e. outside the Community), whether or not the product was originally manufactured in the Community.
- A new requirement[3] for distributors that import medicinal products from other Member States to notify the marketing authorisation holder and the competent authority of the Member State to which the product is imported of the intention to import.
- New powers[4] for the competent authority to carry out unannounced inspections at the premises of manufacturers of starting materials, or at the premises of marketing authorisation holders or any firms employed by the marketing authorisation holder where there are grounds for suspecting non-compliance with GMP principles.
- Changes to the system of licensing for third country imports. The importation of products from third countries now requires a manufacturing authorisation for import, rather than, as previously, a wholesale dealer's import licence.

UK legislation

New regulations[5] were introduced on 30 October 2005 to replace the Standard Provisions Regulations,[6] in relation to relevant medicinal products, i.e. medicinal products to which Directive 2001/83/EC as amended, apply. The previous Standard Provision Regulations, themselves, had

---

[1] Articles 1(33)–(35) of Directive 2004/27/EC amending Articles 46, 46a and 47 of Directive 2001/83/EC.

[2] Articles 1(36)–(38) of Directive 2004/27/EC amending Articles 49–50 of Directive 2001/83/EC.

[3] Article 1(55) of Directive 2004/27/EC amending Article 76 of Directive 2001/83/EC.

[4] Article 1(77) of Directive 2004/27/EC amending Article 111 of Directive 2001/83/EC.

[5] The Medicines for Human Use (Manufacturing, Wholesale Dealing and Miscellaneous Amendments) Regulations 2005 (SI 2005 No. 2789).

[6] The Medicines (Standard Provisions for Licences and Certificates) Regulations 1971 (SI 1971/972)

been amended nine times over the years. The Medicines for Human use (Manufacturing, Wholesale Dealing and Miscellaneous Amendments) Regulations 2005 match the amended European Directive requirements on medicines for human use.

Changes to the EU Guide to GMP

Following a restructuring of the GMP Guide publication, guidance on Basic Requirements for Active Substances used as Starting Materials (formerly Annex 18) now becomes the new Part II to the EC GMP Guide.

New/revised chapters

Chapter 1 has been revised to include new text on Product Quality Review, October 2005. A revised version, containing details of significant quality system-related responsibilities for monitoring, reporting, reviewing and trending requirements came into operation 1 January 2006.

Chapter 6 the revised version (October 2005) includes the on-going stability programme, which came into operation on 1 June 2006.

Chapter 8 was revised in December 2005 to include new requirements on counterfeit products, plus other minor modifications. The revised version came into operation on 1 February 2006.

New/revised annexes

Annex 1 (Manufacture of Sterile Medicinal Products): minor revisions made in September 2003.

Annex 13 (Manufacture of Investigational Medicinal Products): updated, with major revisions, July 2003.

Annex 19 (Reference and Retention Samples): a new annex, with detailed requirements, came into operation in June 2006.

Changes on the horizon

Two new sections are planned to the EC Guide to GMP. These relate to ICH Q9 and Q10, i.e. Quality Risk Management and Quality Systems. These may form new annexes to the Guide (Annexes 20 and 21, respectively) or they may form a separate part (Part III). Adoption is expected during 2007 or 2008.

In addition, further changes are expected during 2007 or 2008 relating to Chapter 4 and in respect of the following annexes: 2, 3, 6, 7, 11, 13 and 16.

The "*Orange Guide*" 2007

Many of the European Directives on medicinal products issued over the last thirty-five years were consolidated into two Directives during 2001, one for products used in humans and one for veterinary products. This makes the requirements more accessible. Although it is UK legislation, implementing the Directives, that bears directly on activities in the UK, it is often helpful for manufacturers and wholesalers to be aware of the original EU obligations. This is particularly so when trading across boundaries of Member States. Therefore, as before, the "Titles" or sections of Directive 2001/83/EC, as amended, dealing with manufacture and wholesale distribution of products for human use are included in this edition.

The UK's Code of Practice for Qualified Persons has been updated by the professional bodies in consultation with the MHRA; this is included.

Recommendations on meeting the important requirement to ensure the "proper conservation and distribution" of medicines requiring storage below ambient temperature ("cold-chain distribution") have been developed between representatives of wholesalers and the MHRA. These were published originally in the Pharmaceutical Journal,[7] were summarised in MAIL,[8] and are reproduced here in updated form.

Finally, there is a new section on the activities and services of the Inspection and Standards Division of the MHRA, which will be of interest to manufacturers and wholesalers.

Although much of the text in this book is available in its original form in other places, including various websites, we are pleased that the "Orange Guide" continues to satisfy a demand for information in one authoritative and convenient place. In particular, the detailed index to the Orange Guide adds value and simplifies the navigation of these complex documents. Readers are invited to suggest further updates to the Index, to the MHRA, for future improvements in navigation and cross-referencing.

For the 2007 version, we have, for the first time made the entire Orange Guide available online, as part of "MedicinesComplete" – a subscription-based database of leading medicines and healthcare references – and via CD-ROM. Also available is a separate GDP booklet for the wholesale dealing market. We hope that this new edition and the new formats will continue to be useful.

Gerald Heddell
Director, Inspection and Standards Division
December 2006

---

[7] Taylor J. Recommendations on the control and monitoring of storage and transportation temperatures of medicinal products. *Pharm J* 2001; 267: 128–131.

[8] MCA Newsletter MAIL, Issue 131, May/June 2002.

Acknowledgements

To the European Commission for permission to reproduce the text of the Directives, the EC Guide to GMP and the guidelines on Good Distribution Practice.

To the Institute of Biology, the Royal Pharmaceutical Society of Great Britain and the Royal Society of Chemistry for permission to reproduce the texts of the Code of Practice for Qualified Persons.

Feedback

Comments on the content or presentation of the Orange Guide are encouraged and will be used to develop further editions. Your views are valued and both MHRA and Pharmaceutical Press would appreciate you taking the time to contact us. Please use the reply card enclosed with this edition or contact us directly by post, telephone, fax or email.

"The Orange Guide"
The MHRA Information Centre
Room 10-2
Medicines and Healthcare products Regulatory Agency
Market Towers
1 Nine Elms Lane
London SW8 5NQ
UK
Tel: +44 (0)20 7084 2352
Fax: +44 (0)20 7084 2353
E-mail: orange.guide@mhra.gsi.gov.uk

Introduction

This publication brings together the main pharmaceutical regulations, directives and guidance which manufacturers and wholesalers are expected to follow when making and distributing medicinal products in the European Union and European Economic Area.[1] It is of particular relevance to all holders of manufacturer's licences and wholesale dealer's licences and to their Qualified Persons (QPs) and Responsible Persons (RPs), who have a responsibility for ensuring compliance with many of these regulatory requirements.

The obligation on governments of all Member States of the European Union to ensure that pharmaceutical manufacturers are authorised is stated in Title IV of Directive 2001/83/EC, as amended (products for human use) and of Directive 2001/82/EC (veterinary products). These titles, or sections, are also the source of requirements for compliance with Good Manufacturing Practice (GMP), employment of QPs and repeated inspections by the regulatory authorities. Title VII of the same Directive requires all wholesale distributors to be authorised, to have available RPs and comply with the guidelines on Good Distribution Practice (GDP).

The principles and guidelines of GMP are set out in two Commission Directives: 2003/94/EC for medicinal products for human use (replacing Directive 91/356/EEC) and 91/412/EEC for veterinary medicinal products. In the United Kingdom, the provisions for manufacturers and wholesale dealers have been implemented by requirements and undertakings incorporated in regulations[2] made under the Medicines Act 1968. Compliance with the principles and guidelines of GMP is a statutory requirement. The European Community (EC) Guide to GMP[3] (including its annexes)

---

[1] The member states of the European Community plus Iceland, Liechtenstein and Norway.

[2] The Medicines for Human Use (Manufacturing, Wholesale dealing and Miscellaneous Amendments) Regulations 2005 [S.I. 2005/2789].

[3] Commission of the European Communities. The rules governing medicinal products in the European Community. Vol IV. Good Manufacturing Practice for medicinal products.

provides detailed guidance which interprets and expands on the statutory principles and guidelines. Changes in technical knowledge and in regulations are reflected by additional and revised annexes.

GMP includes elements of the International Standard for Quality Management Systems ISO 9001:2000 with additional requirements specific to medicines. The UK first produced a national guide to GMP (known traditionally as the Orange Guide) in 1971. Guidance on good pharmaceutical wholesaling practice was added in the 1977 edition and a further edition was produced in 1983. The EC guidance, first issued for GMP in 1989 and for GDP in 1993, supersedes this and all other national guides of Member States, although much that was familiar in the old UK Guide can still be recognised in the EC guidance. The Pharmaceutical Inspection Co-operation Scheme has adopted the text of the EC Guide to GMP ensuring harmonisation of guidelines by its member inspectorates throughout the world. Mutual Recognition Agreements between the EC and several third countries have recognised the equivalence of GMP requirements of the parties concerned.

Manufacturers are required to name a QP on their manufacturer's licence. No batch of medicinal product may be released to the market within the EU unless a nominated QP has certified that it has been manufactured and checked in compliance with the laws in force. Guidance to QPs in fulfilling their responsibilities is given in the EC Guide to GMP and in the Code of Practice[4] for Qualified Persons which they are expected to follow. In similar spirit, wholesalers are required to appoint a RP who has the knowledge and responsibility to ensure that correct procedures are followed during distribution. Notes on the qualifications and duties of RPs are given to assist this.

The aim of GMP and GDP is to assure the quality of the medicinal product for the safety, well-being and protection of the patient. In achieving this aim it is impossible to over-emphasise the importance of people, at all levels, in the assurance of the quality of medicinal products. This is emphasised in the first principle in the EC Guide to GMP. The great majority of reported defective medicinal products has resulted from human error or carelessness, not from failures in technology. All the people involved with the production, Quality Control or distribution of medicinal products, whether key personnel, production or control or warehouse staff, inspectors of a regulatory authority or others involved in the many activities which lead to a patient taking a medicine, should bear this constantly in mind when performing their duties.

---

[4] The Institute of Biology, The Royal Pharmaceutical Society of Great Britain, The Royal Society of Chemistry. Code of Practice for Qualified Persons. In: Register of Qualified Persons. London: Institute of Biology, Royal Pharmaceutical Society of Great Britain, Royal Society of Chemistry, 2004.

MEDICINES AND HEALTHCARE PRODUCTS REGULATORY AGENCY (MHRA)

1

MHRA: Licensing, Inspection and Enforcement for Human Medicines

Contents

Overview of MHRA

In 2003, Ministers announced that the Medicines Control Agency and the Medical Devices Agency would be merged to form a new agency. The new agency is known as the Medicines and Healthcare products Regulatory Agency (MHRA). Its key objective is to protect the health of the public by ensuring that medicines, healthcare products and medical equipment are safe.

All licensed medicines available in the UK are subject to rigorous scrutiny by the MHRA before they can be used by patients. This ensures that medicines meet acceptable standards on safety, quality and efficacy. It is the responsibility of the MHRA and the expert advisory bodies set up by the Medicines Act to ensure that the sometimes difficult balance between safety and effectiveness is achieved. MHRA experts assess all applications for new medicines to ensure they meet the required standards. This is followed up by a system of inspection and testing which continues throughout the lifetime of the medicine.

The roles of the MHRA are to:

- provide a system of post-marketing surveillance for reporting, investigating and monitoring of adverse drug reactions to medicines and medical devices;

- assess and, where appropriate evidence exists, authorise medical products for sale and supply in UK;
- oversee the Notified Bodies that audit medical device manufacturers;
- operate a quality surveillance system to sample and test medicines
  - to address quality defects
  - to monitor the safety and quality of unlicensed products
  - investigate internet sales and potential counterfeiting of medicines
- regulate clinical trials of medicines and medical devices;
- monitor and ensure compliance with statutory obligations relating to medicines and medical devices;
- promote safe use of medicines and devices;
- manage the GPRD, British Pharmacopoeia and the Devices Evaluation Service.

The MHRA also hosts and supports a number of expert advisory bodies, including the Commission on Human Medicines (which replaced the Committee on the Safety of Medicines in 2005), and the British Pharmacopoeia Commission. In addition, as part of the European system of medicines approval, the MHRA or other national bodies may be the Rapporteur or Co-rapporteur for any given pharmaceutical application, taking on the bulk of the verification work on behalf of all members, while the documents are still sent to other members as and where requested.

Inspection and Standards Division

The MHRA's Inspection and Standards Division is responsible for ensuring compliance with the regulations and standards that apply to the manufacture, control and supply of medicines on the UK market.

Inspectorate

The Inspectorate Group in the MHRA's Inspection and Standards Division is comprised of dedicated units for Good Manufacturing Practice (GMP), Good Distribution Practice (GDP), Good Laboratory Practice (GLP), Good Clinical Practice (GCP) and Good Pharmacovigilance Practice (GPvP).

Good Manufacturing Practice (GMP)

GMP Inspectors conduct inspections of pharmaceutical manufacturers and other organisations to assess compliance with EC guidance on Good Manufacturing Practice and the relevant details contained in marketing authorisations and Clinical Trials Authorisations (Investigational Medicinal Products). They ensure that medicines supplied in the UK meet consistent high standards of quality, safety and efficacy. Overseas sites to be named as manufacturing sites for products on UK marketing authorisations are also required to pass an inspection prior to approval of the marketing authorisation application.

GMP Inspectors are also responsible for inspecting and authorising blood product establishments, biologicals products, investigational medicinal products, NHS manufacturing units and a range of manufacturing sites for active pharmaceutical ingredients. GMP Inspectors serve on a number of UK, EU and PIC/S technical and standards committees and provide help and advice to senior managers, Ministers and colleagues across the agency, as necessary.

Good Distribution Practice (GDP)

GDP Inspectors conduct inspections of sites used by wholesale dealers for the storage and distribution of medicinal products. Inspections are undertaken against the requirements of the Medicines for Human Use (Manufacturing and Wholesale Dealing and Miscellaneous Amendments) Regulations 2005 as well as the detailed guidelines contained in the EC Guide on Good Distribution Practice for Medicinal Products for Human Use.

Good Laboratory Practice (GLP)

GLP Inspectors conduct inspections of facilities that carry out non-clinical studies for submission to regulatory authorities to assess the safety of new chemicals to humans, animals and the environment. These inspections assure the integrity of the data being submitted. The range of test facilities to be monitored include those involved in the testing of human and veterinary pharmaceuticals, agrochemicals, cosmetics, food and feed additives and industrial chemicals.

Good Clinical Practice (GCP)

GCP Inspectors assess compliance with the requirements of European guidelines and regulations relating to clinical trials by conducting inspections at the sites of pharmaceutical sponsor companies, contract research organisations, academic research organisations, investigational trial sites, clinical trial laboratories and non-commercial clinical trial sites.

Good Pharmacovigilance Practice (GPvP)

By conducting inspections at the sites of marketing authorisation holders Pharmacovigilance Inspectors assess compliance with the requirements of

European legislation and guidelines relating to the process of monitoring medicines post marketing for safety in clinical practice.

Licensing Office

Manufacture of and wholesale dealing in medicinal products are licensable activities under UK and EU legislation. Applications for new licences and variations to existing licences are processed by the Licensing Office in the Inspection and Standards Division at Market Towers. Licensing Office staff make extensive use of computer technology to carry out their work, which deals with a range of licences and covers activities including pharmaceutical manufacturing (including the manufacture of investigational medicinal products) pharmaceutical wholesaling, authorisation of blood establishments and administrative tasks for clinical trials and pharmacovigilance. Licensing Office staff are also responsible for issuing certificates in support of the World Health Organization scheme on the quality of pharmaceutical products moving in international commerce (often referred to as export certificates). When carrying out their role, staff in the Licensing Office work closely with colleagues in the Inspectorate.

Defective Medicines Report Centre (DMRC)

Manufacturers and importers are obliged to report to the Licensing Authority (MHRA) any quality defect in a medicinal product which could result in a recall or restriction on supply. Other users and distributors of medicinal products are encouraged to do this. The MHRA's Inspection and Standards Division operates a Defective Medicines Report Centre (DMRC) to receive reports on products for human use and to co-ordinate the necessary assessment and action. (The Veterinary Medicines Directorate operates a comparable system in relation to veterinary medicinal products.)

Where a defect is considered to be a risk to public health, the marketing authorisation holder withdraws the affected product from use and the MHRA issues a "drug alert" letter. This alert is classified from 1 to 4 depending upon the risk presented to the public health by the defective product. Class 1 is the most critical, for example serious mislabelling, microbial contamination or incorrect ingredients, and requires immediate recall; Class 4 is the least critical and advises "caution in use".

The DMRC is also part of the European Rapid Alert System, which disseminates information on drug quality issues within EU Member States.

Enforcement and Intelligence Group

The Enforcement and Intelligence (E&I) Group investigates any reported breach of medicines legislation. The Agency's primary objective is to ensure that companies and individuals within the pharmaceutical industry comply with regulatory requirements. Enforcement officers have powers conferred by the Medicines Act 1968 and from regulations flowing from the Act. These include rights of entry, powers of inspection, seizure, sampling and production of documents. Officers investigate cases and, where appropriate, bring criminal prosecutions. MHRA investigators may also investigate offences under other legislation such as the Theft Act, Trademarks Act and the Offences Against the Person Act.

The aim of the Intelligence Unit is to drive forward the implementation of intelligence-led enforcement and enable a more proactive approach to the acquisition and development of information. The Unit acts as a co-ordination point for all information-gathering activities and works in conjunction with a wide network of public and professional bodies and trade associations, e.g. HM Revenue and Customs, Department of Health, Trading Standards and Port Health Authorities; the Police Service; and professional organisations such as the Royal Pharmaceutical Society, General Medical Council and the Association of the British Pharmaceutical Industry (ABPI). Additionally, there is a network of other regulatory agencies and law enforcement bodies within the European Community and in other countries through which the E&I Group can exchange information and follow trends in pharmaceutical crime. The E&I Group provides support to the investigation teams, as well as monitoring trends and acting as a liaison point for outside organisations.

The E&I Group monitors trends in pharmaceutical crime and co-ordinates initiatives to counteract criminal activity. In particular, the availability of counterfeit medicines is a key priority area and an anti-counterfeiting strategy has been agreed and implemented.

Advice

The MHRA publishes a series of Guidance Notes relating to its statutory functions. Those of particular interest to manufacturers and wholesale dealers include:

GN 5   Manufacturer's Licences
GN 6   Wholesale Dealer's Licences
GN 8   Borderline Products
GN 14 Supply of unlicensed relevant medicinal products "Specials".

These Guidance Notes and a list of others available may be obtained from the MHRA's website or from the Agency's Central Enquiry Point.

Contact details are as follows:

Address:
Information Centre, 10-2 Market Towers, 1 Nine Elms Lane, London, SW8 5NQ, UK.
Telephone: +44 (0)20 7084 2000 (weekdays 0900–1700)
Telephone: +44 (0)20 7210 3000 (other times)
Fax: +44 (0)20 7084 2353
E-mail: info@mhra.gsi.gov.uk
Website: www.mhra.gov.uk

GUIDANCE ON GOOD MANUFACTURING PRACTICE (GMP)

The MHRA Index to the EU Guide to GMP

Locators indicate chapter and paragraph numbers.
A = annex; Ch. = chapter; Gls. = glossary; PII = Part II of EC Guide

2

EU Guidance on Good Manufacturing Practice

PART I: Basic Requirements for Medicinal Products

> **Editor's note** The Introduction (below) to the EU Guidance on GMP which was written by the Commission makes reference to a "glossary" of some terms used in the Guide for GMP. This glossary appears immediately after the annexes.
>
> In addition to this glossary a number of the annexes themselves also contain a glossary of some of the terms used in the particular annex to which they are attached. This includes Annex 18, which is now covered under Part II of the EU Guidance on GMP.
>
> In this publication the Introduction (below) to the EU Guidance on GMP, the annexes including Annex 18 as described above and the glossary referred to in the Introduction have been presented as the Commission intended.

Contents of Part I

Contents continue

Contents continue

Introduction

The pharmaceutical industry of the European Union maintains high standards of quality assurance in the development, manufacture and control of medicinal products. A system of marketing authorisations ensures that all medicinal products are assessed by a competent authority to ensure compliance with contemporary requirements of safety, quality and efficacy. A system of manufacturing authorisations ensures that all products authorised on the European market are manufactured only by authorised manufacturers, whose activities are regularly inspected by the competent authorities. Manufacturing authorisations are required by all pharmaceutical manufacturers in the European Community whether the products are sold within or outside of the Community.

Two directives laying down principles and guidelines of good manufacturing practice (GMP) for medicinal products were adopted by the Commission. Directive 2003/94/EC applies to medicinal products for human use and Directive 91/412/EEC for veterinary use. Detailed guidelines in accordance with those principles are published in the Guide to Good Manufacturing Practice, which will be used in assessing applications for manufacturing authorisations and as a basis for inspection of manufacturers of medicinal products.

The principles of GMP and the detailed guidelines are applicable to all operations which require the authorisation referred to in Article 40 of Directive 2001/83/EC and in Article 44 of Directive 2001/82/EC, as amended by Directives 2004/27/EC and 2004/28/EC, respectively. They are also relevant for all other large scale pharmaceutical manufacturing processes, such as that undertaken in hospitals, and for the preparation of products for use in clinical trials.

All Member States and the industry agreed that the GMP requirements applicable to the manufacture of veterinary medicinal products are the same as those applicable to the manufacture of medicinal products for human use. Certain detailed adjustments to the GMP guidelines are set out in two annexes specific to veterinary medicinal products and to immunological veterinary medicinal products.

The Guide is presented in two parts of basic requirements and specific annexes. Part I covers GMP principles for the manufacture of medicinal products. Part II covers GMP for active substances used as starting materials.

Chapters of Part I on "basic requirements" are headed by principles as defined in Directives 2003/94/EC and 91/412/EEC. Chapter 1 on Quality Management outlines the fundamental concept of quality assurance as applied to the manufacture of medicinal products. Thereafter, each chapter has a principle outlining the quality assurance objectives of that chapter and a text which provides sufficient detail for manufacturers to be made aware of the essential matters to be considered when implementing the principle.

Part II was newly established on the basis of a guideline developed on the level of ICH and published as ICH Q7a on "active pharmaceutical ingredients", which was implemented as GMP Annex 18 for voluntary application in 2001. According to the revised Article 47 and Article 51, respectively, of the Directive 2001/83/EC and Directive 2001/82/EC, as amended, detailed guidelines on the principles of GMP for active substances used as starting materials shall be adopted and published by the Commission. The former Annex 18 has been replaced by the new Part II of the GMP Guide, which has an extended application both for the human and the veterinary sector.

In addition to the general matters of Good Manufacturing Practice outlined in Parts I and II, a series of annexes providing detail about specific areas of activity is included. For some manufacturing processes, different annexes will apply simultaneously (e.g. annex on sterile preparations and on radiopharmaceuticals and/or on biological medicinal products).

A glossary of some terms used in the Guide has been incorporated after the annexes.

The Guide is not intended to cover security aspects for the personnel engaged in manufacture. This may be particularly important in the manufacture of certain medicinal products such as highly active, biological and radioactive medicinal products. However, those aspects are governed by other provisions of Community or national law.

Throughout the Guide it is assumed that the requirements of the Marketing Authorisation relating to the safety, quality and efficacy of the products are systematically incorporated into all the manufacturing, control and release for sale arrangements of the holder of the Manufacturing Authorisation.

The manufacture of medicinal products has for many years taken place in accordance with guidelines for Good Manufacturing Practice and the manufacture of medicinal products is not governed by CEN/ISO standards. Harmonised standards as adopted by the European standardisation organisations CEN/ISO may be used at industry's discretion as a tool for implementing a quality system in the pharmaceutical sector. The CEN/ISO standards have been considered but the terminology of these standards has not been implemented in this third edition of the Guide.

It is recognised that there are acceptable methods, other than those described in the Guide, which are capable of achieving the principles of Quality Assurance. The Guide is not intended to place any restraint upon the development of any new concepts or new technologies which have been validated and which provide a level of Quality Assurance at least equivalent to those set out in this Guide. It will be regularly revised.

1   QUALITY MANAGEMENT

Principle

The holder of a Manufacturing Authorisation must manufacture medicinal products so as to ensure that they are fit for their intended use, comply with the requirements of the Marketing Authorisation and do not place patients at risk due to inadequate safety, quality or efficacy. The attainment of this quality objective is the responsibility of senior management and requires the participation and commitment by staff in many different departments and at all levels within the company, by the company's suppliers and by the distributors. To achieve the quality objective in a reliable manner, there must be a comprehensively designed and correctly implemented system of Quality Assurance incorporating Good Manufacturing Practice and thus Quality Control. It should be fully documented and its effectiveness monitored. All parts of the Quality Assurance system should be adequately resourced with competent personnel, and suitable and sufficient premises, equipment and facilities. There are additional legal responsibilities for the holder of the Manufacturing Authorisation and for the Qualified Person(s).

1.1   The basic concepts of Quality Assurance, Good Manufacturing Practice and Quality Control are inter-related. They are described here in order to emphasise their relationships and their fundamental importance to the production and control of medicinal products.

Quality Assurance

1.2   Quality Assurance is a wide ranging concept which covers all matters which individually or collectively influence the quality of a product. It is the total sum of the organised arrangements made with the object of ensuring that medicinal products are of the quality required for their intended use. Quality Assurance therefore incorporates Good Manufacturing Practice plus other factors outside the scope of this Guide. The system of Quality Assurance appropriate for the manufacture of medicinal products should ensure that:

(i)   medicinal products are designed and developed in a way that takes account of the requirements of Good Manufacturing Practice and Good Laboratory Practice;

(ii)   production and control operations are clearly specified and Good Manufacturing Practice adopted;

(iii)   managerial responsibilities are clearly specified;

(iv)   arrangements are made for the manufacture, supply and use of the correct starting and packaging materials;

(v)   all necessary controls on intermediate products, and any other in-process controls and validations are carried out;

(vi)   the finished product is correctly processed and checked, according to the defined procedures;

(vii) medicinal products are not sold or supplied before a Qualified Person has certified that each production batch has been produced and controlled in accordance with the requirements of the Marketing Authorisation and any other regulations relevant to the production, control and release of medicinal products;

(viii) satisfactory arrangements exist to ensure, as far as possible, that the medicinal products are stored, distributed and subsequently handled so that quality is maintained throughout their shelf life;

(ix)   there is a procedure for Self-Inspection and/or quality audit which regularly appraises the effectiveness and applicability of the Quality Assurance system.

Good Manufacturing Practice for Medicinal Products (GMP)

1.3   Good Manufacturing Practice is that part of Quality Assurance which ensures that products are consistently produced and controlled to the quality standards appropriate to their intended use and as required by the Marketing Authorisation or product specification.

Good Manufacturing Practice is concerned with both production and quality control. The basic requirements of GMP are that:

(i)   all manufacturing processes are clearly defined, systematically reviewed in the light of experience and shown to be capable of consistently manufacturing medicinal products of the required quality and complying with their specifications;

(ii)   critical steps of manufacturing processes and significant changes to the process are validated;

(iii) all necessary facilities for GMP are provided including:

(iv)   appropriately qualified and trained personnel;

(v)   adequate premises and space;

(vi)   suitable equipment and services;

(vii) correct materials, containers and labels;

(viii) approved procedures and instructions;

(ix)   suitable storage and transport;

(x)   instructions and procedures are written in an instructional form in clear and unambiguous language, specifically applicable to the facilities provided;

(xi) operators are trained to carry out procedures correctly;

(xii) records are made, manually and/or by recording instruments, during manufacture which demonstrate that all the steps required by the defined procedures and instructions were in fact taken and that the quantity and quality of the product was as expected. Any significant deviations are fully recorded and investigated;

(xiii) records of manufacture including distribution which enable the complete history of a batch to be traced, are retained in a comprehensible and accessible form;

(xiv) the distribution (wholesaling) of the products minimises any risk to their quality;

(xv) a system is available to recall any batch of product, from sale or supply;

(xvi) complaints about marketed products are examined, the causes of quality defects investigated and appropriate measures taken in respect of the defective products and to prevent reoccurrence.

Quality Control

1.4 Quality Control is that part of Good Manufacturing Practice which is concerned with sampling, specifications and testing, and with the organisation, documentation and release procedures which ensure that the necessary and relevant tests are actually carried out and that materials are not released for use, nor products released for sale or supply, until their quality has been judged to be satisfactory. The basic requirements of Quality Control are that:

(i) adequate facilities, trained personnel and approved procedures are available for sampling, inspecting and testing starting materials, packaging materials, intermediate, bulk, and finished products, and where appropriate for monitoring environmental conditions for GMP purposes;

(ii) samples of starting materials, packaging materials, intermediate products, bulk products and finished products are taken by personnel and by methods approved by Quality Control;

(iii) test methods are validated;

(iv) records are made, manually and/or by recording instruments, which demonstrate that all the required sampling, inspecting and testing procedures were actually carried out. Any deviations are fully recorded and investigated;

(v) the finished products contain active ingredients complying with the qualitative and quantitative composition of the Marketing

Authorisation, are of the purity required, and are enclosed within their proper containers and correctly labelled;

(vi)   records are made of the results of inspection and that testing of materials, intermediate, bulk, and finished products is formally assessed against specification. Product assessment includes a review and evaluation of relevant production documentation and an assessment of deviations from specified procedures;

(vii) no batch of product is released for sale or supply prior to certification by a Qualified Person that it is in accordance with the requirements of the Marketing Authorisation;

(viii) sufficient reference samples of starting materials and products are retained to permit future examination of the product if necessary and that the product is retained in its final pack unless exceptionally large packs are produced.

Product Quality Review

1.5   Regular periodic or rolling quality reviews of all licensed medicinal products, including export only products, should be conducted with the objective of verifying the consistency of the existing process, the appropriateness of current specifications for both starting materials and finished product to highlight any trends and to identify product and process improvements. Such reviews should normally be conducted and documented annually, taking into account previous reviews, and should include at least:

(i)   A review of starting materials and packaging materials used for the product, especially those from new sources;

(ii)   A review of critical in-process controls and finished product results;

(iii) A review of all batches that failed to meet established specification(s) and their investigation;

(iv)   A review of all significant deviations or non-conformances, their related investigations, and the effectiveness of resultant corrective and preventative actions taken;

(v)   A review of all changes carried out to the processes or analytical methods;

(vi)   A review of Marketing Authorisation variations submitted/granted/refused, including those for third country (export only) dossiers;

(vii) A review of the results of the stability monitoring programme and any adverse trends;

(viii) A review of all quality-related returns, complaints and recalls and the investigations performed at the time;

(ix)   A review of adequacy of any other previous product process or equipment corrective actions;

(x)   For new marketing authorisations and variations to marketing autho-
      risations, a review of post-marketing commitments;

(xi) The qualification status of relevant equipment and utilities, e.g.
      HVAC, water, compressed gases, etc;

(xii) A review of Technical Agreements to ensure that they are up to date.

The manufacturer and marketing authorisation holder, where different, should evaluate the results of this review and an assessment should be made whether corrective and preventative action or any revalidation should be undertaken. Reasons for such corrective actions should be documented. Agreed corrective and preventative actions should be completed in a timely and effective manner. There should be management procedures for the ongoing management and review of these actions and the effectiveness of these procedures verified during self inspection. Quality reviews may be grouped by product type, e.g. solid dosage forms, liquid dosage forms, sterile products, etc. where scientifically justified.

Where the marketing authorisation holder is not the manufacturer, there should be a technical agreement in place between the various parties that defines their respective responsibilities in producing the quality review. The Qualified Person responsible for final batch certification together with the marketing authorisation holder should ensure that the quality review is performed in a timely manner and is accurate.

2   PERSONNEL

Principle

The establishment and maintenance of a satisfactory system of quality assurance and the correct manufacture of medicinal products relies upon people. For this reason there must be sufficient qualified personnel to carry out all the tasks which are the responsibility of the manufacturer. Individual responsibilities should be clearly understood by the individuals and recorded. All personnel should be aware of the principles of Good Manufacturing Practice that affect them and receive initial and continuing training, including hygiene instructions, relevant to their needs.

General

2.1   The manufacturer should have an adequate number of personnel with the necessary qualifications and practical experience. The responsibilities placed on any one individual should not be so extensive as to present any risk to quality.

2.2   The manufacturer must have an organisation chart. People in responsible positions should have specific duties recorded in written job descriptions and adequate authority to carry out their responsibilities. Their duties may be delegated to designated deputies of a satisfactory qualification level. There should be no gaps or unexplained overlaps in the responsibilities of those personnel concerned with the application of Good Manufacturing Practice.

Key Personnel

2.3   Key Personnel include the head of Production, the head of Quality Control, and if at least one of these persons is not responsible for the duties described in Article 51 of Directive 2001/83/EC,[1] the Qualified Person(s) designated for the purpose. Normally key posts should be occupied by full-time personnel. The heads of Production and Quality Control must be independent from each other. In large organisations, it may be necessary to delegate some of the functions listed in 2.5, 2.6 and 2.7.

2.4   The duties of the Qualified Person(s) are fully described in Article 51 of Directive 2001/83/EC, and can be summarised as follows:

---

[1] Article 55 of Directive 2001/82/EC.

(a) for medicinal products manufactured within the European Community, a Qualified Person must ensure that each batch has been produced and tested/checked in accordance with the directives and the marketing authorisation;[2]

(b) for medicinal products manufactured outside the European Community, a Qualified Person must ensure that each imported batch has undergone, in the importing country, the testing specified in paragraph 1 (b) of Article 51;

(c) a Qualified Person must certify in a register or equivalent document, as operations are carried out and before any release, that each production batch satisfies the provisions of Article 51.

The persons responsible for these duties must meet the qualification requirements laid down in Article 49[3] of the same Directive, they shall be permanently and continuously at the disposal of the holder of the Manufacturing Authorisation to carry out their responsibilities. Their responsibilities may be delegated, but only to other Qualified Person(s).

2.5   The head of the Production Department generally has the following responsibilities:

(i)   to ensure that products are produced and stored according to the appropriate documentation in order to obtain the required quality;

(ii)   to approve the instructions relating to production operations and to ensure their strict implementation;

(iii) to ensure that the production records are evaluated and signed by an authorised person before they are sent to the Quality Control Department;

(iv) to check the maintenance of his department, premises and equipment;

(v)   to ensure that the appropriate validations are done;

(vi) to ensure that the required initial and continuing training of his department personnel is carried out and adapted according to need.

2.6   The head of the Quality Control Department generally has the following responsibilities:

(i)   to approve or reject, as he sees fit, starting materials, packaging materials, and intermediate, bulk and finished products;

(ii)   to evaluate batch records;

---

[2] According to Directive 75/319/EEC (now codified Directive 2001/83/EC) and the ruling of the Court of Justice of the European Communities, medicinal products which have been properly controlled in the EU by a Qualified Person do not have to be recontrolled or rechecked in any other Member State of the Community.

[3] Article 53 of Directive 2001/82/EC.

(iii) to ensure that all necessary testing is carried out;

(iv) to approve specifications, sampling instructions, test methods and other Quality Control procedures;

(v) to approve and monitor any contract analysts;

(vi) to check the maintenance of his department, premises and equipment;

(vii) to ensure that the appropriate validations are done;

(viii) to ensure that the required initial and continuing training of his department personnel is carried out and adapted according to need.

Other duties of the Quality Control Department are summarised in Chapter 6.

2.7 The heads of Production and Quality Control generally have some shared, or jointly exercised, responsibilities relating to quality. These may include, subject to any national regulations:

- the authorisation of written procedures and other documents, including amendments;
- the monitoring and control of the manufacturing environment;
- plant hygiene;
- process validation;
- training;
- the approval and monitoring of suppliers of materials;
- the approval and monitoring of contract manufacturers;
- the designation and monitoring of storage conditions for materials and products;
- the retention of records;
- the monitoring of compliance with the requirements of Good Manufacturing Practice;
- the inspection, investigation, and taking of samples, in order to monitor factors which may affect product quality.

Training

2.8 The manufacturer should provide training for all the personnel whose duties take them into production areas or into control laboratories (including the technical, maintenance and cleaning personnel), and for other personnel whose activities could affect the quality of the product.

2.9 Besides the basic training on the theory and practice of Good Manufacturing Practice, newly recruited personnel should receive training appropriate to the duties assigned to them. Continuing training should also be given, and its practical effectiveness should be periodically assessed. Training programmes should be available, approved by either the head of Production or the head of Quality Control, as appropriate. Training records should be kept.

2.10 Personnel working in areas where contamination is a hazard, e.g. clean areas or areas where highly active, toxic, infectious or sensitising materials are handled, should be given specific training.

2.11 Visitors or untrained personnel should, preferably, not be taken into the Production and Quality Control areas. If this is unavoidable, they should be given information in advance, particularly about personal hygiene and the prescribed protective clothing. They should be closely supervised.

2.12 The concept of Quality Assurance and all the measures capable of improving its understanding and implementation should be fully discussed during the training sessions.

Personnel Hygiene

2.13 Detailed hygiene programmes should be established and adapted to the different needs within the factory. They should include procedures relating to the health, hygiene practices and clothing of personnel. These procedures should be understood and followed in a very strict way by every person whose duties take him into the production and control areas. Hygiene programmes should be promoted by management and widely discussed during training sessions.

2.14 All personnel should receive medical examination upon recruitment. It must be the manufacturer's responsibility that there are instructions ensuring that health conditions that can be of relevance to the quality of products come to the manufacturer's knowledge. After the first medical examination, examinations should be carried out when necessary for the work and personal health.

2.15 Steps should be taken to ensure as far as is practicable that no person affected by an infectious disease or having open lesions on the exposed surface of the body is engaged in the manufacture of medicinal products.

2.16 Every person entering the manufacturing areas should wear protective garments appropriate to the operations to be carried out.

2.17 Eating, drinking, chewing or smoking, or the storage of food, drink, smoking materials or personal medication in the production and storage areas should be prohibited. In general, any unhygienic practice within the manufacturing areas or in any other area where the product might be adversely affected, should be forbidden.

2.18   Direct contact should be avoided between the operator's hands and the exposed product as well as with any part of the equipment that comes into contact with the products.

2.19   Personnel should be instructed to use the hand-washing facilities.

2.20   Any specific requirements for the manufacture of special groups of products, for example sterile preparations, are covered in the annexes.

3   PREMISES AND EQUIPMENT

Principle

Premises and equipment must be located, designed, constructed, adapted and maintained to suit the operations to be carried out. Their layout and design must aim to minimise the risk of errors and permit effective cleaning and maintenance in order to avoid cross-contamination, build up of dust or dirt and, in general, any adverse effect on the quality of products.

Premises

General

3.1   Premises should be situated in an environment which, when considered together with measures to protect the manufacture, presents minimal risk of causing contamination of materials or products.

3.2   Premises should be carefully maintained, ensuring that repair and main-tenance operations do not present any hazard to the quality of products. They should be cleaned and, where applicable, disinfected according to detailed written procedures.

3.3   Lighting, temperature, humidity and ventilation should be appropriate and such that they do not adversely affect, directly or indirectly, either the medicinal products during their manufacture and storage, or the accurate functioning of equipment.

3.4   Premises should be designed and equipped so as to afford maximum pro-tection against the entry of insects or other animals.

3.5   Steps should be taken in order to prevent the entry of unauthorised people. Production, storage and quality control areas should not be used as a right of way by personnel who do not work in them.

Production Area

3.6   In order to minimise the risk of a serious medical hazard due to cross-contamination, dedicated and self contained facilities must be available for the production of particular medicinal products, such as highly sen-sitising materials (e.g. penicillins) or biological preparations (e.g. from live micro-organisms). The production of certain additional products, such as certain antibiotics, certain hormones, certain cytotoxics, certain highly active drugs and non-medicinal products should not be conducted in the same facilities. For those products, in exceptional cases, the principle of campaign working in the same facilities can be accepted provided that specific precautions are taken and the necessary validations are made. The manufacture of technical poisons, such as pesticides and herbicides, should not be allowed in premises used for the manufacture of medicinal products.

3.7   Premises should preferably be laid out in such a way as to allow the production to take place in areas connected in a logical order corresponding to the sequence of the operations and to the requisite cleanliness levels.

3.8   The adequacy of the working and in-process storage space should permit the orderly and logical positioning of equipment and materials so as to minimise the risk of confusion between different medicinal products or their components, to avoid cross-contamination and to minimise the risk of omission or wrong application of any of the manufacturing or control steps.

3.9   Where starting and primary packaging materials, intermediate or bulk products are exposed to the environment, interior surfaces (walls, floors and ceilings) should be smooth, free from cracks and open joints, and should not shed particulate matter and should permit easy and effective cleaning and, if necessary, disinfection.

3.10   Pipework, light fittings, ventilation points and other services should be designed and sited to avoid the creation of recesses which are difficult to clean. As far as possible, for maintenance purposes, they should be accessible from outside the manufacturing areas.

3.11   Drains should be of adequate size, and have trapped gullies. Open channels should be avoided where possible, but if necessary, they should be shallow to facilitate cleaning and disinfection.

3.12   Production areas should be effectively ventilated, with air control facilities (including temperature and, where necessary, humidity and filtration) appropriate both to the products handled, to the operations undertaken within them and to the external environment.

3.13   Weighing of starting materials usually should be carried out in a separate weighing room designed for that use.

3.14   In cases where dust is generated (e.g. during sampling, weighing, mixing and processing operations, packaging of dry products), specific provisions should be taken to avoid cross-contamination and facilitate cleaning.

3.15   Premises for the packaging of medicinal products should be specifically designed and laid out so as to avoid mix-ups or cross-contamination.

3.16   Production areas should be well lit, particularly where visual on-line controls are carried out.

3.17   In-process controls may be carried out within the production area provided they do not carry any risk for the production.

Storage Areas

3.18   Storage areas should be of sufficient capacity to allow orderly storage of the various categories of materials and products: starting and packaging materials, intermediate, bulk and finished products, products in quarantine, released, rejected, returned or recalled.

3.19   Storage areas should be designed or adapted to ensure good storage conditions. In particular, they should be clean and dry and maintained within acceptable temperature limits. Where special storage conditions are required (e.g. temperature, humidity) these should be provided, checked and monitored.

3.20   Receiving and dispatch bays should protect materials and products from the weather. Reception areas should be designed and equipped to allow containers of incoming materials to be cleaned where necessary before storage.

3.21   Where quarantine status is ensured by storage in separate areas, these areas must be clearly marked and their access restricted to authorised personnel. Any system replacing the physical quarantine should give equivalent security.

3.22   There should normally be a separate sampling area for starting materials. If sampling is performed in the storage area, it should be conducted in such a way as to prevent contamination or cross-contamination.

3.23   Segregated areas should be provided for the storage of rejected, recalled or returned materials or products.

3.24   Highly active materials or products should be stored in safe and secure areas.

3.25   Printed packaging materials are considered critical to the conformity of the medicinal product and special attention should be paid to the safe and secure storage of these materials.

Quality Control Areas

3.26   Normally, Quality Control laboratories should be separated from production areas. This is particularly important for laboratories for the control of biologicals, microbiologicals and radioisotopes, which should also be separated from each other.

3.27   Control laboratories should be designed to suit the operations to be carried out in them. Sufficient space should be given to avoid mix-ups and cross-contamination. There should be adequate suitable storage space for samples and records.

3.28   Separate rooms may be necessary to protect sensitive instruments from vibration, electrical interference, humidity, etc.

3.29   Special requirements are needed in laboratories handling particular substances, such as biological or radioactive samples.

Ancillary Areas

3.30   Rest and refreshment rooms should be separate from other areas.

3.31   Facilities for changing clothes, and for washing and toilet purposes should be easily accessible and appropriate for the number of users. Toilets should not directly communicate with production or storage areas.

3.32   Maintenance workshops should as far as possible be separated from production areas. Whenever parts and tools are stored in the production area, they should be kept in rooms or lockers reserved for that use.

3.33   Animal houses should be well isolated from other areas, with separate entrance (animal access) and air handling facilities.

Equipment

3.34   Manufacturing equipment should be designed, located and maintained to suit its intended purpose.

3.35   Repair and maintenance operations should not present any hazard to the quality of the products.

3.36   Manufacturing equipment should be designed so that it can be easily and thoroughly cleaned. It should be cleaned according to detailed and written procedures and stored only in a clean and dry condition.

3.37   Washing and cleaning equipment should be chosen and used in order not to be a source of contamination.

3.38   Equipment should be installed in such a way as to prevent any risk of error or of contamination.

3.39 Production equipment should not present any hazard to the products. The parts of the production equipment that come into contact with the product must not be reactive, additive or absorptive to such an extent that it will affect the quality of the product and thus present any hazard.

3.40 Balances and measuring equipment of an appropriate range and precision should be available for production and control operations.

3.41 Measuring, weighing, recording and control equipment should be calibrated and checked at defined intervals by appropriate methods. Adequate records of such tests should be maintained.

3.42 Fixed pipework should be clearly labelled to indicate the contents and, where applicable, the direction of flow.

3.43 Distilled, deionized and, where appropriate, other water pipes should be sanitised according to written procedures that detail the action limits for microbiological contamination and the measures to be taken.

3.44 Defective equipment should, if possible, be removed from production and quality control areas, or at least be clearly labelled as defective.

4   DOCUMENTATION

Principle

Good documentation constitutes an essential part of the quality assurance system. Clearly written documentation prevents errors from spoken communication and permits tracing of batch history. Specifications, Manufacturing Formulae and instructions, procedures, and records must be free from errors and available in writing. The legibility of documents is of paramount importance.

General

4.1   *Specifications* describe in detail the requirements with which the products or materials used or obtained during manufacture have to conform. They serve as a basis for quality evaluation.

Manufacturing Formulae, Processing and Packaging Instructions state all the starting materials used and lay down all processing and packaging operations.

Procedures give directions for performing certain operations e.g. cleaning, clothing, environmental control, sampling, testing, equipment operation.

Records provide a history of each batch of product, including its distribution, and also of all other relevant circumstances pertinent to the quality of the final product.

4.2   Documents should be designed, prepared, reviewed and distributed with care. They should comply with the relevant parts of the manufacturing and marketing authorisation dossiers.

4.3   Documents should be approved, signed and dated by appropriate and authorised persons.

4.4   Documents should have unambiguous contents; title, nature and purpose should be clearly stated. They should be laid out in an orderly fashion and be easy to check. Reproduced documents should be clear and legible. The reproduction of working documents from master documents must not allow any error to be introduced through the reproduction process.

4.5   Documents should be regularly reviewed and kept up-to-date. When a document has been revised, systems should be operated to prevent inadvertent use of superseded documents.

4.6   Documents should not be handwritten; although, where documents require the entry of data, these entries may be made in clear, legible, indelible handwriting. Sufficient space should be provided for such entries.

4.7   Any alteration made to the entry on a document should be signed and dated; the alteration should permit the reading of the original information. Where appropriate, the reason for the alteration should be recorded.

4.8   The records should be made or completed at the time each action is taken and in such a way that all significant activities concerning the manufacture of medicinal products are traceable. They should be retained for at least one year after the expiry date of the finished product.

4.9   Data may be recorded by electronic data processing systems, photographic or other reliable means, but detailed procedures relating to the system in use should be available and the accuracy of the records should be checked. If documentation is handled by electronic data processing methods, only authorised persons should be able to enter or modify data in the computer and there should be a record of changes and deletions; access should be restricted by passwords or other means and the result of entry of critical data should be independently checked. Batch records electronically stored should be protected by back-up transfer on magnetic tape, microfilm, paper or other means. It is particularly important that the data are readily available throughout the period of retention.

Documents Required

Specifications

4.10   There should be appropriately authorised and dated specifications for starting and packaging materials, and finished products; where appropriate, they should be also available for intermediate or bulk products.

Specifications for Starting and Packaging Materials

4.11   Specifications for starting and primary or printed packaging materials should include, if applicable:

(a) a description of the materials, including:
- the designated name and the internal code reference,
- the reference, if any, to a pharmacopoeial monograph,
- the approved suppliers and, if possible, the original producer of the products,
- a specimen of printed materials;

(b) directions for sampling and testing or reference to procedures;

(c) qualitative and quantitative requirements with acceptance limits;

(d) storage conditions and precautions;

(e) the maximum period of storage before re-examination.

Specifications for Intermediate and Bulk Products

4.12   Specifications for intermediate and bulk products should be available if these are purchased or dispatched, or if data obtained from intermediate products are used for the evaluation of the finished product. The specifications should be similar to specifications for starting materials or for finished products, as appropriate.

Specifications for Finished Products

4.13   Specifications for finished products should include:

(a) the designated name of the product and the code reference where applicable;

(b) the formula or a reference to;

(c) a description of the pharmaceutical form and package details;

(d) directions for sampling and testing or a reference to procedures;

(e) the qualitative and quantitative requirements, with the acceptance limits;

(f) the storage conditions and any special handling precautions, where applicable;

(g) the shelf-life.

Manufacturing Formula and Processing Instructions

Formally authorised Manufacturing Formula and Processing Instructions should exist for each product and batch size to be manufactured. They are often combined in one document.

4.14   The Manufacturing Formula should include:

(a) the name of the product, with a product reference code relating to its specification;

(b) a description of the pharmaceutical form, strength of the product and batch size;

(c) a list of all starting materials to be used, with the amount of each, described using the designated name and a reference which is unique to that material; mention should be made of any substance that may disappear in the course of processing;

(d) a statement of the expected final yield with the acceptable limits, and of relevant intermediate yields, where applicable.

4.15 The Processing Instructions should include:

(a) a statement of the processing location and the principal equipment to be used;

(b) the methods, or reference to the methods, to be used for preparing the critical equipment (e.g. cleaning, assembling, calibrating, sterilising);

(c) detailed stepwise processing instructions (e.g. checks on materials, pre-treatments, sequence for adding materials, mixing times, temperatures);

(d) the instructions for any in-process controls with their limits;

(e) where necessary, the requirements for bulk storage of the products; including the container, labelling and special storage conditions where applicable;

(f) any special precautions to be observed.

Packaging Instructions

4.16 There should be formally authorised Packaging Instructions for each product, pack size and type. These should normally include, or have a reference to, the following:

(a) name of the product;

(b) description of its pharmaceutical form, and strength where applicable;

(c) the pack size expressed in terms of the number, weight or volume of the product in the final container;

(d) a complete list of all the packaging materials required for a standard batch size, including quantities, sizes and types, with the code or reference number relating to the specifications of each packaging material;

(e) where appropriate, an example or reproduction of the relevant printed packaging materials, and specimens indicating where to apply batch number references, and shelf life of the product;

(f) special precautions to be observed, including a careful examination of the area and equipment in order to ascertain the line clearance before operations begin;

(g) a description of the packaging operation, including any significant subsidiary operations, and equipment to be used;

(h) details of in-process controls with instructions for sampling and acceptance limits.

Batch Processing Records

4.17   A Batch Processing Record should be kept for each batch processed. It should be based on the relevant parts of the currently approved Manufacturing Formula and Processing Instructions. The method of preparation of such records should be designed to avoid transcription errors. The record should carry the number of the batch being manufactured.

Before any processing begins, there should be recorded checks that the equipment and work station are clear of previous products, documents or materials not required for the planned process, and that equipment is clean and suitable for use.

During processing, the following information should be recorded at the time each action is taken and, after completion, the record should be dated and signed in agreement by the person responsible for the processing operations:

(a) the name of the product;
(b) dates and times of commencement, of significant intermediate stages and of completion of production;
(c) name of the person responsible for each stage of production;
(d) initials of the operator of different significant steps of production and, where appropriate, of the person who checked each of these operations (e.g. weighing);
(e) the batch number and/or analytical control number as well as the quantities of each starting material actually weighed (including the batch number and amount of any recovered or reprocessed material added);
(f) any relevant processing operation or event and major equipment used;
(g) a record of the in-process controls and the initials of the person(s) carrying them out, and the results obtained;
(h) the product yield obtained at different and pertinent stages of manufacture;
(i) notes on special problems including details, with signed authorisation for any deviation from the Manufacturing Formula and Processing Instructions.

Batch Packaging Records

4.18   A Batch Packaging Record should be kept for each batch or part batch processed. It should be based on the relevant parts of the Packaging Instructions and the method of preparation of such records should be designed to avoid transcription errors. The record should carry the batch number and the quantity of bulk product to be packed, as well as the batch number and the planned quantity of finished product that will be obtained.

Before any packaging operation begins, there should be recorded checks that the equipment and work station are clear of previous products, documents or materials not required for the planned packaging operations, and that equipment is clean and suitable for use.

The following information should be entered at the time each action is taken and, after completion, the record should be dated and signed in agreement by the person(s) responsible for the packaging operations:

(a) the name of the product;
(b) the date(s) and times of the packaging operations;
(c) the name of the responsible person carrying out the packaging operation;
(d) the initials of the operators of the different significant steps;
(e) records of checks for identity and conformity with the packaging instructions including the results of in-process controls;
(f) details of the packaging operations carried out, including references to equipment and the packaging lines used;
(g) whenever possible, samples of printed packaging materials used, including specimens of the batch coding, expiry dating and any additional overprinting;
(h) notes on any special problems or unusual events including details, with signed authorisation for any deviation from the Manufacturing Formula and Processing Instructions;
(i) the quantities and reference number or identification of all printed packaging materials and bulk product issued, used, destroyed or returned to stock and the quantities of obtained product, in order to provide for an adequate reconciliation.

Procedures and Records

Receipt

4.19 There should be written procedures and records for the receipt of each delivery of each starting and primary and printed packaging material.

4.20 The records of the receipts should include:

(a) the name of the material on the delivery note and the containers;
(b) the "in-house" name and/or code of material (if different from a);
(c) date of receipt;
(d) supplier's name and, if possible, manufacturer's name;
(e) manufacturer's batch or reference number
(f) total quantity, and number of containers received;
(g) the batch number assigned after receipt;
(h) any relevant comment (e.g. state of the containers).

4.21 There should be written procedures for the internal labelling, quarantine and storage of starting materials, packaging materials and other materials, as appropriate.

Sampling

4.22 There should be written procedures for sampling, which include the person(s) authorised to take samples, the methods and equipment to be used, the amounts to be taken and any precautions to be observed to avoid contamination of the material or any deterioration in its quality (see Section II, Chapter 6, item 13).

Testing

4.23 There should be written procedures for testing materials and products at different stages of manufacture, describing the methods and equipment to be used. The tests performed should be recorded (see Section II, Chapter 6, item 17).

Other

4.24 Written release and rejection procedures should be available for materials and products, and in particular for the release for sale of the finished product by the Qualified Person(s) in accordance with the requirements of Article 51 of Directive 2001/83/EC.[1]

4.25 Records should be maintained of the distribution of each batch of a product in order to facilitate the recall of the batch if necessary (see Section II, Chapter 8).

4.26 There should be written procedures and the associated records of actions taken or conclusions reached, where appropriate, for:

- validation;
- equipment assembly and calibration;
- maintenance, cleaning and sanitation;
- personnel matters including training, clothing, hygiene;
- environmental monitoring;
- pest control;
- complaints;
- recalls;
- returns.

---

[1] Article 55 of the Directive 2001/82/EC.

4.27   Clear operating procedures should be available for major items of manufacturing and test equipment.

4.28   Log books should be kept for major or critical equipment recording, as appropriate, any validations, calibrations, maintenance, cleaning or repair operations, including the dates and identity of people who carried these operations out.

4.29   Log books should also record in chronological order the use of major or critical equipment and the areas where the products have been processed.

5   PRODUCTION

Principle

Production operations must follow clearly defined procedures; they must comply with the principles of Good Manufacturing Practice in order to obtain products of the requisite quality and be in accordance with the relevant manufacturing and marketing authorisations.

General

5.1   Production should be performed and supervised by competent people.

5.2   All handling of materials and products, such as receipt and quarantine, sampling, storage, labelling, dispensing, processing, packaging and distribution should be done in accordance with written procedures or instructions and, where necessary, recorded.

5.3   All incoming materials should be checked to ensure that the consignment corresponds to the order. Containers should be cleaned where necessary and labelled with the prescribed data.

5.4   Damage to containers and any other problems which might adversely affect the quality of a material should be investigated, recorded and reported to the Quality Control Department.

5.5   Incoming materials and finished products should be physically or administratively quarantined immediately after receipt or processing, until they have been released for use or distribution.

5.6   Intermediate and bulk products purchased as such should be handled on receipt as though they were starting materials.

5.7   All materials and products should be stored under the appropriate conditions established by the manufacturer and in an orderly fashion to permit batch segregation and stock rotation.

5.8   Checks on yields, and reconciliation of quantities, should be carried out as necessary to ensure that there are no discrepancies outside acceptable limits.

5.9   Operations on different products should not be carried out simultaneously or consecutively in the same room unless there is no risk of mix-up or cross-contamination.

5.10   At every stage of processing, products and materials should be protected from microbial and other contamination.

5.11   When working with dry materials and products, special precautions should be taken to prevent the generation and dissemination of dust. This applies particularly to the handling of highly active or sensitising materials.

5.12   At all times during processing, all materials, bulk containers, major items of equipment and where appropriate rooms used should be labelled or otherwise identified with an indication of the product or material being processed, its strength (where applicable) and batch number. Where applicable, this indication should also mention the stage of production.

5.13   Labels applied to containers, equipment or premises should be clear, unambiguous and in the company's agreed format. It is often helpful in addition to the wording on the labels to use colours to indicate status (for example, quarantined, accepted, rejected, clean, . . .).

5.14   Checks should be carried out to ensure that pipelines and other pieces of equipment used for the transportation of products from one area to another are connected in a correct manner.

5.15   Any deviation from instructions or procedures should be avoided as far as possible. If a deviation occurs, it should be approved in writing by a competent person, with the involvement of the Quality Control Department when appropriate.

5.16   Access to production premises should be restricted to authorised personnel.

5.17   Normally, the production of non-medicinal products should be avoided in areas and with the equipment destined for the production of medicinal products.

Prevention of Cross-contamination in Production

5.18   Contamination of a starting material or of a product by another material or product must be avoided. This risk of accidental cross-contamination arises from the uncontrolled release of dust, gases, vapours, sprays or organisms from materials and products in process, from residues on equipment, and from operators' clothing. The significance of this risk varies with the type of contaminant and of product being contaminated. Amongst the most hazardous contaminants are highly sensitising materials, biological preparations containing living organisms, certain hormones, cytotoxics and other highly active materials. Products in which contamination is likely to be most significant are those administered by injection, those given in large doses and/or over a long time.

5.19   Cross-contamination should be avoided by appropriate technical or organisational measures, for example:

(a) production in segregated areas (required for products such as penicillins, live vaccines, live bacterial preparations and some other biologicals), or by campaign (separation in time) followed by appropriate cleaning;

(b) providing appropriate air-locks and air extraction;

(c) minimising the risk of contamination caused by recirculation or re-entry of untreated or insufficiently treated air;

(d) keeping protective clothing inside areas where products with special risk of cross-contamination are processed;

(e) using cleaning and decontamination procedures of known effectiveness, as ineffective cleaning of equipment is a common source of cross-contamination;

(f) using "closed systems" of production;

(g) testing for residues and use of cleaning status labels on equipment.

5.20   Measures to prevent cross-contamination and their effectiveness should be checked periodically according to set procedures.

Validation

5.21   Validation studies should reinforce Good Manufacturing Practice and be conducted in accordance with defined procedures. Results and conclusions should be recorded.

5.22   When any new manufacturing formula or method of preparation is adopted, steps should be taken to demonstrate its suitability for routine processing. The defined process, using the materials and equipment specified, should be shown to yield a product consistently of the required quality.

5.23   Significant amendments to the manufacturing process, including any change in equipment or materials, which may affect product quality and/or the reproducibility of the process should be validated.

5.24   Processes and procedures should undergo periodic critical re-validation to ensure that they remain capable of achieving the intended results.

Starting Materials

5.25   The purchase of starting materials is an important operation which should involve staff who have a particular and thorough knowledge of the suppliers.

5.26   Starting materials should only be purchased from approved suppliers named in the relevant specification and, where possible, directly from the producer. It is recommended that the specifications established by the manufacturer for the starting materials be discussed with the suppliers. It is of benefit that all aspects of the production and control of the starting material in question, including handling, labelling and packaging requirements, as well as complaints and rejection procedures are discussed with the manufacturer and the supplier.

5.27   For each delivery, the containers should be checked for integrity of package and seal and for correspondence between the delivery note and the supplier's labels.

5.28   If one material delivery is made up of different batches, each batch must be considered as separate for sampling, testing and release.

5.29   Starting materials in the storage area should be appropriately labelled (see Section II, Chapter 5, item 13). Labels should bear at least the following information:

- the designated name of the product and the internal code reference where applicable;
- a batch number given at receipt;
- where appropriate, the status of the contents (e.g. in quarantine, on test, released, rejected);
- where appropriate, an expiry date or a date beyond which retesting is necessary.

When fully computerised storage systems are used, all the above information need not necessarily be in a legible form on the label.

5.30   There should be appropriate procedures or measures to assure the identity of the contents of each container of starting material. Bulk containers from which samples have been drawn should be identified (see Section II, Chapter 6, item 13).

5.31   Only starting materials which have been released by the Quality Control Department and which are within their shelf life should be used.

5.32   Starting materials should only be dispensed by designated persons, following a written procedure, to ensure that the correct materials are accurately weighed or measured into clean and properly labelled containers.

5.33   Each dispensed material and its weight or volume should be independently checked and the check recorded.

5.34   Materials dispensed for each batch should be kept together and conspicuously labelled as such.

Processing Operations: intermediate and bulk products

5.35   Before any processing operation is started, steps should be taken to ensure that the work area and equipment are clean and free from any starting materials, products, product residues or documents not required for the current operation.

5.36   Intermediate and bulk products should be kept under appropriate conditions.

5.37   Critical processes should be validated (see "VALIDATION" in this chapter).

5.38   Any necessary in-process controls and environmental controls should be carried out and recorded.

5.39   Any significant deviation from the expected yield should be recorded and investigated.

Packaging Materials

5.40   The purchase, handling and control of primary and printed packaging materials shall be accorded attention similar to that given to starting materials.

5.41   Particular attention should be paid to printed materials. They should be stored in adequately secure conditions such as to exclude unauthorised access. Cut labels and other loose printed materials should be stored and transported in separate closed containers so as to avoid mix-ups. Packaging materials should be issued for use only by authorised personnel following an approved and documented procedure.

5.42   Each delivery or batch of printed or primary packaging material should be given a specific reference number or identification mark.

5.43   Outdated or obsolete primary packaging material or printed packaging material should be destroyed and this disposal recorded.

Packaging Operations

5.44   When setting up a programme for the packaging operations, particular attention should be given to minimising the risk of cross-contamination, mix-ups or substitutions. Different products should not be packaged in close proximity unless there is physical segregation.

5.45 Before packaging operations are begun, steps should be taken to ensure that the work area, packaging lines, printing machines and other equipment are clean and free from any products, materials or documents previously used, if these are not required for the current operation. The line-clearance should be performed according to an appropriate check-list.

5.46 The name and batch number of the product being handled should be displayed at each packaging station or line.

5.47 All products and packaging materials to be used should be checked on delivery to the packaging department for quantity, identity and conformity with the Packaging Instructions.

5.48 Containers for filling should be clean before filling. Attention should be given to avoiding and removing any contaminants such as glass fragments and metal particles.

5.49 Normally, filling and sealing should be followed as quickly as possible by labelling. If it is not the case, appropriate procedures should be applied to ensure that no mix-ups or mislabelling can occur.

5.50 The correct performance of any printing operation (for example code numbers, expiry dates) to be done separately or in the course of the packaging should be checked and recorded. Attention should be paid to printing by hand which should be re-checked at regular intervals.

5.51 Special care should be taken when using cut-labels and when over-printing is carried out off-line. Roll-feed labels are normally preferable to cut-labels, in helping to avoid mix-ups.

5.52 Checks should be made to ensure that any electronic code readers, label counters or similar devices are operating correctly.

5.53 Printed and embossed information on packaging materials should be distinct and resistant to fading or erasing.

5.54 On-line control of the product during packaging should include at least checking the following:

(a) general appearance of the packages;
(b) whether the packages are complete;
(c) whether the correct products and packaging materials are used;
(d) whether any over-printing is correct;
(e) correct functioning of line monitors.

Samples taken away from the packaging line should not be returned.

5.55 Products which have been involved in an unusual event should only be reintroduced into the process after special inspection, investigation and approval by authorised personnel. Detailed record should be kept of this operation.

5.56 Any significant or unusual discrepancy observed during reconciliation of the amount of bulk product and printed packaging materials and the number of units produced should be investigated and satisfactorily accounted for before release.

5.57 Upon completion of a packaging operation, any unused batch-coded packaging materials should be destroyed and the destruction recorded. A documented procedure should be followed if uncoded printed materials are returned to stock.

Finished Products

5.58 Finished products should be held in quarantine until their final release under conditions established by the manufacturer.

5.59 The evaluation of finished products and documentation which is necessary before release of product for sale are described in Chapter 6 (Quality Control).

5.60 After release, finished products should be stored as usable stock under conditions established by the manufacturer.

Rejected, Recovered and Returned Materials

5.61 Rejected materials and products should be clearly marked as such and stored separately in restricted areas. They should either be returned to the suppliers or, where appropriate, reprocessed or destroyed. Whatever action is taken should be approved and recorded by authorised personnel.

5.62 The reprocessing of rejected products should be exceptional. It is only permitted if the quality of the final product is not affected, if the specifications are met and if it is done in accordance with a defined and authorised procedure after evaluation of the risks involved. Record should be kept of the reprocessing.

5.63 The recovery of all or part of earlier batches which conform to the required quality by incorporation into a batch of the same product at a defined stage of manufacture should be authorised beforehand. This recovery should be carried out in accordance with a defined procedure after evaluation of the risks involved, including any possible effect on shelf life. The recovery should be recorded.

5.64 The need for additional testing of any finished product which has been reprocessed, or into which a recovered product has been incorporated, should be considered by the Quality Control Department.

5.65 Products returned from the market and which have left the control of the manufacturer should be destroyed unless without doubt their quality is satisfactory; they may be considered for re-sale, re-labelling or recovery in a subsequent batch only after they have been critically assessed by the Quality Control Department in accordance with a written procedure. The nature of the product, any special storage conditions it requires, its condition and history, and the time elapsed since it was issued should all be taken into account in this assessment. Where any doubt arises over the quality of the product, it should not be considered suitable for re-issue or re-use, although basic chemical reprocessing to recover active ingredient may be possible. Any action taken should be appropriately recorded.

6 QUALITY CONTROL

| Editor's note | Came into force 1 June 2006. |

Principle

Quality Control is concerned with sampling, specifications and testing as well as the organisation, documentation and release procedures which ensure that the necessary and relevant tests are carried out, and that materials are not released for use, nor products released for sale or supply, until their quality has been judged satisfactory. Quality Control is not confined to laboratory operations, but must be involved in all decisions which may concern the quality of the product. The independence of Quality Control from Production is considered fundamental to the satisfactory operation of Quality Control. (see also Section II, Chapter 1).

General

6.1 Each holder of a manufacturing authorisation should have a Quality Control Department. This department should be independent from other departments, and under the authority of a person with appropriate qualifications and experience, who has one or several control laboratories at his disposal. Adequate resources must be available to ensure that all the Quality Control arrangements are effectively and reliably carried out.

6.2 The principal duties of the head of Quality Control are summarised in Chapter 2. The Quality Control Department as a whole will also have other duties, such as to establish, validate and implement all quality control procedures, keep the reference samples of materials and products, ensure the correct labelling of containers of materials and products, ensure the monitoring of the stability of the products, participate in the investigation of complaints related to the quality of the product, etc. All these operations should be carried out in accordance with written procedures and, where necessary, recorded.

6.3 Finished product assessment should embrace all relevant factors, including production conditions, results of in-process testing, a review of manufacturing (including packaging) documentation, compliance with Finished Product Specification and examination of the final finished pack.

6.4   Quality Control personnel should have access to production areas for sampling and investigation as appropriate.

Good Quality Control Laboratory Practice

6.5   Control laboratory premises and equipment should meet the general and specific requirements for Quality Control areas given in Chapter 3.

6.6   The personnel, premises, and equipment in the laboratories should be appropriate to the tasks imposed by the nature and the scale of the manufacturing operations. The use of outside laboratories, in conformity with the principles detailed in Chapter 7, Contract Analysis, can be accepted for particular reasons, but this should be stated in the Quality Control records.

Documentation

6.7   Laboratory documentation should follow the principles given in Chapter 4. An important part of this documentation deals with Quality Control and the following details should be readily available to the Quality Control Department:

- specifications;
- sampling procedures;
- testing procedures and records (including analytical worksheets and/or laboratory notebooks);
- analytical reports and/or certificates;
- data from environmental monitoring, where required;
- validation records of test methods, where applicable;
- procedures for and records of the calibration of instruments and maintenance of equipment.

6.8   Any Quality Control documentation relating to a batch record should be retained for one year after the expiry date of the batch and at least 5 years after the certification referred to in Article 51(3) of Directive 2001/83/EC.

6.9   For some kinds of data (e.g. analytical tests results, yields, environmental controls) it is recommended that records are kept in a manner permitting trend evaluation.

6.10 In addition to the information which is part of the batch record, other original data such as laboratory notebooks and/or records should be retained and readily available.

Sampling

6.11 The sample taking should be done in accordance with approved written procedures that describe:

- the method of sampling;
- the equipment to be used;
- the amount of the sample to be taken;
- instructions for any required sub-division of the sample;
- the type and condition of the sample container to be used;
- the identification of containers sampled;
- any special precautions to be observed, especially with regard to the sampling of sterile or noxious materials;
- the storage conditions;
- instructions for the cleaning and storage of sampling equipment.

6.12 Reference samples should be representative of the batch of materials or products from which they are taken. Other samples may also be taken to monitor the most stressed part of a process (e.g. beginning or end of a process).

6.13 Sample containers should bear a label indicating the contents, with the batch number, the date of sampling and the containers from which samples have been drawn.

6.14 Further guidance on reference and retention samples is given in Annex 19.

Testing

6.15 Analytical methods should be validated. All testing operations described in the marketing authorisation should be carried out according to the approved methods.

6.16 The results obtained should be recorded and checked to make sure that they are consistent with each other. Any calculations should be critically examined.

6.17 The tests performed should be recorded and the records should include at least the following data:

(a) name of the material or product and, where applicable, dosage form;
(b) batch number and, where appropriate, the manufacturer and/or supplier;
(c) references to the relevant specifications and testing procedures;
(d) test results, including observations and calculations, and reference to any certificates of analysis;
(e) dates of testing;

(f) initials of the persons who performed the testing;

(g) initials of the persons who verified the testing and the calculations, where appropriate;

(h) a clear statement of release or rejection (or other status decision) and the dated signature of the designated responsible person.

6.18   All the in-process controls, including those made in the production area by production personnel, should be performed according to methods approved by Quality Control and the results recorded.

6.19   Special attention should be given to the quality of laboratory reagents, volumetric glassware and solutions, reference standards and culture media. They should be prepared in accordance with written procedures.

6.20   Laboratory reagents intended for prolonged use should be marked with the preparation date and the signature of the person who prepared them. The expiry date of unstable reagents and culture media should be indicated on the label, together with specific storage conditions. In addition, for volumetric solutions, the last date of standardisation and the last current factor should be indicated.

6.21   Where necessary, the date of receipt of any substance used for testing operations (e.g. reagents and reference standards) should be indicated on the container. Instructions for use and storage should be followed. In certain cases it may be necessary to carry out an identification test and/or other testing of reagent materials upon receipt or before use.

6.22   Animals used for testing components, materials or products, should, where appropriate, be quarantined before use. They should be maintained and controlled in a manner that assures their suitability for the intended use. They should be identified, and adequate records should be maintained, showing the history of their use.

On-going stability programme

6.23   After marketing, the stability of the medicinal product should be monitored according to a continuous appropriate programme that will permit the detection of any stability issue (e.g. changes in levels of impurities or dissolution profile) associated with the formulation in the marketed package.

6.24   The purpose of the on-going stability programme is to monitor the product over its shelf life and to determine that the product remains, and can be expected to remain, within specifications under the labelled storage conditions.

6.25   This mainly applies to the medicinal product in the package in which it is sold, but consideration should also be given to the inclusion in the programme of bulk product. For example, when the bulk product is stored for a long period before being packaged and/or shipped from a manufacturing site to a packaging site, the impact on the stability of the packaged product should be evaluated and studied under ambient conditions. In addition, consideration should be given to intermediates that are stored and used over prolonged periods. Stability studies on reconstituted product are performed during product development and need not be monitored on an on-going basis. However, when relevant, the stability of reconstituted product can also be monitored.

6.26   The on-going stability programme should be described in a written protocol following the general rules of Chapter 4 and results formalised as a report. The equipment used for the on-going stability programme (stability chambers among others) should be qualified and maintained following the general rules of Chapter 3 and Annex 15.

6.27   The protocol for an on-going stability programme should extend to the end of the shelf life period and should include, but not be limited to, the following parameters:

- number of batch(es) per strength and different batch sizes, if applicable;
- relevant physical, chemical, microbiological and biological test methods;
- acceptance criteria;
- reference to test methods;
- description of the container closure system(s);
- testing intervals (time points);
- description of the conditions of storage (standardised ICH conditions for long-term testing, consistent with the product labelling, should be used);
- other applicable parameters specific to the medicinal product.

6.28   The protocol for the on-going stability programme can be different from that of the initial long-term stability study as submitted in the marketing authorisation dossier provided that this is justified and documented in the protocol (for example the frequency of testing, or when updating to ICH recommendations).

6.29   The number of batches and frequency of testing should provide a sufficient amount of data to allow for trend analysis. Unless otherwise justified, at least one batch per year of product manufactured in every strength and every primary packaging type, if relevant, should be included in the stability programme (unless none are produced during that year). For products where on-going stability monitoring would normally require testing using animals and no appropriate alternative, validated techniques are available, the frequency of testing may take account of a risk-benefit approach. The principle of bracketing and matrixing designs may be applied if scientifically justified in the protocol.

6.30   In certain situations, additional batches should be included in the on-going stability programme. For example, an on-going stability study should be conducted after any significant change or significant deviation to the process or package. Any reworking, reprocessing or recovery operation should also be considered for inclusion.

6.31   Results of on-going stability studies should be made available to key personnel and, in particular, to the Qualified Person(s). Where on-going stability studies are carried out at a site other than the site of manufacture of the bulk or finished product, there should be a written agreement between the parties concerned. Results of on-going stability studies should be available at the site of manufacture for review by the competent authority.

6.32   Out of specification or significant atypical trends should be investigated. Any confirmed out of specification result, or significant negative trend, should be reported to the relevant competent authorities. The possible impact on batches on the market should be considered in accordance with Chapter 8 of the GMP Guide and in consultation with the relevant competent authorities.

6.33   A summary of all the data generated, including any interim conclusions on the programme, should be written and maintained. This summary should be subjected to periodic review.

7 CONTRACT MANUFACTURE AND ANALYSIS

Principle

Contract manufacture and analysis must be correctly defined, agreed and controlled in order to avoid misunderstandings which could result in a product or work of unsatisfactory quality. There must be a written contract between the Contract Giver and the Contract Acceptor which clearly establishes the duties of each party. The contract must clearly state the way in which the Qualified Person releasing each batch of product for sale exercises his full responsibility.

Note: *This chapter deals with the responsibilities of manufacturers towards the Competent Authorities of the Member States with respect to the granting of marketing and manufacturing authorisations. It is not intended in any way to affect the respective liability of contract acceptors and contract givers to consumers; this is governed by other provisions of Community and national law.*

General

7.1 There should be a written contract covering the manufacture and/or analysis arranged under contract and any technical arrangements made in connection with it.

7.2 All arrangements for contract manufacture and analysis including any proposed changes in technical or other arrangements should be in accordance with the marketing authorisation for the product concerned.

The Contract Giver

7.3 The Contract Giver is responsible for assessing the competence of the Contract Acceptor to carry out successfully the work required and for ensuring by means of the contract that the principles and guidelines of GMP as interpreted in this Guide are followed.

7.4 The Contract Giver should provide the Contract Acceptor with all the information necessary to carry out the contracted operations correctly in accordance with the marketing authorisation and any other legal requirements. The Contract Giver should ensure that the Contract Acceptor is fully aware of any problems associated with the product or the work which might pose a hazard to his premises, equipment, personnel, other materials or other products.

7.5   The Contract Giver should ensure that all processed products and materials delivered to him by the Contract Acceptor comply with their specifications or that the products have been released by a Qualified Person.

The Contract Acceptor

7.6   The Contract Acceptor must have adequate premises and equipment, knowledge and experience, and competent personnel to carry out satisfactorily the work ordered by the Contract Giver. Contract manufacture may be undertaken only by a manufacturer who is the holder of a manufacturing authorisation.

7.7   The Contract Acceptor should ensure that all products or materials delivered to him are suitable for their intended purpose.

7.8   The Contract Acceptor should not pass to a third party any of the work entrusted to him under the contract without the Contract Giver's prior evaluation and approval of the arrangements. Arrangements made between the Contract Acceptor and any third party should ensure that the manufacturing and analytical information is made available in the same way as between the original Contract Giver and Contract Acceptor.

7.9   The Contract Acceptor should refrain from any activity which may adversely affect the quality of the product manufactured and/or analysed for the Contract Giver.

The Contract

7.10   A contract should be drawn up between the Contract Giver and the Contract Acceptor which specifies their respective responsibilities relating to the manufacture and control of the product. Technical aspects of the contract should be drawn up by competent persons suitably knowledgeable in pharmaceutical technology, analysis and Good Manufacturing Practice. All arrangements for manufacture and analysis must be in accordance with the marketing authorisation and agreed by both parties.

7.11   The contract should specify the way in which the Qualified Person releasing the batch for sale ensures that each batch has been manufactured and checked for compliance with the requirements of Marketing Authorisation.

7.12   The contract should describe clearly who is responsible for purchasing materials, testing and releasing materials, undertaking production and quality controls, including in-process controls, and who has responsibility for sampling and analysis. In the case of contract analysis, the contract should state whether or not the Contract Acceptor should take samples at the premises of the manufacturer.

7.13   Manufacturing, analytical and distribution records, and reference samples should be kept by, or be available to, the Contract Giver. Any records relevant to assessing the quality of a product in the event of complaints or a suspected defect must be accessible and specified in the defect/recall procedures of the Contract Giver.

7.14   The contract should permit the Contract Giver to visit the facilities of the Contract Acceptor.

7.15   In the case of contract analysis, the Contract Acceptor should understand that he is subject to Inspection by the competent Authorities.

8 COMPLAINTS AND PRODUCT RECALL

Editor's note — Revised December 2005, came into operation February 2006.

Principle

All complaints and other information concerning potentially defective products must be reviewed carefully according to written procedures. In order to provide for all contingencies, and in accordance with Article 117 of Directive 2001/83/EC and Article 84 of Directive 2001/82/EC, a system should be designed to recall, if necessary, promptly and effectively products known or suspected to be defective from the market.

Complaints

8.1 A person should be designated responsible for handling the complaints and deciding the measures to be taken together with sufficient supporting staff to assist him. If this person is not the Qualified Person, the latter should be made aware of any complaint, investigation or recall.

8.2 There should be written procedures describing the action to be taken, including the need to consider a recall, in the case of a complaint concerning a possible product defect.

8.3 Any complaint concerning a product defect should be recorded with all the original details and thoroughly investigated. The person responsible for Quality Control should normally be involved in the study of such problems.

8.4 If a product defect is discovered or suspected in a batch, consideration should be given to checking other batches in order to determine whether they are also affected. In particular, other batches which may contain reworks of the defective batch should be investigated.

8.5 All the decisions and measures taken as a result of a complaint should be recorded and referenced to the corresponding batch records.

8.6 Complaints records should be reviewed regularly for any indication of specific or recurring problems requiring attention and possibly the recall of marketed products.

8.7 Special attention should be given to establishing whether a complaint was caused because of counterfeiting.

8.8   The competent authorities should be informed if a manufacturer is considering action following possibly faulty manufacture, product deterioration, detection of counterfeiting or any other serious quality problems with a product.

Recalls

8.9   A person should be designated as responsible for execution and co-ordination of recalls and should be supported by sufficient staff to handle all the aspects of the recalls with the appropriate degree of urgency. This responsible person should normally be independent of the sales and marketing organisation. If this person is not the Qualified Person, the latter should be made aware of any recall operation.

8.10   There should be established written procedures, regularly checked and updated when necessary, in order to organise any recall activity.

8.11   Recall operations should be capable of being initiated promptly and at any time.

8.12   All Competent Authorities of all countries to which products may have been distributed should be informed promptly if products are intended to be recalled because they are, or are suspected of being defective.

8.13   The distribution records should be readily available to the person(s) responsible for recalls, and should contain sufficient information on wholesalers and directly supplied customers (with addresses, phone and/or fax numbers inside and outside working hours, batches and amounts delivered), including those for exported products and medical samples.

8.14   Recalled products should be identified and stored separately in a secure area while awaiting a decision on their fate.

8.15   The progress of the recall process should be recorded and a final report issued, including a reconciliation between the delivered and recovered quantities of the products.

8.16   The effectiveness of the arrangements for recalls should be evaluated regularly.

9   SELF INSPECTION

Principle

Self inspections should be conducted in order to monitor the implementation and compliance with Good Manufacturing Practice principles and to propose necessary corrective measures.

9.1   Personnel matters, premises, equipment, documentation, production, quality control, distribution of the medicinal products, arrangements for dealing with complaints and recalls, and self inspection, should be examined at intervals following a pre-arranged programme in order to verify their conformity with the principles of Quality Assurance.

9.2   Self inspections should be conducted in an independent and detailed way by designated competent person(s) from the company. Independent audits by external experts may also be useful.

9.3   All self inspections should be recorded. Reports should contain all the observations made during the inspections and, where applicable, proposals for corrective measures. Statements on the actions subsequently taken should also be recorded.

ANNEX 1 MANUFACTURE OF STERILE MEDICINAL PRODUCTS

Note: *Annex 1 of the EU Guide to Good Manufacturing Practice (GMP) provides supplementary guidance on the application of the principles and guidelines of GMP to sterile medicinal products. The guidance includes recommendations on standards of environmental cleanliness for clean rooms. The guidance has been reviewed in the light of the international standard EN/ISO 14644-1 and amended in the interests of harmonisation but taking into account specific concerns unique to the production of sterile medicinal products.*

The changes affect Section 3 of the annex together with a minor change to Section 20. The remainder of the annex remains unchanged.

Principle

The manufacture of sterile products is subject to special requirements in order to minimise risks of microbiological contamination, and of particulate and pyrogen contamination. Much depends on the skill, training and attitudes of the personnel involved. Quality Assurance is particularly important, and this type of manufacture must strictly follow carefully established and validated methods of preparation and procedure. Sole reliance for sterility or other quality aspects must not be placed on any terminal process or finished product test.

Note: *This guidance does not lay down detailed methods for determining the microbiological and particulate cleanliness of air, surfaces, etc. Reference should be made to other documents such as the EN/ISO Standards.*

General

1   The manufacture of sterile products should be carried out in clean areas entry to which should be through airlocks for personnel and/or for equipment and materials. Clean areas should be maintained to an appropriate cleanliness standard and supplied with air which has passed through filters of an appropriate efficiency.

2   The various operations of component preparation, product preparation and filling should be carried out in separate areas within the clean area. Manufacturing operations are divided into two categories; firstly those where the product is terminally sterilised, and secondly those which are conducted aseptically at some or all stages.

3   Clean areas for the manufacture of sterile products are classified according to the required characteristics of the environment. Each manufacturing

operation requires an appropriate environmental cleanliness level in the operational state in order to minimise the risks of particulate or microbial contamination of the product or materials being handled.

In order to meet "in operation" conditions these areas should be designed to reach certain specified air-cleanliness levels in the "at rest" occupancy state. The "at-rest" state is the condition where the installation is installed and operating, complete with production equipment but with no operating personnel present. The "in operation" state is the condition where the installation is functioning in the defined operating mode with the specified number of personnel working.

The "in operation" and "at rest" states should be defined for each clean room or suite of clean rooms. For the manufacture of sterile medicinal products 4 grades can be distinguished:

Grade A: The local zone for high risk operations, e.g. filling zone, stopper bowls, open ampoules and vials, making aseptic connections. Normally such conditions are provided by a laminar air flow work station. Laminar air flow systems should provide a homogeneous air speed in a range of 0.36–0.54 m/s (guidance value) at the working position in open clean room applications. The maintenance of laminarity should be demonstrated and validated. A uni-directional air flow and lower velocities may be used in closed isolators and glove boxes.

Grade B: For aseptic preparation and filling, this is the background environment for the grade A zone.

Grade C and D: Clean areas for carrying out less critical stages in the manufacture of sterile products. The airborne particulate classification for these grades is given in the following table.

Grade	at rest (b)		in operation (b)	
	maximum permitted number of particles/m³ equal to or above (a)			
	0.5 μm (d)	5 μm	0.5 μm (d)	5 μm
A	3 500	1 (e)	3 500	1 (e)
B (c)	3 500	1 (e)	350 000	2 000
C (c)	350 000	2 000	3 500 000	20 000
D (c)	3 500 000	20 000	not defined (f)	Not defined (f)

Notes:
(a) Particle measurement based on the use of a discrete airborne particle counter to measure the concentration of particles at designated sizes equal to or greater than the threshold stated. A continuous measurement system should be used for monitoring the concentration of particles in the grade A zone, and is recommended for the surrounding grade B areas.

For routine testing the total sample volume should not be less than 1 m³ for grade A and B areas and preferably also in grade C areas.

(b) The particulate conditions given in the table for the "at rest" state should be achieved after a short "clean up" period of 15–20 minutes (guidance value) in an unmanned state after completion of operations.

The particulate conditions for grade A "in operation" given in the table should be maintained in the zone immediately surrounding the product whenever the product or open container is exposed to the environment. It is accepted that it may not always be possible to demonstrate conformity with particulate standards at the point of fill when filling is in progress, due to the generation of particles or droplets from the product itself.

(c) In order to reach the B, C and D air grades, the number of air changes should be related to the size of the room and the equipment and personnel present in the room. The air system should be provided with appropriate terminal filters such as HEPA for grades A, B and C.

(d) The guidance given for the maximum permitted number of particles in the "at rest" and "in operation" conditions correspond approximately to the cleanliness classes in the EN/ISO 14644-1 at a particle size of 0.5 μm.

(e) These areas are expected to be completely free from particles of size greater than or equal to 5 μm. As it is impossible to demonstrate the absence of particles with any statistical significance the limits are set to 1 particle/m^3. During the clean room qualification it should be shown that the areas can be maintained within the defined limits.

(f) The requirements and limits will depend on the nature of the operations carried out. Other characteristics such as temperature and relative humidity depend on the product and nature of the operations carried out. These parameters should not interfere with the defined cleanliness standard.

Examples of operations to be carried out in the various grades are given in the table below. (see also par. 11 and par.12)

Grade	Examples of operations for terminally sterilised products. (see par. 11)
A	Filling of products, when unusually at risk
C	Preparation of solutions, when unusually at risk. Filling of products
D	Preparation of solutions and components for subsequent filling

Grade	Examples of operations for aseptic preparations. (see par. 12)
A	Aseptic preparation and filling
C	Preparation of solutions to be filtered
D	Handling of components after washing

4   The areas should be monitored during operation, in order to control the particulate cleanliness of the various grades.

5   Where aseptic operations are performed monitoring should be frequent using methods such as settle plates, volumetric air and surface sampling (e.g. swabs and contact plates). Sampling methods used in operation should not interfere with zone protection. Results from monitoring should be considered when reviewing batch documentation for finished product release. Surfaces and personnel should be monitored after critical operations.

Additional microbiological monitoring is also required outside production operations, e.g. after validation of systems, cleaning and sanitisation.

Recommended limits for microbiological monitoring of clean areas during operation.

	Recommended limits for microbial contamination (a)			
Grade	air sample cfu/m^3	settle plates (diam. 90 mm), cfu/4 hours (b)	contact plates (diam. 55 mm), cfu/plate	glove print 5 fingers cfu/glove
A	< 1	< 1	< 1	< 1
B	10	5	5	5
C	100	50	25	–
D	200	100	50	–

Notes:
(a) These are average values.
(b) Individual settle plates may be exposed for less than 4 hours.

6   Appropriate alert and action limits should be set for the results of particulate and microbiological monitoring. If these limits are exceeded operating procedures should prescribe corrective action.

Isolator Technology

7   The utilisation of isolator technology to minimise human interventions in processing areas may result in a significant decrease in the risk of microbiological contamination of aseptically manufactured products from the environment. There are many possible designs of isolators and transfer devices. The isolator and the background environment should be designed so that the required air quality for the respective zones can be realised. Isolators are constructed of various materials more or less prone to puncture and leakage. Transfer devices may vary from a single door to double door designs to fully sealed systems incorporating sterilisation mechanisms.

   The transfer of materials into and out of the unit is one of the greatest potential sources of contamination. In general the area inside the isolator is the local zone for high risk manipulations, although it is recognised that laminar air flow may not exist in the working zone of all such devices.

   The air classification required for the background environment depends on the design of the isolator and its application. It should be controlled and for aseptic processing it should be at least grade D.

8   Isolators should be introduced only after appropriate validation. Validation should take into account all critical factors of isolator technology, for example the quality of the air inside and outside (background) the isolator, sanitisation of the isolator, the transfer process and isolator integrity.

9   Monitoring should be carried out routinely and should include frequent leak testing of the isolator and glove/sleeve system.

Blow/Fill/Seal Technology

10   Blow/fill/seal units are purpose built machines in which, in one continuous operation, containers are formed from a thermoplastic granulate, filled and then sealed, all by the one automatic machine. Blow/fill/seal equipment used for aseptic production which is fitted with an effective grade A air shower may be installed in at least a grade C environment, provided that grade A/B clothing is used. The environment should comply with the viable and non viable limits at rest and the viable limit only when in operation. Blow/fill/seal equipment used for the production of products which are terminally sterilised should be installed in at least a grade D environment.

    Because of this special technology particular attention should be paid to, at least the following: equipment design and qualification, validation and reproducibility of cleaning-in-place and sterilisation-in-place, background cleanroom environment in which the equipment is located, operator training and clothing, and interventions in the critical zone of the equipment including any aseptic assembly prior to the commencement of filling.

Terminally Sterilised Products

11   Preparation of components and most products should be done in at least a grade D environment in order to give low risk of microbial and particulate contamination, suitable for filtration and sterilisation. Where the product is at a high or unusual risk of microbial contamination, (for example, because the product actively supports microbial growth or must be held for a long period before sterilisation or is necessarily processed not mainly in closed vessels), then preparation should be carried out in a grade C environment.

    Filling of products for terminal sterilisation should be carried out in at least a grade C environment.

    Where the product is at unusual risk of contamination from the environment, for example because the filling operation is slow or the containers are wide-necked or are necessarily exposed for more than a few seconds before sealing, the filling should be done in a grade A zone with at least a grade C background. Preparation and filling of ointments, creams, suspensions and emulsions should generally be carried out in a grade C environment before terminal sterilisation.

Aseptic Preparation

12   Components after washing should be handled in at least a grade D environment. Handling of sterile starting materials and components, unless

subjected to sterilisation or filtration through a micro-organism-retaining filter later in the process, should be done in a grade A environment with grade B background. Preparation of solutions which are to be sterile filtered during the process should be done in a grade C environment; if not filtered, the preparation of materials and products should be done in a grade A environment with a grade B background.

Handling and filling of aseptically prepared products should be done in a grade A environment with a grade B background.

Prior to the completion of stoppering, transfer of partially closed containers, as used in freeze drying should be done either in a grade A environment with grade B background or in sealed transfer trays in a grade B environment.

Preparation and filling of sterile ointments, creams, suspensions and emulsions should be done in a grade A environment, with a grade B background, when the product is exposed and is not subsequently filtered.

Personnel

13   Only the minimum number of personnel required should be present in clean areas; this is particularly important during aseptic processing. Inspections and controls should be conducted outside the clean areas as far as possible.

14   All personnel (including those concerned with cleaning and maintenance) employed in such areas should receive regular training in disciplines relevant to the correct manufacture of sterile products. This training should include reference to hygiene and to the basic elements of microbiology. When outside staff who have not received such training (e.g. building or maintenance contractors) need to be brought in, particular care should be taken over their instruction and supervision.

15   Staff who have been engaged in the processing of animal tissue materials or of cultures of micro-organisms other than those used in the current manufacturing process should not enter sterile-product areas unless rigorous and clearly defined entry procedures have been followed.

16   High standards of personal hygiene and cleanliness are essential. Personnel involved in the manufacture of sterile preparations should be instructed to report any condition which may cause the shedding of abnormal numbers or types of contaminants; periodic health checks for such conditions are desirable. Actions to be taken about personnel who could be introducing undue microbiological hazard should be decided by a designated competent person.

17   Changing and washing should follow a written procedure designed to minimise contamination of clean area clothing or carry-through of contaminants to the clean areas.

18   Wristwatches, make-up and jewellery should not be worn in clean areas.

19   The clothing and its quality should be appropriate for the process and the grade of the working area. It should be worn in such a way as to protect the product from contamination.

The description of clothing required for each grade is given below:

Grade D: Hair and, where relevant, beard should be covered. A general protective suit and appropriate shoes or overshoes should be worn. Appropriate measures should be taken to avoid any contamination coming from outside the clean area.

Grade C: Hair and where relevant beard and moustache should be covered. A single or two-piece trouser suit, gathered at the wrists and with high neck and appropriate shoes or overshoes should be worn. They should shed virtually no fibres or particulate matter.

Grade A/B: Headgear should totally enclose hair and, where relevant, beard and moustache; it should be tucked into the neck of the suit; a face mask should be worn to prevent the shedding of droplets. Appropriate sterilised, non-powdered rubber or plastic gloves and sterilised or disinfected footwear should be worn. Trouser-legs should be tucked inside the footwear and garment sleeves into the gloves. The protective clothing should shed virtually no fibres or particulate matter and retain particles shed by the body.

20   Outdoor clothing should not be brought into changing rooms leading to grade B and C rooms. For every worker in a grade A/B area, clean sterile (sterilised or adequately sanitised) protective garments should be provided at each work session. Gloves should be regularly disinfected during operations.

Masks and gloves should be changed at least for every working session.

21   Clean area clothing should be cleaned and handled in such a way that it does not gather additional contaminants which can later be shed. These operations should follow written procedures. Separate laundry facilities for such clothing are desirable. Inappropriate treatment of clothing will damage fibres and may increase the risk of shedding of particles.

Premises

22   In clean areas, all exposed surfaces should be smooth, impervious and unbroken in order to minimise the shedding or accumulation of particles or micro-organisms and to permit the repeated application of cleaning agents, and disinfectants where used.

23   To reduce accumulation of dust and to facilitate cleaning there should be no uncleanable recesses and a minimum of projecting ledges, shelves, cupboards and equipment. Doors should be designed to avoid those uncleanable recesses; sliding doors may be undesirable for this reason.

24   False ceilings should be sealed to prevent contamination from the space above them.

25   Pipes and ducts and other utilities should be installed so that they do not create recesses, unsealed openings and surfaces which are difficult to clean.

26   Sinks and drains should be prohibited in grade A/B areas used for aseptic manufacture. In other areas air breaks should be fitted between the machine or sink and the drains. Floor drains in lower grade clean rooms should be fitted with traps or water seals to prevent back-flow.

27   Changing rooms should be designed as airlocks and used to provide physical separation of the different stages of changing and so minimise microbial and particulate contamination of protective clothing. They should be flushed effectively with filtered air. The final stage of the changing room should, in the at-rest state, be the same grade as the area into which it leads.
      The use of separate changing rooms for entering and leaving clean areas is sometimes desirable. In general hand washing facilities should be provided only in the first stage of the changing rooms.

28   Both airlock doors should not be opened simultaneously. An interlocking system or a visual and/or audible warning system should be operated to prevent the opening of more than one door at a time.

29   A filtered air supply should maintain a positive pressure and an air flow relative to surrounding areas of a lower grade under all operational conditions and should flush the area effectively. Adjacent rooms of different grades should have a pressure differential of 10–15 pascals (guidance values). Particular attention should be paid to the protection of the zone of greatest risk, that is, the immediate environment to which a product and cleaned components which contact the product are exposed. The various recommendations regarding air supplies and pressure differentials may need to be modified where it becomes necessary to contain some materials, e.g. pathogenic, highly toxic, radioactive or live viral or bacterial materials or products. Decontamination of facilities and treatment of air leaving a clean area may be necessary for some operations.

30   It should be demonstrated that air-flow patterns do not present a contamination risk, e.g. care should be taken to ensure that air flows do not distribute particles from a particle-generating person, operation or machine to a zone of higher product risk.

31   A warning system should be provided to indicate failure in the air supply. Indicators of pressure differences should be fitted between areas where these differences are important. These pressure differences should be recorded regularly or otherwise documented.

Equipment

32   A conveyor belt should not pass through a partition between a grade A or B area and a processing area of lower air cleanliness, unless the belt itself is continually sterilised (e.g. in a sterilising tunnel).

33   As far as practicable equipment, fittings and services should be designed and installed so that operations, maintenance and repairs can be carried out outside the clean area. If sterilisation is required, it should be carried out, wherever possible, after complete reassembly.

34   When equipment maintenance has been carried out within the clean area, the area should be cleaned, disinfected and/or sterilised where appropriate, before processing recommences if the required standards of cleanliness and/or asepsis have not been maintained during the work.

35   Water treatment plants and distribution systems should be designed, constructed and maintained so as to ensure a reliable source of water of an appropriate quality. They should not be operated beyond their designed capacity. Water for injections should be produced, stored and distributed in a manner which prevents microbial growth, for example by constant circulation at a temperature above 70°C.

36   All equipment such as sterilisers, air handling and filtration systems, air vent and gas filters, water treatment, generation, storage and distribution systems should be subject to validation and planned maintenance; their return to use should be approved.

Sanitation

37   The sanitation of clean areas is particularly important. They should be cleaned thoroughly in accordance with a written programme. Where disinfectants are used, more than one type should be employed. Monitoring should be undertaken regularly in order to detect the development of resistant strains.

38   Disinfectants and detergents should be monitored for microbial contamination; dilutions should be kept in previously cleaned containers and

should only be stored for defined periods unless sterilised. Disinfectants and detergents used in grades A and B areas should be sterile prior to use.

39   Fumigation of clean areas may be useful for reducing microbiological contamination in inaccessible places.

Processing

40   Precautions to minimise contamination should be taken during all processing stages including the stages before sterilisation.

41   Preparations of microbiological origin should not be made or filled in areas used for the processing of other medicinal products; however, vaccines of dead organisms or of bacterial extracts may be filled, after inactivation, in the same premises as other sterile medicinal products.

42   Validation of aseptic processing should include a process simulation test using a nutrient medium (media fill). Selection of the nutrient medium should be made based on dosage form of the product and selectivity, clarity, concentration and suitability for sterilisation of the nutrient medium. The process simulation test should imitate as closely as possible the routine aseptic manufacturing process and include all the critical subsequent manufacturing steps. It should also take into account various interventions known to occur during normal production as well as worst case situations. Process simulation tests should be performed as initial validation with three consecutive satisfactory simulation tests per shift and repeated at defined intervals and after any significant modification to the HVAC-system, equipment, process and number of shifts.
   Normally process simulation tests should be repeated twice a year per shift and process. The number of containers used for media fills should be sufficient to enable a valid evaluation. For small batches, the number of containers for media fills should at least equal the size of the product batch. The target should be zero growth but a contamination rate of less than 0.1% with 95% confidence limit is acceptable. The manufacturer should establish alert and action limits.
   Any contamination should be investigated.

43   Care should be taken that any validation does not compromise the processes.

44   Water sources, water treatment equipment and treated water should be monitored regularly for chemical and biological contamination and, as

appropriate, for endotoxins. Records should be maintained of the results of the monitoring and of any action taken.

45   Activities in clean areas and especially when aseptic operations are in progress should be kept to a minimum and movement of personnel should be controlled and methodical, to avoid excessive shedding of particles and organisms due to over-vigorous activity. The ambient temperature and humidity should not be uncomfortably high because of the nature of the garments worn.

46   Microbiological contamination of starting materials should be minimal. Specifications should include requirements for microbiological quality when the need for this has been indicated by monitoring.

47   Containers and materials liable to generate fibres should be minimised in clean areas.

48   Where appropriate, measures should be taken to minimise the particulate contamination of the end product.

49   Components, containers and equipment should be handled after the final cleaning process in such a way that they are not recontaminated.

50   The interval between the washing and drying and the sterilisation of components, containers and equipment as well as between their sterilisation and use should be minimised and subject to a time-limit appropriate to the storage conditions.

51   The time between the start of the preparation of a solution and its sterilisation or filtration through a micro-organism-retaining filter should be minimised. There should be a set maximum permissible time for each product that takes into account its composition and the prescribed method of storage.

52   The bioburden should be monitored before sterilisation. There should be working limits on contamination immediately before sterilisation which are related to the efficiency of the method to be used. Where appropriate the absence of pyrogens should be monitored. All solutions, in particular large volume infusion fluids, should be passed through a micro-organism-retaining filter, if possible sited immediately before filling.

53   Components, containers, equipment and any other article required in a clean area where aseptic work takes place should be sterilised and passed into the area through double-ended sterilisers sealed into the wall, or by a procedure which achieves the same objective of not introducing contamination. Non-combustible gases should be passed through micro-organism-retentive filters.

54   The efficacy of any new procedure should be validated, and the validation verified at scheduled intervals based on performance history or when any significant change is made in the process or equipment.

Sterilisation

55   All sterilisation processes should be validated. Particular attention should be given when the adopted sterilisation method is not described in the current edition of the European Pharmacopoeia, or when it is used for a product which is not a simple aqueous or oily solution. Where possible, heat sterilisation is the method of choice. In any case, the sterilisation process must be in accordance with the marketing and manufacturing authorisations.

56   Before any sterilisation process is adopted its suitability for the product and its efficacy in achieving the desired sterilising conditions in all parts of each type of load to be processed should be demonstrated by physical measurements and by biological indicators where appropriate. The validity of the process should be verified at scheduled intervals, at least annually, and whenever significant modifications have been made to the equipment. Records should be kept of the results.

57   For effective sterilisation the whole of the material must be subjected to the required treatment and the process should be designed to ensure that this is achieved.

58   Validated loading patterns should be established for all sterilisation processes.

59   Biological indicators should be considered as an additional method for monitoring the sterilisation. They should be stored and used according to the manufacturers instructions, and their quality checked by positive controls. If biological indicators are used, strict precautions should be taken to avoid transferring microbial contamination from them.

60   There should be a clear means of differentiating products which have not been sterilised from those which have. Each basket, tray or other carrier of products or components should be clearly labelled with the material name, its batch number and an indication of whether or not it has been sterilised. Indicators such as autoclave tape may be used, where appropriate, to indicate whether or not a batch (or sub-batch) has passed through a sterilisation process, but they do not give a reliable indication that the lot is, in fact, sterile.

61   Sterilisation records should be available for each sterilisation run. They should be approved as part of the batch release procedure.

Sterilisation by Heat

62   Each heat sterilisation cycle should be recorded on a time/temperature chart with a sufficiently large scale or by other appropriate equipment with suitable accuracy and precision. The position of the temperature probes used for controlling and/or recording should have been determined during the validation, and where applicable also checked against a second independent temperature probe located at the same position.

63   Chemical or biological indicators may also be used, but should not take the place of physical measurements.

64   Sufficient time must be allowed for the whole of the load to reach the required temperature before measurement of the sterilising time-period is commenced. This time must be determined for each type of load to be processed.

65   After the high temperature phase of a heat sterilisation cycle, precautions should be taken against contamination of a sterilised load during cooling. Any cooling fluid or gas in contact with the product should be sterilised unless it can be shown that any leaking container would not be approved for use.

Moist Heat

66   Both temperature and pressure should be used to monitor the process. Control instrumentation should normally be independent of monitoring instrumentation and recording charts. Where automated control and monitoring systems are used for these applications they should be validated to ensure that critical process requirements are met. System and cycle faults should be registered by the system and observed by the operator. The reading of the independent temperature indicator should be routinely checked against the chart recorder during the sterilisation period. For sterilisers fitted with a drain at the bottom of the chamber, it may also be necessary to record the temperature at this position, throughout the sterilisation period. There should be frequent leak tests on the chamber when a vacuum phase is part of the cycle.

67   The items to be sterilised, other than products in sealed containers, should be wrapped in a material which allows removal of air and penetration of steam but which prevents recontamination after sterilisation. All parts of the load should be in contact with the sterilising agent at the required temperature for the required time.

68   Care should be taken to ensure that steam used for sterilisation is of suitable quality and does not contain additives at a level which could cause contamination of product or equipment.

Dry Heat

69   The process used should include air circulation within the chamber and the maintenance of a positive pressure to prevent the entry of non-sterile air. Any air admitted should be passed through a HEPA filter. Where this process is also intended to remove pyrogens, challenge tests using endotoxins should be used as part of the validation.

Sterilisation by Radiation

70   Radiation sterilisation is used mainly for the sterilisation of heat-sensitive materials and products. Many medicinal products and some packaging materials are radiation-sensitive, so this method is permissible only when the absence of deleterious effects on the product has been confirmed experimentally. Ultraviolet irradiation is not normally an acceptable method of sterilisation.

71   During the sterilisation procedure the radiation dose should be measured. For this purpose, dosimetry indicators which are independent of dose rate should be used, giving a quantitative measurement of the dose received by the product itself. Dosimeters should be inserted in the load in sufficient number and close enough together to ensure that there is always a dosimeter in the irradiator. Where plastic dosimeters are used they should be used within the time-limit of their calibration. Dosimeter absorbances should be read within a short period after exposure to radiation.

72   Biological indicators may be used as an additional control.

73   Validation procedures should ensure that the effects of variations in density of the packages are considered.

74   Materials handling procedures should prevent mix-up between irradiated and non-irradiated materials. Radiation sensitive colour disks should also be used on each package to differentiate between packages which have been subjected to irradiation and those which have not.

75   The total radiation dose should be administered within a predetermined time span.

Sterilisation with Ethylene Oxide

76   This method should only be used when no other method is practicable. During process validation it should be shown that there is no damaging effect on the product and that the conditions and time allowed for degassing are such as to reduce any residual gas and reaction products to defined acceptable limits for the type of product or material.

77   Direct contact between gas and microbial cells is essential; precautions should be taken to avoid the presence of organisms likely to be enclosed in material such as crystals or dried protein. The nature and quantity of packaging materials can significantly affect the process.

78   Before exposure to the gas, materials should be brought into equilibrium with the humidity and temperature required by the process. The time required for this should be balanced against the opposing need to minimise the time before sterilisation.

79   Each sterilisation cycle should be monitored with suitable biological indicators, using the appropriate number of test pieces distributed throughout the load. The information so obtained should form part of the batch record.

80   For each sterilisation cycle, records should be made of the time taken to complete the cycle, of the pressure, temperature and humidity within the chamber during the process and of the gas concentration and of the total amount of gas used. The pressure and temperature should be recorded throughout the cycle on a chart. The record(s) should form part of the batch record.

81   After sterilisation, the load should be stored in a controlled manner under ventilated conditions to allow residual gas and reaction products to reduce to the defined level. This process should be validated.

Filtration of Medicinal Products which cannot be Sterilised in their Final Container

82   Filtration alone is not considered sufficient when sterilisation in the final container is possible. With regard to methods currently available, steam sterilisation is to be preferred. If the product cannot be sterilised in the final container, solutions or liquids can be filtered through a sterile filter of nominal pore size of 0.22 micron (or less), or with at least equivalent micro-organism retaining properties, into a previously sterilised container. Such filters can remove most bacteria and moulds, but not all viruses or

mycoplasmas. Consideration should be given to complementing the filtration process with some degree of heat treatment.

83 Due to the potential additional risks of the filtration method as compared with other sterilisation processes, a second filtration via a further sterilised micro-organism retaining filter, immediately prior to filling, may be advisable. The final sterile filtration should be carried out as close as possible to the filling point.

84 Fibre shedding characteristics of filters should be minimal.

85 The integrity of the sterilised filter should be verified before use and should be confirmed immediately after use by an appropriate method such as a bubble point, diffusive flow or pressure hold test. The time taken to filter a known volume of bulk solution and the pressure difference to be used across the filter should be determined during validation and any significant differences from this during routine manufacturing, should be noted and investigated. Results of these checks should be included in the batch record. The integrity of critical gas and air vent filters should be confirmed after use. The integrity of other filters should be confirmed at appropriate intervals.

86 The same filter should not be used for more than one working day unless such use has been validated.

87 The filter should not affect the product by removal of ingredients from it or by release of substances into it.

Finishing of Sterile Products

88 Containers should be closed by appropriately validated methods. Containers closed by fusion, e.g. glass or plastic ampoules should be subject to 100% integrity testing. Samples of other containers should be checked for integrity according to appropriate procedures.

89 Containers sealed under vacuum should be tested for maintenance of that vacuum after an appropriate, pre-determined period.

90 Filled containers of parenteral products should be inspected individually for extraneous contamination or other defects. When inspection is done visually, it should be done under suitable and controlled conditions of illumination and background. Operators doing the inspection should pass regular eye-sight checks, with spectacles if worn, and be allowed frequent breaks from inspection. Where other methods of inspection are used, the process should be validated and the performance of the equipment checked at intervals. Results should be recorded.

Quality Control

91 The sterility test applied to the finished product should only be regarded as the last in a series of control measures by which sterility is assured. The test should be validated for the product(s) concerned.

92 In those cases where parametric release has been authorised, special attention should be paid to the validation and the monitoring of the entire manufacturing process.

93 Samples taken for sterility testing should be representative of the whole of the batch, but should in particular include samples taken from parts of the batch considered to be most at risk of contamination, e.g.:

   a. for products which have been filled aseptically, samples should include containers filled at the beginning and end of the batch and after any significant intervention,

   b. or products which have been heat sterilised in their final containers, consideration should be given to taking samples from the potentially coolest part of the load.

ANNEX 2 MANUFACTURE OF BIOLOGICAL MEDICINAL PRODUCTS FOR HUMAN USE

Scope

The methods employed in the manufacture of biological medicinal products are a critical factor in shaping the appropriate regulatory control. Biological medicinal products can be defined therefore largely by reference to their method of manufacture. Biological medicinal products prepared by the following methods of manufacture will fall under the scope of this annex[1].

Biological medicinal products manufactured by these methods include: vaccines, immunosera, antigens, hormones, cytokines, enzymes and other products of fermentation (including monoclonal antibodies and products derived from r-DNA).

(a) Microbial cultures, excluding those resulting from r-DNA techniques;
(b) Microbial and cell cultures, including those resulting from recombinant DNA or hybridoma techniques;
(c) Extraction from biological tissues
(d) Propagation of live agents in embryos or animals

(Not all of the aspects of this annex may necessarily apply to products in Category a.)

Note: *In drawing up this guidance, due consideration has been given to the general requirements for manufacturing establishments and control laboratories proposed by the WHO.*

The present guidance does not lay down detailed requirements for specific classes of biological products, and attention is, therefore, directed to other guidelines issued by the Committee for Proprietary Medicinal Products (CPMP), for example the note for guidance on monoclonal antibodies and the note for guidance on products of recombinant DNA technology ("The rules governing medicinal products in the European Community", Volume 3).

Principle

The manufacture of biological medicinal products involves certain specific considerations arising from the nature of the products and the processes. The way in which biological medicinal products are produced, controlled and administered make some particular precautions necessary.

---

[1] Biological medicinal products manufactured by these methods include: vaccines, immunosera, antigens, hormones, cytokines, enzymes and other products of fermentation (including monoclonal antibodies and products derived from r-DNA).

Unlike conventional medicinal products, which are reproduced using chemical and physical techniques capable of a high degree of consistency, the production of biological medicinal products involves biological processes and materials, such as cultivation of cells or extraction of material from living organisms. These biological processes may display inherent variability, so that the range and nature of by-products are variable. Moreover, the materials used in these cultivation processes provide good substrates for growth of microbial contaminants.

Control of biological medicinal products usually involves biological analytical techniques which have a greater variability than physico-chemical determinations. In-process controls therefore take on a great importance in the manufacture of biological medicinal products.

Personnel

1   All personnel (including those concerned with cleaning, maintenance or quality control) employed in areas where biological medicinal products are manufactured should receive additional training specific to the products manufactured and to their work. Personnel should be given relevant information and training in hygiene and microbiology.

2   Persons responsible for production and quality control should have an adequate background in relevant scientific disciplines, such as bacteriology, biology, biometry, chemistry, medicine, pharmacy, pharmacology, virology, immunology and veterinary medicine, together with sufficient practical experience to enable them to exercise their management function for the process concerned.

3   The immunological status of personnel may have to be taken into consideration for product safety. All personnel engaged in production, maintenance, testing and animal care (and inspectors) should be vaccinated where necessary with appropriate specific vaccines and have regular health checks. Apart from the obvious problem of exposure of staff to infectious agents, potent toxins or allergens, it is necessary to avoid the risk of contamination of a production batch with infectious agents. Visitors should generally be excluded from production areas.

4   Any changes in the immunological status of personnel which could adversely affect the quality of the product should preclude work in the production area. Production of BCG vaccine and tuberculin products should be restricted to staff who are carefully monitored by regular checks of immunological status or chest X-ray.

5   In the course of a working day, personnel should not pass from areas where exposure to live organisms or animals is possible to areas where other

products or different organisms are handled. If such passage is unavoidable, clearly defined decontamination measures, including change of clothing and shoes and, where necessary, showering should be followed by staff involved in any such production.

Premises and Equipment

6   The degree of environmental control of particulate and microbial contamination of the production premises should be adapted to the product and the production step, bearing in mind the level of contamination of the starting materials and the risk to the finished product.

7   The risk of cross-contamination between biological medicinal products, especially during those stages of the manufacturing process in which live organisms are used, may require additional precautions with respect to facilities and equipment, such as the use of dedicated facilities and equipment, production on a campaign basis and the use of closed systems. The nature of the product as well as the equipment used will determine the level of segregation needed to avoid cross-contamination.

8   In principle, dedicated facilities should be used for the production of BCG vaccine and for the handling of live organisms used in production of tuberculin products.

9   Dedicated facilities should be used for the handling of *Bacillus anthracis*, of *Clostridium botulinum* and of *Clostridium tetani* until the inactivation process is accomplished.

10   Production on a campaign basis may be acceptable for other spore-forming organisms provided that the facilities are dedicated to this group of products and not more than one product is processed at any one time.

11   Simultaneous production in the same area using closed systems of biofermenters may be acceptable for products such as monoclonal antibodies and products prepared by DNA techniques.

12   Processing steps after harvesting may be carried out simultaneously in the same production area provided that adequate precautions are taken to prevent cross-contamination. For killed vaccines and toxoids, such parallel processing should only be performed after inactivation of the culture or after detoxification.

13   Positive pressure areas should be used to process sterile products but negative pressure in specific areas at point of exposure of pathogens is acceptable for containment reasons.

   Where negative pressure areas or safety cabinets are used for aseptic processing of pathogens, they should be surrounded by a positive pressure sterile zone.

14 Air filtration units should be specific to the processing area concerned and recirculation of air should not occur from areas handling live pathogenic organisms.

15 The layout and design of production areas and equipment should permit effective cleaning and decontamination (e.g. by fumigation). The adequacy of cleaning and decontamination procedures should be validated.

16 Equipment used during handling of live organisms should be designed to maintain cultures in a pure state and uncontaminated by external sources during processing.

17 Pipework systems, valves and vent filters should be properly designed to facilitate cleaning and sterilisation. The use of "clean in place" and "sterilise in place" systems should be encouraged. Valves on fermentation vessels should be completely steam sterilisable. Air vent filters should be hydrophobic and validated for their scheduled life span.

18 Primary containment should be designed and tested to demonstrate freedom from leakage risk.

19 Effluents which may contain pathogenic micro-organisms should be effectively decontaminated.

20 Due to the variability of biological products or processes, some additives or ingredients have to be measured or weighed during the production process (e.g. buffers). In these cases, small stocks of these substances may be kept in the production area.

Animal Quarters and Care

21 Animals are used for the manufacture of a number of biological products, for example polio vaccine (monkeys), snake antivenoms (horses and goats), rabies vaccine (rabbits, mice and hamsters) and serum gonadotrophin (horses). In addition, animals may also be used in the quality control of most sera and vaccines, e.g. pertussis vaccine (mice), pyrogenicity (rabbits), BCG vaccine (guinea-pigs).

22 General requirements for animal quarters, care and quarantine are laid down in Directive 86/609/EEC[2]. Quarters for animals used in production

---

[2] Directive 2003/65/EC of the European Parliament and of the Council of 22 July 2003 amending Council Directive 86/609/EEC on the approximation of laws, regulations and administrative provisions of the Member States regarding the protection of animals used for experimental and other scientific purposes (OJ L 230, 16.09.2003, p. 32–33).

and control of biological products should be separated from production and control areas. The health status of animals from which some starting materials are derived and of those used for quality control and safety testing should be monitored and recorded. Staff employed in such areas must be provided with special clothing and changing facilities. Where monkeys are used for the production or quality control of biological medicinal products, special consideration is required as laid down in the current WHO Requirements for Biological Substances N° 7.

Documentation

23 Specifications for biological starting materials may need additional documentation on the source, origin, method of manufacture and controls applied, particularly microbiological controls.

24 Specifications are routinely required for intermediate and bulk biological medicinal products.

Production

Starting materials

25 The source, origin and suitability of starting materials should be clearly defined. Where the necessary tests take a long time, it may be permissible to process starting materials before the results of the tests are available. In such cases, release of a finished product is conditional on satisfactory results of these tests.

26 Where sterilisation of starting materials is required, it should be carried out where possible by heat. Where necessary, other appropriate methods may also be used for inactivation of biological materials (e.g. irradiation).

Seed lot and cell bank system

27 In order to prevent the unwanted drift of properties which might ensue from repeated subcultures or multiple generations, the production of biological medicinal products obtained by microbial culture, cell culture or propagation in embryos and animals should be based on a system of master and working seed lots and/or cell banks.

28 The number of generations (doublings, passages) between the seed lot or cell bank and the finished product should be consistent with the marketing authorisation dossier. Scaling up of the process should not change this fundamental relationship.

29   Seed lots and cell banks should be adequately characterised and tested for contaminants. Their suitability for use should be further demonstrated by the consistency of the characteristics and quality of the successive batches of product. Seed lots and cell banks should be established, stored and used in such a way as to minimise the risks of contamination or alteration.

30   Establishment of the seed lot and cell bank should be performed in a suitably controlled environment to protect the seed lot and the cell bank and, if applicable, the personnel handling it. During the establishment of the seed lot and cell bank, no other living or infectious material (e.g. virus, cell lines or cell strains) should be handled simultaneously in the same area or by the same persons.

31   Evidence of the stability and recovery of the seeds and banks should be documented. Storage containers should be hermetically sealed, clearly labelled and kept at an appropriate temperature. An inventory should be meticulously kept. Storage temperature should be recorded continuously for freezers and properly monitored for liquid nitrogen. Any deviation from set limits and any corrective action taken should be recorded.

32   Only authorised personnel should be allowed to handle the material and this handling should be done under the supervision of a responsible person. Access to stored material should be controlled. Different seed lots or cell banks should be stored in such a way to avoid confusion or cross-contamination. It is desirable to split the seed lots and cell banks and to store the parts at different locations so as to minimise the risks of total loss.

33   All containers of master or working cell banks and seed lots should be treated identically during storage. Once removed from storage, the containers should not be returned to the stock.

Operating principles

34   The growth promoting properties of culture media should be demonstrated.

35   Addition of materials or cultures to fermenters and other vessels and the taking of samples should be carried out under carefully controlled conditions to ensure that absence of contamination is maintained. Care should be taken to ensure that vessels are correctly connected when addition or sampling take place.

36   Centrifugation and blending of products can lead to aerosol formation, and containment of such activities to prevent transfer of live micro-organisms is necessary.

37   If possible, media should be sterilised in situ. In-line sterilising filters for routine addition of gases, media, acids or alkalis, defoaming agents etc. to fermenters should be used where possible.

38   Careful consideration should be given to the validation of any necessary virus removal or inactivation undertaken (see CPMP notes for guidance).

39   In cases where a virus inactivation or removal process is performed during manufacture, measures should be taken to avoid the risk of recontamination of treated products by non-treated products.

40   A wide variety of equipment is used for chromatography, and in general such equipment should be dedicated to the purification of one product and should be sterilised or sanitised between batches. The use of the same equipment at different stages of processing should be discouraged. Acceptance criteria, life span and sanitation or sterilisation method of columns should be defined.

Quality Control

41   In-process controls play a specially important role in ensuring the consistency of the quality of biological medicinal products. Those controls, which are crucial for quality (e.g. virus removal) but which cannot be carried out on the finished product, should be performed at an appropriate stage of production.

42   It may be necessary to retain samples of intermediate products in sufficient quantities and under appropriate storage conditions to allow the repetition or confirmation of a batch control.

43   Continuous monitoring of certain production processes is necessary, for example fermentation. Such data should form part of the batch record.

44   Where continuous culture is used, special consideration should be given to the quality control requirements arising from this type of production method.

ANNEX 3 MANUFACTURE OF RADIOPHARMACEUTICALS

Principle

The manufacturing and handling of radiopharmaceuticals is potentially hazardous. The level of risk depends in particular upon the types of radiation emitted and the half-lives of the radioactive isotopes. Particular attention must be paid to the prevention of cross-contamination, to the retention of radionuclide contaminants, and to waste disposal.

Special consideration may be necessary with reference to the small batch sizes made frequently for many radiopharmaceuticals. Due to their short half-life, some radiopharmaceuticals are released before completion of certain Quality Control tests. In this case, the continuous assessment of the effectiveness of the Quality Assurance system becomes very important.

Note: *Manufacture must comply with the requirements of EURATOM Directives laying down the basic standards for the health protection of the general public and workers against the dangers of ionising radiation, as well as complying with other relevant national requirements.*

Personnel

1   All personnel (including those concerned with cleaning and maintenance) employed in areas where radioactive products are manufactured should receive additional training specific to this class of products. In particular, they should be given detailed information and appropriate training on radiation protection.

Premises and Equipment

2   Radioactive products should be stored, processed, packaged and controlled in dedicated and self-contained facilities. The equipment used for manufacturing operations should be reserved exclusively for radiopharmaceuticals.

3   In order to contain the radioactive particles, it may be necessary for the air pressure to be lower where products are exposed than in surrounding areas. However, it is still necessary to protect the product from environmental contamination.

4   For sterile products the working zone where products or containers may be exposed should comply with the environmental requirements described in the Supplement on Sterile Products. This may be achieved by the provision within the work station of a laminar flow of HEPA-filtered air and by fitting

air-locks to entry ports. Total containment work stations may provide these requirements. They should be in an environment conforming to at least grade D.

5   Air extracted from areas where radioactive products are handled should not be re-circulated; air outlets should be designed to avoid possible environmental contamination by radioactive particles and gases.

There should be a system to prevent air entering the clean area through extract ducts e.g. when the extract fan is not operating.

Production

6   Production of different radioactive products in the same work stations and at the same time should be avoided in order to minimise the risk of cross-contamination or mix-up.

7   Process validation, in-process controls and monitoring of process parameters and environment, assume particular importance in cases where it is necessary to take the decision to release or reject a batch or a product before all tests are completed.

Quality Control

8   When products have to be dispatched before all tests are completed, this does not obviate the need for a formal recorded decision to be taken by the Qualified Person on the conformity of the batch. In this case there should be a written procedure detailing all production and Quality Control data which should be considered before the batch is dispatched. A procedure should also describe the measures to be taken by the Qualified Person if unsatisfactory test results are obtained after dispatch.

9   Unless otherwise specified in the marketing authorisation, reference samples of every batch should be retained.

Distribution and Recalls

10   Detailed distribution records should be maintained and there should be procedures which describe the measures to be taken for stopping the use of defective radiopharmaceuticals. Recall operations should be shown to be operable within a very short time.

ANNEX 4 MANUFACTURE OF VETERINARY MEDICINAL PRODUCTS OTHER THAN IMMUNOLOGICAL VETERINARY MEDICINAL PRODUCTS

Note: *This annex applies to all veterinary medicinal products falling within the scope of Directive 2001/82/EC other than immunological veterinary medicinal products, which are the subject of a separate annex.*

Manufacture of Premixes for Medicated Feedingstuffs

For the purposes of these paragraphs,

- *a medicated feedingstuff* is any mixture of a veterinary medicinal product or products and feed or feeds which is ready prepared for marketing and intended to be fed to animals without further processing because of its curative or preventative properties or other properties as a medicinal product covered by Article 1(2) of Directive 2001/82/EC;
- *a pre-mix for medicated feedingstuffs* is any veterinary medicinal product prepared in advance with a view to the subsequent manufacture of medicated feedingstuffs.

1   The manufacture of premixes for medicated feedingstuffs requires the use of large quantities of vegetable matter which is likely to attract insects and rodents. Premises should be designed, equipped and operated to minimise this risk (point 3.4) and should also be subject to a regular pest control programme.

2   Because of the large volume of dust generated during the production of bulk material for premixes, specific attention should be given to the need to avoid cross-contamination and facilitate cleaning (point 3.14), for example through the installation of sealed transport systems and dust extraction, whenever possible. The installation of such systems does not, however, eliminate the need for regular cleaning of production areas.

3   Parts of the process likely to have a significant adverse influence on the stability of the active ingredient(s) (e.g. use of steam in pellet manufacture) should be carried out in an uniform manner from batch to batch.

4   Consideration should be given to undertake the manufacture of premixes in dedicated areas which, if at all possible, do not form part of a main manufacturing plant. Alternatively, such dedicated areas should be surrounded by a buffer zone in order to minimise the risk of contamination of other manufacturing areas.

Manufacture of Ectoparasiticides

5   In derogation from point 3.6, ectoparasiticides for external application to animals, which are veterinary medicinal products, and subject to marketing authorisation, may be produced and filled on a campaign basis in pesticide specific areas. However other categories of veterinary medicinal products should not be produced in such areas.

6   Adequate validated cleaning procedures should be employed to prevent cross-contamination, and steps should be taken to ensure the secure storage of the veterinary medicinal product in accordance with the guide.

Manufacture of Veterinary Medicinal Products Containing Penicillins

7   The use of penicillins in veterinary medicine does not present the same risks of hypersensitivity in animals as in humans. Although incidents of hypersensitivity have been recorded in horses and dogs, there are other materials which are toxic to certain species, e.g. the ionophore antibiotics in horses. Although desirable, the requirements that such products be manufactured in dedicated, self-contained facilities (point 3.6) may be dispensed with in the case of facilities dedicated to the manufacture of veterinary medicinal products only. However, all necessary measures should be taken to avoid cross-contamination and any risk to operator safety in accordance with the guide. In such circumstances, penicillin-containing products should be manufactured on a campaign basis and should be followed by appropriate, validated decontamination and cleaning procedures.

Retention of Samples (point 1.4 viii and point 6.14)

8   It is recognised that because of the large volume of certain veterinary medicinal products in their final packaging, in particular premixes, it may not be feasible for manufacturers to retain samples from each batch in its final packaging. However, manufacturers should ensure that sufficient representative samples of each batch are retained and stored in accordance with the guide.

9   In all cases, the container used for storage should be composed of the same material as the market primary container in which the product is marketed.

Sterile Veterinary Medicinal Products

10   Where this has been accepted by the competent authorities, terminally sterilised veterinary medicinal products may be manufactured in a clean area of a lower grade than the grade required in the annex on "Sterile preparations," but at least in a grade D environment.

ANNEX 5 MANUFACTURE OF IMMUNOLOGICAL VETERINARY MEDICINAL PRODUCTS

Principle

The manufacture of immunological veterinary medicinal products has special characteristics which should be taken into consideration when implementing and assessing the quality assurance system.

Due to the large number of animal species and related pathogenic agents, the variety of products manufactured is very wide and the volume of manufacture is often low; hence, work on a campaign basis is common. Moreover, because of the very nature of this manufacture (cultivation steps, lack of terminal sterilisation, etc.), the products must be particularly well-protected against contamination and cross-contamination. The environment also must be protected especially when the manufacture involves the use of pathogenic or exotic biological agents and the worker must be particularly well-protected when the manufacture involves the use of biological agents pathogenic to man.

These factors, together with the inherent variability of immunological products and the relative inefficiency in particular of final product quality control tests in providing adequate information about products, means that the role of the quality assurance system is of the utmost importance. The need to maintain control over all of the following aspects of GMP, as well as those outlined in this Guide, cannot be overemphasised. In particular, it is important that the data generated by the monitoring of the various aspects of GMP (equipment, premises, product, etc.) are rigorously assessed and informed decisions, leading to appropriate action, are made and recorded.

Personnel

1   All personnel (including those concerned with cleaning and maintenance) employed in areas where immunological products are manufactured should be given training in and information on hygiene and microbiology. They should receive additional training specific to the products with which they work.

2   Responsible personnel should be formally trained in some or all of the following fields: bacteriology, biology, biometry, chemistry, immunology, medicine, parasitology, pharmacy, pharmacology, virology and veterinary medicine and should also have an adequate knowledge of environmental protection measures.

3   Personnel should be protected against possible infection with the biological agents used in manufacture. In the case of biological agents known to cause disease in humans, adequate measures should be taken to prevent infection of personnel working with the agent or with experimental animals.

Where relevant, the personnel should be vaccinated and subject to medical examination.

4   Adequate measures should be taken to prevent biological agents being taken outside the manufacturing plant by personnel acting as a carrier. Dependent on the type of biological agent, such measures may include complete change of clothes and compulsory showering before leaving the production area.

5   For immunological products, the risk of contamination or cross-contamination by personnel is particularly important.

Prevention of *contamination* by personnel should be achieved by a set of measures and procedures to ensure that appropriate protective clothing is used during the different stages of the production process.

Prevention of *cross-contamination* by personnel involved in production should be achieved by a set of measures and procedures to ensure that they do not pass from one area to another unless they have taken appropriate measures to eliminate the risk of contamination. In the course of a working day, personnel should not pass from areas where contamination with live micro-organisms is likely or where animals are housed to premises where other products or organisms are handled. If such passage is unavoidable, clearly defined decontamination procedures, including change of clothing and shoes, and, where necessary, showering, should be followed by staff involved in any such production.

Personnel entering a contained area where organisms had not been handled in open circuit operations in the previous twelve hours to check on cultures in sealed, surface decontaminated flasks would not be regarded as being at risk of contamination, unless the organism involved was an exotic.

Premises

6   Premises should be designed in such a way as to control both the risk to the product and to the environment.

This can be achieved by the use of containment, clean, clean/contained or controlled areas.

7   Live biological agents should be handled in contained areas. The level of containment should depend on the pathogenicity of the micro-organism

and whether it has been classified as exotic. (Other relevant legislation, such as Directives 90/219/EEC[1] and 90/220/EEC,[2] also applies).

8   Inactivated biological agents should be handled in clean areas. Clean areas should also be used when handling non-infected cells isolated from multi-cellular organisms and, in some cases, filtration-sterilised media.

9   Open circuit operations involving products or components not subsequently sterilised should be carried out within a laminar air flow work station (grade A) in a grade B area.

10   Other operations where live biological agents are handled (quality control, research and diagnostic services, etc.) should be appropriately contained and separated if production operations are carried out in the same building. The level of containment should depend on the pathogenicity of the biological agent and whether they have been classified as exotic. Whenever diagnostic activities are carried out, there is the risk of introducing highly pathogenic organisms. Therefore, the level of containment should be adequate to cope with all such risks. Containment may also be required if quality control or other activities are carried out in buildings in close proximity to those used for production.

11   Containment premises should be easily disinfected and should have the following characteristics:

(a) the absence of direct venting to the outside;
(b) a ventilation with air at negative pressure. Air should be extracted through HEPA filters and not be re circulated except to the same area, and provided further HEPA filtration is used (normally this condition would be met by routing the re circulated air through the normal supply HEPAs for that area). However, recycling of air between areas may be permissible provided that it passes through two exhaust HEPAs, the first of which is continuously monitored for integrity, and there are adequate measures for safe venting of exhaust air should this filter fail;
(c) air from manufacturing areas used for the handling of exotic organisms should be vented through 2 sets of HEPA filters in series, and that from production areas not re-circulated;

---

[1] Council Directive 98/81/EC of 26 October 1998 amending Directive 90/219/EEC on the contained use of genetically modified micro-organisms (OJ L 330, 05.12.1998, p. 13–31).

[2] Directive 2001/18/EC of the European Parliament and of the Council of 12 March 2001 on the deliberate release into the environment of genetically modified organisms and repealing Council Directive 90/220/EEC – Commission Declaration (OJ L 106, 17.04.2001, p. 01–39).

(d) a system for the collection and disinfection of liquid effluents including contaminated condensate from sterilizers, biogenerators, etc. Solid wastes, including animal carcasses, should be disinfected, sterilized or incinerated as appropriate. Contaminated filters should be removed using a safe method;

(e) changing rooms designed and used as air locks, and equipped with washing and showering facilities if appropriate. Air pressure differentials should be such that there is no flow of air between the work area and the external environment or risk of contamination of outer clothing worn outside the area;

(f) an air lock system for the passage of equipment, which is constructed so that there is no flow of contaminated air between the work area and the external environment or risk of contamination of equipment within the lock. The air lock should be of a size which enables the effective surface decontamination of materials being passed through it. Consideration should be given to having a timing device on the door interlock to allow sufficient time for the decontamination process to be effective.

(g) in many instances, a barrier double-door autoclave for the secure removal of waste materials and introduction of sterile items.

12 Equipment passes and changing rooms should have an interlock mechanism or other appropriate system to prevent the opening of more than one door at a time. Changing rooms should be supplied with air filtered to the same standard as that for the work area, and equipped with air extraction facilities to produce an adequate air circulation independent of that of the work area. Equipment passes should normally be ventilated in the same way, but unventilated passes, or those equipped with supply air only, may be acceptable.

13 Production operations such as cell maintenance, media preparation, virus culture, etc. likely to cause contamination should be performed in separate areas. Animals and animal products should be handled with appropriate precautions.

14 Production areas where biological agents particularly resistant to disinfection (e.g. spore-forming bacteria) are handled should be separated and dedicated to that particular purpose until the biological agents have been inactivated.

15 With the exception of blending and subsequent filling operations, one biological agent only should be handled at a time within an area.

16 Production areas should be designed to permit disinfection between campaigns, using validated methods.

17 Production of biological agents may take place in controlled areas provided it is carried out in totally enclosed and heat sterilised equipment,

all connections being also heat sterilised after making and before breaking. It may be acceptable for connections to be made under local laminar air flow provided these are few in number and proper aseptic techniques are used and there is no risk of leakage. The sterilisation parameters used before breaking the connections must be validated for the organisms being used. Different products may be placed in different biogenerators, within the same area, provided that there is no risk of accidental cross-contamination. However, organisms generally subject to special requirements for containment should be in areas dedicated to such products.

18   Animal houses where animals intended or used for production are accommodated, should be provided with the appropriate containment and/or clean area measures, and should be separate from other animal accommodation.

   Animal houses where animals used for quality control, involving the use of pathogenic biological agents, are accommodated, should be adequately contained.

19   Access to manufacturing areas should be restricted to authorised personnel. Clear and concise written procedures should be posted as appropriate.

20   Documentation relating to the premises should be readily available in a plant master file.

   The manufacturing site and buildings should be described in sufficient detail (by means of plans and written explanations) so that the designation and conditions of use of all the rooms are correctly identified as well as the biological agents which are handled in them. The flow of people and product should also be clearly marked.

   The animal species accommodated in the animal houses or otherwise on the site should be identified.

   The activities carried out in the vicinity of the site should also be indicated. Plans of contained and/or clean area premises, should describe the ventilation system indicating inlets and outlets, filters and their specifications, the number of air changes per hour, and pressure gradients. They should indicate which pressure gradients are monitored by pressure indicator.

Equipment

21   The equipment used should be designed and constructed so that it meets the particular requirements for the manufacture of each product.

   Before being put into operation the equipment should be qualified and validated and subsequently be regularly maintained and validated.

22   Where appropriate, the equipment should ensure satisfactory primary containment of the biological agents.

Where appropriate, the equipment should be designed and constructed as to allow easy and effective decontamination and/or sterilisation.

23   Closed equipment used for the primary containment of the biological agents should be designed and constructed as to prevent any leakage or the formation of droplets and aerosols.

Inlets and outlets for gases should be protected so as to achieve adequate containment e.g. by the use of sterilising hydrophobic filters.

The introduction or removal of material should take place using a sterilisable closed system, or possibly in an appropriate laminar air flow.

24   Equipment where necessary should be properly sterilised before use, preferably by pressurised dry steam. Other methods can be accepted if steam sterilisation cannot be used because of the nature of the equipment. It is important not to overlook such individual items as bench centrifuges and water baths.

Equipment used for purification, separation or concentration should be sterilised or disinfected at least between use for different products. The effect of the sterilisation methods on the effectiveness and validity of the equipment should be studied in order to determine the life span of the equipment.

All sterilisation procedures should be validated.

25   Equipment should be designed so as to prevent any mix-up between different organisms or products. Pipes, valves and filters should be identified as to their function.

Separate incubators should be used for infected and non infected containers and also generally for different organisms or cells. Incubators containing more than one organism or cell type will only be acceptable if adequate steps are taken to seal, surface decontaminate and segregate the containers. Culture vessels, etc. should be individually labelled. The cleaning and disinfection of the items can be particularly difficult and should receive special attention.

Equipment used for the storage of biological agents or products should be designed and used in such a manner as to prevent any possible mix-up. All stored items should be clearly and unambiguously labelled and in leak-proof containers. Items such as cells and organisms seed stock should be stored in dedicated equipment.

26   Relevant equipment, such as that requiring temperature control, should be fitted with recording and/or alarm systems.

To avoid breakdowns, a system of preventive maintenance, together with trend analysis of recorded data, should be implemented.

27   The loading of freeze dryers requires an appropriate clean/contained area.

Unloading freeze dryers contaminates the immediate environment. Therefore, for single-ended freeze dryers, the clean room should be decontaminated before a further manufacturing batch is introduced into the area, unless this contains the same organisms, and double door freeze dryers should be sterilised after each cycle unless opened in a clean area.

Sterilisation of freeze dryers should be done in accordance with item 24. In case of campaign working, they should at least be sterilised after each campaign.

Animals and Animal Houses

28   General requirements for animal quarters, care and quarantine are laid down in Directive 86/609/EEC[3].

29   Animal houses should be separated from the other production premises and suitably designed.

30   The sanitary status of the animals used for production should be defined, monitored, and recorded. Some animals should be handled as defined in specific monographs (e.g. Specific Pathogen Free flocks).

31   Animals, biological agents, and tests carried out should be the subject of an identification system so as to prevent any risk of confusion and to control all possible hazards.

Disinfection–Waste Disposal

32   Disinfection and/or wastes and effluents disposal may be particularly important in the case of manufacture of immunological products. Careful consideration should therefore be given to procedures and equipment aiming at avoiding environmental contamination as well as to their validation or qualification.

---

[3] Directive 2003/65/EC of the European Parliament and of the Council of 22 July 2003 amending Council Directive 86/609/EEC on the approximation of laws, regulations and administrative provisions of the Member States regarding the protection of animals used for experimental and other scientific purposes (OJ L 230 , 16.09.2003, p. 32–33).

Production

33 Because of the wide variety of products, the frequently large number of stages involved in the manufacture of immunological veterinary medicinal products and the nature of the biological processes, careful attention must be paid to adherence to validated operating procedures, to the constant monitoring of production at all stages and to in-process controls.

Additionally, special consideration should be given to starting materials, media and the use of a seed lot system.

Starting Materials

34 The suitability of starting materials should be clearly defined in written specifications. These should include details of the supplier, the method of manufacture, the geographical origin and the animal species from which the materials are derived. The controls to be applied to starting materials must be included. Microbiological controls are particularly important.

35 The results of tests on starting materials must comply with the specifications. Where the tests take a long time (e.g. eggs from SPF flocks) it may be necessary to process starting materials before the results of analytical controls are available. In such cases, the release of a finished product is conditional upon satisfactory results of the tests on starting materials.

36 Special attention should be paid to a knowledge of the supplier's quality assurance system in assessing the suitability of a source and the extent of quality control testing required.

37 Where possible, heat is the preferred method for sterilising starting materials. If necessary, other validated methods, such as irradiation, may be used.

Media

38 The ability of media to support the desired growth should be properly validated in advance.

39 Media should preferably be sterilised in situ or in line. Heat is the preferred method. Gases, media, acids, alkalis, de-foaming agents and other materials introduced into sterile biogenerators should themselves be sterile.

Seed lot and cell bank system

40 In order to prevent the unwanted drift of properties which might ensue from repeated subcultures or multiple generations, the production of

immunological veterinary medicinal products obtained by microbial, cell or tissue culture, or propagation in embryos and animals, should be based on a system of seed lots or cell banks.

41   The number of generations (doublings, passages) between the seed lot or cell bank and the finished product should be consistent with the dossier of authorisation for marketing.

42   Seed lots and cell banks should be adequately characterised and tested for contaminants. Acceptance criteria for new seed lots should be established. Seed lots and cell banks shall be established, stored and used in such a way as to minimise the risks of contamination, or any alteration. During the establishment of the seed lot and cell bank, no other living or infectious material (e.g. virus or cell lines) shall be handled simultaneously in the same area or by the same person.

43   Establishment of the seed lot and cell bank should be performed in a suitable environment to protect the seed lot and the cell bank and, if applicable, the personnel handling it and the external environment.

44   The origin, form and storage conditions of seed material should be described in full. Evidence of the stability and recovery of the seeds and cells should be provided. Storage containers should be hermetically sealed, clearly labelled and stored at an appropriate temperature. Storage conditions shall be properly monitored. An inventory should be kept and each container accounted for.

45   Only authorised personnel should be allowed to handle the material and this handling should be done under the supervision of a responsible person. Different seed lots or cell banks shall be stored in such a way to avoid confusion or cross-contamination errors. It is desirable to split the seed lots and cell banks and to store the parts at different locations so as to minimise the risk of total loss.

Operating principles

46   The formation of droplets and the production of foam should be avoided or minimised during manufacturing processes. Centrifugation and blending procedures which can lead to droplet formation should be carried out in appropriate contained or clean/contained areas to prevent transfer of live organisms.

47   Accidental spillages, especially of live organisms, must be dealt with quickly and safely. Validated decontamination measures should be available for each organism. Where different strains of single bacteria species or very similar viruses are involved, the process need be validated against only one

of them, unless there is reason to believe that they may vary significantly in their resistance to the agent(s) involved.

48   Operations involving the transfer of materials such as sterile media, cultures or product should be carried out in pre-sterilised closed systems wherever possible. Where this is not possible, transfer operations must be protected by laminar airflow work stations.

49   Addition of media or cultures to biogenerators and other vessels should be carried out under carefully controlled conditions to ensure that contamination is not introduced. Care must be taken to ensure that vessels are correctly connected when addition of cultures takes place.

50   Where necessary, for instance when two or more fermenters are within a single area, sampling and addition ports, and connectors (after connection, before the flow of product, and again before disconnection) should be sterilised with steam. In other circumstances, chemical disinfection of ports and laminar air flow protection of connections may be acceptable.

51   Equipment, glassware, the external surfaces of product containers and other such materials must be disinfected before transfer from a contained area using a validated method (see item 47 above). Batch documentation can be a particular problem. Only the absolute minimum required to allow operations to GMP standards should enter and leave the area. If obviously contaminated, such as by spills or aerosols, or if the organism involved is an exotic, the paperwork must be adequately disinfected through an equipment pass, or the information transferred out by such means as photocopy or fax.

52   Liquid or solid wastes such as the debris after harvesting eggs, disposable culture bottles, unwanted cultures or biological agents, are best sterilised or disinfected before transfer from a contained area. However, alternatives such as sealed containers or piping may be appropriate in some cases.

53   Articles and materials, including documentation, entering a production room should be carefully controlled to ensure that only articles and materials concerned with production are introduced. There should be a system which ensures that articles and materials entering a room are reconciled with those leaving so that their accumulation within the room does not occur.

54   Heat stable articles and materials entering a clean area or clean/contained area should do so through a double-ended autoclave or oven. Heat labile articles and materials should enter through an air-lock with interlocked doors where they are disinfected. Sterilisation of articles and materials elsewhere is acceptable provided that they are double wrapped and enter through an airlock with the appropriate precautions.

55 Precautions must be taken to avoid contamination or confusion during incubation. There should be a cleaning and disinfection procedure for incubators. Containers in incubators should be carefully and clearly labelled.

56 With the exception of blending and subsequent filling operations (or when totally enclosed systems are used) only one live biological agent may be handled within a production room at any given time. Production rooms must be effectively disinfected between the handling of different live biological agents.

57 Products should be inactivated by the addition of inactivant accompanied by sufficient agitation. The mixture should then be transferred to a second sterile vessel, unless the container is of such a size and shape as to be easily inverted and shaken so as to wet all internal surfaces with the final culture/inactivant mixture.

58 Vessels containing inactivated products should not be opened or sampled in areas containing live biological agents. All subsequent processing of inactivated products should take place in clean areas grade A-B or enclosed equipment dedicated to inactivated products.

59 Careful consideration should be given to the validation of methods for sterilisation, disinfection, virus removal and inactivation.

60 Filling should be carried out as soon as possible following production. Containers of bulk product prior to filling should be sealed, appropriately labelled and stored under specified conditions of temperature.

61 There should be a system to assure the integrity and closure of containers after filling.

62 The capping of vials containing live biological agents must be performed in such a way that ensures that contamination of other products or escape of the live agents into other areas or the external environment does not occur.

63 For various reasons there may be a delay between the filling of final containers and their labelling and packaging. Procedures should be specified for the storage of unlabelled containers in order to prevent confusion and to ensure satisfactory storage conditions. Special attention should be paid to the storage of heat labile or photosensitive products. Storage temperatures should be specified.

64 For each stage of production, the yield of product should be reconciled with that expected from that process. Any significant discrepancies should be investigated.

Quality control

65 In-process controls play a specially important role in ensuring the consistency of the quality of biological medicinal products. Those controls which are crucial for the quality (e.g. virus removal) but which cannot be carried out on the finished product, should be performed at an appropriate stage of production.

66 It may be necessary to retain samples of intermediate products in sufficient amount and under appropriate storage conditions to allow repetition or confirmation of a batch control.

67 There may be a requirement for the continuous monitoring of data during a production process, for example monitoring of physical parameters during fermentation.

68 Continuous culture of biological products is a common practice and special consideration needs to be given to the quality control requirements arising from this type of production method.

ANNEX 6 MANUFACTURE OF MEDICINAL GASES

1   Principle

This annex deals with industrial manufacturing of medicinal gases, which is a specialised industrial process not normally undertaken by pharmaceutical companies. It does not cover manufacturing and handling of medicinal gases in hospitals, which will be subject to national legislation. However relevant parts of this annex may be used as a basis for such activities.

The manufacture of medicinal gases is generally carried out in closed equipment. Consequently, environmental contamination of the product is minimal. However, there is a risk of cross-contamination with other gases.

Manufacture of medicinal gases should comply with the basic requirements of GMP, with applicable annexes, Pharmacopoeial standards and the following detailed guidelines.

2   Personnel

2.1   The qualified person responsible for release of medicinal gases should have a thorough knowledge of the production and control of medicinal gases.

2.2   All personnel involved in the manufacture of medicinal gases should understand the GMP requirements relevant to medicinal gases and should be aware of the critically important aspects and potential hazards for patients from products in the form of medicinal gases.

3   Premises and Equipment

3.1   Premises

3.1.1   Medicinal gases should be filled in a separate area from non-medicinal gases and there should be no exchange of containers between these areas. In exceptional cases, the principal of campaign filling in the same area can be accepted provided that specific precautions are taken and necessary validation is done.

3.1.2   Premises should provide sufficient space for manufacturing, testing and storage operations to avoid the risk of mix-up. Premises should be clean and tidy to encourage orderly working and adequate storage.

3.1.3   Filling areas should be of sufficient size and have an orderly layout to provide:

(a) separate marked areas for different gases;

(**b**) clear identification and segregation of empty cylinders and cylinders at various stages of processing (e.g. "awaiting filling", "filled", "quarantine", "approved", "rejected").

The method used to achieve these various levels of segregation will depend on the nature, extent and complexity of the overall operation, but marked-out floor areas, partitions, barriers and signs could be used or other appropriate means.

3.2   Equipment

3.2.1   All equipment for manufacture and analyses should be qualified and calibrated regularly as appropriate.

3.2.2   It is necessary to ensure that the correct gas is put into the correct container. Except for validated automated filling processes there should be no interconnections between pipelines carrying different gases. The manifolds should be equipped with fill connections that correspond only to the valve for that particular gas or particular mixture of gases so that only the correct containers can be attached to the manifold. (The use of manifold and container valve connections may be subject to international or national standards.)

3.2.3   Repair and maintenance operations should not affect the quality of the medicinal gases.

3.2.4   Filling of non-medicinal gases should be avoided in areas and with equipment destined for the production of medicinal gases. Exceptions can be acceptable if the quality of the gas used for non-medicinal purposes is at least equal to the quality of the medicinal gas and GMP-standards are maintained. There should be a validated method of backflow prevention in the line supplying the filling area for non-medicinal gases to prevent contamination of the medicinal gas.

3.2.5   Storage tanks and mobile delivery tanks should be dedicated to one gas and a well-defined quality of this gas. However liquefied medicinal gases may be stored or transported in the same tanks as the same non-medicinal gas provided that the quality of the latter is at least equal to the quality of the medicinal gas.

4   Documentation

4.1   Data included in the records for each batch of cylinders filled must ensure that each filled cylinder is traceable to significant aspects of the relevant filling operations. As appropriate, the following should be entered:

- the name of the product;
- the date and the time of the filling operations;
- a reference to the filling station used;
- equipment used;
- name and reference to the specification of the gas or each gas in a mixture;
- pre filling operations performed (see point 5.3.5);
- the quantity and size of cylinders before and after filling;
- the name of the person carrying out the filling operation;
- the initials of the operators for each significant step (line clearance, receipt of cylinders, emptying of cylinders etc.);
- key parameters that are needed to ensure correct fill at standard conditions;
- the results of quality control tests and where test equipment is calibrated before each test, the reference gas specification and calibration check results;
- results of appropriate checks to ensure the containers have been filled;
- a sample of the batch code label;
- details of any problems or unusual events, and signed authorisation for any deviation from filling instructions;
- to indicate agreement, the date and signature of the supervisor responsible for the filling operation.

5 Production

5.1 All critical steps in the different manufacturing processes should be subject to validation.

5.2 Bulk Production

5.2.1 Bulk gases intended for medicinal use could be prepared by chemical synthesis or obtained from natural resources followed by purification steps if necessary (as for example in an air separation plant). These gases could be regarded as Active Pharmaceutical Ingredients (API) or as bulk pharmaceutical products as decided by the national competent authority.

5.2.2 Documentation should be available specifying the purity, other components and possible impurities that may be present in the source gas and at purification steps, as applicable. Flow charts of each different process should be available.

5.2.3 All separation and purification steps should be designed to operate at optimal effectiveness. For example, impurities that may adversely affect a purification step should be removed before this step is reached.

5.2.4   Separation and purification steps should be validated for effectiveness and monitored according to the results of the validation. Where necessary, in-process controls should include continuous analysis to monitor the process. Maintenance and replacement of expendable equipment components, e.g. purification filters, should be based on the results of monitoring and validation.

5.2.5   If applicable, limits for process temperatures should be documented and in-process monitoring should include temperature measurement.

5.2.6   Computer systems used in controlling or monitoring processes should be validated.

5.2.7   For continuous processes, a definition of a batch should be documented and related to the analysis of the bulk gas.

5.2.8   Gas production should be continuously monitored for quality and impurities.

5.2.9   Water used for cooling during compression of air should be monitored for microbiological quality when in contact with the medicinal gas.

5.2.10   All the transfer operations, including controls before transfers, of liquefied gases from primary storage should be in accordance with written procedures designed to avoid any contamination. The transfer line should be equipped with a non-return valve or other suitable alternative. Particular attention should be paid to purge the flexible connections and to coupling hoses and connectors.

5.2.11   Deliveries of gas may be added to bulk storage tanks containing the same gas from previous deliveries. The results of a sample must show that the quality of the delivered gas is acceptable. Such a sample could be taken from:

 • the delivered gas before the delivery is added; or
 • from the bulk tank after adding and mixing

5.2.12   Bulk gases intended for medicinal use should be defined as a batch, controlled in accordance with relevant Pharmacopoeial monographs and released for filling.

5.3   Filling and labelling

5.3.1   For filling of medicinal gases the batch should be defined.

5.3.2   Containers for medicinal gases should conform to appropriate technical specifications. Valve outlets should be equipped with tamper-evident seals after filling. Cylinders should preferably have minimum retention valves in order to get adequate protection against contamination.

5.3.3 The medicinal gases filling manifold as well as the cylinders should be dedicated to a single medicinal gas or to a given mixture of medicinal gases (see also point 3.2.2). There should be a system in place ensuring traceability of cylinders and valves.

5.3.4 Cleaning and purging of filling equipment and pipelines should be carried out according to written procedures. This is especially important after maintenance or breaches of system integrity. Checks for the absence of contaminants should be carried out before the line is released for use. Records should be maintained.

5.3.5 Cylinders should be subject to an internal visual inspection when:

- they are new
- in connection with any hydrostatic pressure test or equivalent test

After fitting of the valve, the valve should be maintained in a closed position to prevent any contamination from entering the cylinder.

5.3.6 Checks to be performed before filling should include:

- a check to determine the residual pressure (> 3 to 5 bar) to ensure that the cylinder is not emptied;
- cylinders with no residual pressure should be put aside for additional measures to make sure they are not contaminated with water or other contaminants. These could include cleaning with validated methods or visual inspection as justified;
- assuring that all batch labels and other labels if damaged have been removed;
- visual external inspection of each valve and container for dents, arc burns, debris, other damage and contamination with oil or grease; cylinders should be cleaned, tested and maintained in an appropriate manner;
- a check of each cylinder or cryogenic vessel valve connection to determine that it is the proper type for the particular medicinal gas involved;
- a check of the cylinder "test code date" to determine that the hydrostatic pressure test or equivalent test has been conducted and still is valid as required by national or international guidelines;
- a check to determine that each container is colour-coded according to the relevant standard

5.3.7 Cylinders which have been returned for refilling should be prepared with great care in order to minimise risks for contamination. For compressed gases a maximum theoretical impurity of 500 ppm v/v should be obtained for a filling pressure of 200 bar (and equivalent for other filling pressures). Cylinders could be prepared as follows:

- any gas remaining in the cylinders should be removed by evacuating the container [at least to a remaining absolute pressure of 150 millibar] or
- by blowing down each container, followed by purging using validated methods (partial pressurisation at least to 7 bar and then blowing down).

For cylinders equipped with residual (positive) pressure valves, one evacuation under vacuum at 150 millibar is sufficient if the pressure is positive. As an alternative, full analysis of the remaining gas should be carried out for each individual container.

5.3.8 There should be appropriate checks to ensure that containers have been filled. An indication that it is filling properly could be to ensure that the exterior of the cylinder is warm by touching it lightly during filling.

5.3.9 Each cylinder should be labelled and colour-coded. The batch number and/or filling date and expiry date may be on a separate label.

6 Quality Control

6.1 Water used for hydrostatic pressure testing should be at least of drinking water quality and monitored routinely for microbiological contamination.

6.2 Each medicinal gas should be tested and released according to its specifications. In addition, each medicinal gas should be tested to full relevant pharmacopoeial requirements at sufficient frequency to assure ongoing compliance.

6.3 The bulk gas supply should be released for filling (see point 5.2.12).

6.4 In the case of a single medicinal gas filled via a multi-cylinder manifold, at least one cylinder of product from each manifold filling should be tested for identity, assay and if necessary water content each time the cylinders are changed on the manifold.

6.5 In the case of a single medicinal gas filled into cylinders one at a time by individual filling operations, at least one cylinder of each uninterrupted filling cycle should be tested for identity and assay. An example of an uninterrupted filling operation cycle is one shift's production using the same personnel, equipment, and batch of bulk gas.

6.6 In the case of a medicinal gas produced by mixing two or more different gases in a cylinder from the same manifold, at least one cylinder from each manifold filling operation cycle should be tested for identity, assay and if necessary water content of all of the component gases and for identity of the balance gas in the mixture. When cylinders are filled individually, every cylinder should be tested for identity and assay of all of the component gases and at least one cylinder of each uninterrupted filling cycle should be tested for identity of the balance gas in the mixture.

6.7   When gases are mixed in-line before filling (e.g. nitrous oxide/oxygen mixture) continuous analysis of the mixture being filled is required.

6.8   When a cylinder is filled with more than one gas, the filling process must ensure that the gases are correctly mixed in every cylinder and are fully homogeneous.

6.9   Each filled cylinder should be tested for leaks using an appropriate method, prior to fitting the tamper evident seal. Where sampling and testing is carried out the leak test should be completed after testing.

6.10   In the case of cryogenic gas filled into cryogenic home vessels for delivery to users, each vessel should be tested for identity and assay.

6.11   Cryogenic vessels which are retained by customers and where the medicinal gas is refilled in place from dedicated mobile delivery tanks need not be sampled after filling provided the filling company delivers a certificate of analysis for a sample taken from the mobile delivery tank. Cryogenic vessels retained by customers should be periodically tested to confirm that the contents comply with Pharmacopoeial requirements.

6.12   Retained samples are not required, unless otherwise specified.

7   Storage and Release

7.1   Filled cylinders should be held in quarantine until released by the qualified person.

7.2   Gas cylinders should be stored under cover and not be subjected to extremes of temperature. Storage areas should be clean, dry, well ventilated and free of combustible materials to ensure that cylinders remain clean up to the time of use.

7.3   Storage arrangements should permit segregation of different gases and of full/empty cylinders and permit rotation of stock on a first in - first out basis.

7.4   Gas cylinders should be protected from adverse weather conditions during transportation. Specific conditions for storage and transportation should be employed for gas mixtures for which phase separation occurs on freezing.

Glossary

Definition of terms relating to manufacture of medicinal gases, which are not given in the glossary of the current PIC/S Guide to GMP, but which are used in this Annex are given below.

Air separation plant

Air separation plants take atmospheric air and through processes of purification, cleaning, compression, cooling, liquefaction and distillation separates the air into the gases oxygen, nitrogen and argon

Area

Part of premises that is specific to the manufacture of medicinal gases

Blowing down

Blow the pressure down to atmospheric pressure

Bulk gas

Any gas intended for medicinal use, which has completed all processing up to but not including final packaging

Compressed gas

A gas which when packaged under pressure is entirely gaseous at −50°C. (ISO 10286)

Container

A container is a cryogenic vessel, a tank, a tanker, a cylinder, a cylinder bundle or any other package that is in direct contact with the medicinal gas

Cryogenic gas

Gas which liquefies at 1.013 bar at temperature below −150°C

Cryogenic vessel

A static or mobile thermally insulated container designed to contain liquefied or cryogenic gases; the gas is removed in gaseous or liquid form

Cylinder

A transportable, pressure container with a water capacity not exceeding 150 litres; in this document when using the word cylinder it includes cylinder bundle (or cylinder pack) when appropriate

Cylinder bundle

A set assembly of cylinders, which are fastened together in a frame and interconnected by a manifold, transported and used as a unit

Evacuate

To remove the residual gas in a container by pulling a vacuum on it

Gas

A substance or a mixture of substances that is completely gaseous at 1013 bar (101,325 kPa) and +15°C or has a vapour pressure exceeding 3 bar (300 kPa) at +50°C. (ISO 10286)

Hydrostatic pressure test

Test performed for safety reasons as required by national or international guideline in order to make sure that cylinders or tanks can withhold high pressures

Liquefied gas

A gas which when packaged under pressure, is partially liquid (gas over a liquid) at −50°C

Manifold

Equipment or apparatus designed to enable one or more gas containers to be emptied and filled at a time

Maximum theoretical residual impurity

Gaseous impurity coming from a possible retro-pollution and remaining after the cylinders pre-treatment before filling. The calculation of the maximum theoretical impurity is only relevant for compressed gases and supposes that these gases act as perfect gases

Medicinal gas

Any gas or mixture of gases intended to be administered to patients for therapeutic, diagnostic or prophylactic purposes using pharmacological action and classified as a medicinal product

Minimum pressure retention valve

Valve equipped with a non-return system which maintains a definite pressure (about 3 to 5 bar over atmospheric pressure) in order to prevent contamination during use

Non-return valve

Valve which permits flow in one direction only

Purge

To empty and clean a cylinder

- by blowing down and evacuating
  or
- by blowing down, partial pressurisation with the gas in question and then blowing down

Tank

Static container for the storage of liquefied or cryogenic gas

Tanker

Container fixed on a vehicle for the transport of liquefied or cryogenic gas

Valve

Device for opening and closing containers

ANNEX 7 MANUFACTURE OF HERBAL MEDICINAL PRODUCTS

Principle

Because of their often complex and variable nature, and the number and small quantity of defined active ingredients, control of starting materials, storage and processing assume particular importance in the manufacture of herbal medicinal products.

Premises

Storage areas

1   Crude (i.e. unprocessed) plants should be stored in separate areas. The storage area should be well ventilated and be equipped in such a way as to give protection against the entry of insects or other animals, especially rodents. Effective measures should be taken to prevent the spread of any such animals and micro-organisms brought in with the crude plant and to prevent cross-contamination. Containers should be located in such a way as to allow free air circulation.

2   Special attention should be paid to the cleanliness and good maintenance of the storage areas particularly when dust is generated.

3   Storage of plants, extracts, tinctures and other preparations may require special conditions of humidity, temperature or light protection; these conditions should be provided and monitored.

Production area

4   Specific provisions should be taken during sampling, weighing, mixing and processing operations of crude plants whenever dust is generated, to facilitate cleaning and to avoid cross-contamination, as for example, dust extraction, dedicated premises, etc.

Documentation

Specifications for starting materials

5   Apart from the data described in General Guide (Section II, Chapter 4, point 4.11), specifications for medicinal crude plants should include, as far as possible:

- the botanical name (with, if appropriate, the name of the originator of the classification, e.g. Linnaeus);
- the details of the source of the plant (country or region of origin, and where applicable, cultivation, time of harvesting, collection procedures, possible pesticides used, etc.);
- whether the whole plant or only a part is used;
- when a dried plant is purchased, the drying system should be specified;
- the description of the plant and its macro and microscopical examination;
- the suitable identification tests including, where appropriate, identification tests for known active ingredients, or markers. A reference authentic specimen should be available for identification purposes;
- the assay, where appropriate, of constituents of known therapeutic activity or of markers;
- the methods suitable to determine possible pesticide contamination and limits accepted;
- the tests to determine fungal and/or microbial contamination, including aflatoxins and pest-infestations, and limits accepted;
- the tests for toxic metals and for likely contaminants and adulterants;
- the tests for foreign materials.

Any treatment used to reduce fungal/microbial contamination or other infestation should be documented. Specifications for such procedures should be available and should include details of process, tests and limits for residues.

Processing instructions

6   The processing instructions should describe the different operations carried out upon the crude plant such as drying, crushing and sifting, and include drying time and temperatures, and methods used to control fragment or particle size. It should also describe security sieving or other methods of removing foreign materials.

For the production of a vegetable drug preparation, instructions should include details of base or solvent, time and temperatures of extraction, details of any concentration stages and methods used (see also the note for guidance "Quality of herbal remedies", Volume III of The rules governing medicinal products in the European Union).

Sampling

7   Due to the fact that crude drugs are an aggregate of individual plants and contain an element of heterogeneity, their sampling has to be carried out

with special care by personnel with particular expertise. Each batch should be identified by its own documentation.

Quality Control

8   Quality Control personnel should have particular expertise in herbal medicinal products in order to be able to carry out identification tests and recognise adulteration, the presence of fungal growth, infestations, non-uniformity within a delivery of crude plants, etc.

9   The identity and quality of vegetable drug preparations and of finished product should be tested as described in the note for guidance "Quality of herbal remedies".

ANNEX 8 SAMPLING OF STARTING AND PACKAGING MATERIALS

Principle

Sampling is an important operation in which only a small fraction of a batch is taken. Valid conclusions on the whole cannot be based on tests which have been carried out on non-representative samples. Correct sampling is thus an essential part of a system of Quality Assurance.

Note: *Sampling is dealt with in Chapter 6 of the Guide, items 6.11–6.14. This annex gives additional guidance on the sampling of starting and packaging materials.*

Personnel

1   Personnel who take samples should receive initial and on-going regular training in the disciplines relevant to correct sampling. This training should include:

- sampling plans;
- written sampling procedures;
- the techniques and equipment for sampling;
- the risks of cross-contamination;
- the precautions to be taken with regard to unstable and/or sterile substances;
- the importance of considering the visual appearance of materials, containers and labels;
- the importance of recording any unexpected or unusual circumstances.

Starting Materials

2   The identity of a complete batch of starting materials can normally only be ensured if individual samples are taken from all the containers and an identity test performed on each sample. It is permissible to sample only a proportion of the containers where a validated procedure has been established to ensure that no single container of starting material has been incorrectly labelled.

3   This validation should take account of at least the following aspects:

- the nature and status of the manufacturer and of the supplier and their understanding of the GMP requirements of the Pharmaceutical Industry;

- the Quality Assurance system of the manufacturer of the starting material;
- the manufacturing conditions under which the starting material is produced and controlled;
- the nature of the starting material and the medicinal products in which it will be used.

Under such a system, it is possible that a validated procedure exempting identity testing of each incoming container of starting material could be accepted for:

- starting materials coming from a single product manufacturer or plant;
- starting materials coming directly from a manufacturer or in the manufacturer's sealed container where there is a history of reliability and regular audits of the manufacturer's Quality Assurance system are conducted by the purchaser (the manufacturer of the medicinal product) or by an officially accredited body.

It is improbable that a procedure could be satisfactorily validated for:

- starting materials supplied by intermediaries such as brokers where the source of manufacture is unknown or not audited;
- starting materials for use in parenteral products.

4   The quality of a batch of starting materials may be assessed by taking and testing a representative sample. The samples taken for identity testing could be used for this purpose. The number of samples taken for the preparation of a representative sample should be determined statistically and specified in a sampling plan. The number of individual samples which may be blended to form a composite sample should also be defined, taking into account the nature of the material, knowledge of the supplier and the homogeneity of the composite sample.

Packaging Material

5   The sampling plan for packaging materials should take account of at least the following: the quantity received, the quality required, the nature of the material (e.g. primary packaging materials and/or printed packaging materials), the production methods, and what is known of the Quality Assurance system of the packaging materials manufacturer based on audits. The number of samples taken should be determined statistically and specified in a sampling plan.

ANNEX 9 MANUFACTURE OF LIQUIDS, CREAMS AND OINTMENTS

Principle

Liquids, creams and ointments may be particularly susceptible to microbial and other contamination during manufacture. Therefore special measures must be taken to prevent any contamination.

Premises and Equipment

1   The use of closed systems for processing and transfer is recommended in order to protect the product from contamination. Production areas where the products or open clean containers are exposed should normally be effectively ventilated with filtered air.

2   Tanks, containers, pipework and pumps should be designed and installed so that they may be readily cleaned and if necessary sanitised. In particular, equipment design should include a minimum of dead-legs or sites where residues can accumulate and promote microbial proliferation.

3   The use of glass apparatus should be avoided wherever possible. High quality stainless steel is often the material of choice for parts coming into contact with product.

Production

4   The chemical and microbiological quality of water used in production should be specified and monitored. Care should be taken in the maintenance of water systems in order to avoid the risk of microbial proliferation. After any chemical sanitisation of the water systems, a validated flushing procedure should be followed to ensure that the sanitising agent has been effectively removed.

5   The quality of materials received in bulk tankers should be checked before they are transferred to bulk storage tanks.

6   Care should be taken when transferring materials via pipelines to ensure that they are delivered to their correct destination.

7   Materials likely to shed fibres or other contaminants, like cardboard or wooden pallets, should not enter the areas where products or clean containers are exposed.

8   Care should be taken to maintain the homogeneity of mixtures, suspensions, etc. during filling. Mixing and filling processes should be validated. Special care should be taken at the beginning of a filling process, after stoppages and at the end of the process to ensure that homogeneity is maintained.

9   When the finished product is not immediately packaged, the maximum period of storage and the storage conditions should be specified and adhered to.

ANNEX 10 MANUFACTURE OF PRESSURISED METERED DOSE AEROSOL PREPARATIONS FOR INHALATION

Principle

The manufacture of pressurised aerosol products for inhalation with metering valves requires special consideration because of the particular nature of this form of product. It should be done under conditions which minimise microbial and particulate contamination. Assurance of the quality of the valve components and, in the case of suspensions, of uniformity is also of particular importance.

General

1   There are presently two common manufacturing and filling methods as follows:

   (a) Two-shot system (pressure filling). The active ingredient is suspended in a high boiling point propellant, the dose is put into the container, the valve is crimped on and the lower boiling point propellant is injected through the valve stem to make up the finished product. The suspension of active ingredient in propellant is kept cool to reduce evaporation loss.
   (b) One-shot process (cold filling). The active ingredient is suspended in a mixture of propellants and held either under high pressure or at a low temperature, or both. The suspension is then filled directly into the container in one shot.

Premises and Equipment

2   Manufacture and filling should be carried out as far as possible in a closed system.

3   Where products or clean components are exposed, the area should be fed with filtered air, should comply with the requirements of at least a Grade D environment and should be entered through airlocks.

Production and Quality Control

4   Metering valves for aerosols are more complex pieces of engineering than most items used in pharmaceutical production. Their specifications,

sampling and testing should recognise this. Auditing the Quality Assurance system of the valve manufacturer is of particular importance.

5   All fluids (e.g. liquid or gaseous propellants) should be filtered to remove particles greater than 0.2 micron. An additional filtration where possible immediately before filling is desirable.

6   Containers and valves should be cleaned using a validated procedure appropriate to the use of the product to ensure the absence of any contaminants such as fabrication aids (e.g. lubricants) or undue microbiological contaminants. After cleaning, valves should be kept in clean, closed containers and precautions taken not to introduce contamination during subsequent handling, e.g. taking samples. Containers should be fed to the filling line in a clean condition or cleaned on line immediately before filling.

7   Precautions should be taken to ensure uniformity of suspensions at the point of fill throughout the filling process.

8   When a two-shot filling process is used, it is necessary to ensure that both shots are of the correct weight in order to achieve the correct composition. For this purpose, 100% weight checking at each stage is often desirable.

9   Controls after filling should ensure the absence of undue leakage. Any leakage test should be performed in a way which avoids microbial contamination or residual moisture.

ANNEX 11 COMPUTERISED SYSTEMS

Principle

The introduction of computerised systems into systems of manufacturing, including storage, distribution and quality control does not alter the need to observe the relevant principles given elsewhere in the Guide. Where a computerised system replaces a manual operation, there should be no resultant decrease in product quality or quality assurance. Consideration should be given to the risk of losing aspects of the previous system which could result from reducing the involvement of operators.

Personnel

1   It is essential that there is the closest co-operation between key personnel and those involved with computer systems. Persons in responsible positions should have the appropriate training for the management and use of systems within their field of responsibility which utilises computers. This should include ensuring that appropriate expertise is available and used to provide advice on aspects of design, validation, installation and operation of computerised system.

Validation

2   The extent of validation necessary will depend on a number of factors including the use to which the system is to be put, whether the validation is to be prospective or retrospective and whether or not novel elements are incorporated. Validation should be considered as part of the complete life cycle of a computer system. This cycle includes the stages of planning, specification, programming, testing, commissioning, documentation, operation, monitoring and modifying.

System

3   Attention should be paid to the siting of equipment in suitable conditions where extraneous factors cannot interfere with the system.

4   A written detailed description of the system should be produced (including diagrams as appropriate) and kept up to date. It should describe the principles, objectives, security measures and scope of the system and the main

features of the way in which the computer is used and how it interacts with other systems and procedures.

5   The software is a critical component of a computerised system. The user of such software should take all reasonable steps to ensure that it has been produced in accordance with a system of Quality Assurance.

6   The system should include, where appropriate, built-in checks of the correct entry and processing of data.

7   Before a system using a computer is brought into use, it should be thoroughly tested and confirmed as being capable of achieving the desired results. If a manual system is being replaced, the two should be run in parallel for a time, as a part of this testing and validation.

8   Data should only be entered or amended by persons authorised to do so. Suitable methods of deterring unauthorised entry of data include the use of keys, pass cards, personal codes and restricted access to computer terminals. There should be a defined procedure for the issue, cancellation, and alteration of authorisation to enter and amend data, including the changing of personal passwords. Consideration should be given to systems allowing for recording of attempts to access by unauthorised persons.

9   When critical data are being entered manually (for example the weight and batch number of an ingredient during dispensing), there should be an additional check on the accuracy of the record which is made. This check may be done by a second operator or by validated electronic means.

10   The system should record the identity of operators entering or confirming critical data. Authority to amend entered data should be restricted to nominated persons. Any alteration to an entry of critical data should be authorised and recorded with the reason for the change. Consideration should be given to building into the system the creation of a complete record of all entries and amendments (an "audit trail").

11   Alterations to a system or to a computer program should only be made in accordance with a defined procedure which should include provision for validating, checking, approving and implementing the change. Such an alteration should only be implemented with the agreement of the person responsible for the part of the system concerned, and the alteration should be recorded. Every significant modification should be validated.

12   For quality auditing purposes, it should be possible to obtain clear printed copies of electronically stored data.

13   Data should be secured by physical or electronic means against wilful or accidental damage, in accordance with item 4.9 of the Guide. Stored data should be checked for accessibility, durability and accuracy. If changes

are proposed to the computer equipment or its programs, the above mentioned checks should be performed at a frequency appropriate to the storage medium being used.

14 Data should be protected by backing-up at regular intervals. Back-up data should be stored as long as necessary at a separate and secure location.

15 There should be available adequate alternative arrangements for systems which need to be operated in the event of a breakdown. The time required to bring the alternative arrangements into use should be related to the possible urgency of the need to use them. For example, information required to effect a recall must be available at short notice.

16 The procedures to be followed if the system fails or breaks down should be defined and validated. Any failures and remedial action taken should be recorded.

17 A procedure should be established to record and analyse errors and to enable corrective action to be taken.

18 When outside agencies are used to provide a computer service, there should be a formal agreement including a clear statement of the responsibilities of that outside agency (see Section II, Chapter 7).

19 When the release of batches for sale or supply is carried out using a computerised system, the system should allow for only a Qualified Person to release the batches and it should clearly identify and record the person releasing the batches.

ANNEX 12 USE OF IONISING RADIATION IN THE MANUFACTURE OF MEDICINAL PRODUCTS

Note: *The holder of, or applicant for, a marketing authorisation for a product which includes irradiation as part of its processing should also refer to the note produced by the Committee for Proprietary Medicinal Products giving guidance on "Ionising radiation in the manufacture of medicinal products".*

Introduction

Ionising radiation may be used during the manufacturing process for various purposes including the reduction of bioburden and the sterilisation of starting materials, packaging components or products and the treatment of blood products.

There are two types of irradiation process: Gamma Irradiation from a radioactive source and high-energy Electron Irradiation (Beta radiation) from an accelerator.

Gamma Irradiation: two different processing modes may be employed:

(i) Batch mode: the product is arranged at fixed locations around the radiation source and cannot be loaded or unloaded while the radiation source is exposed.

(ii) Continuous mode: an automatic system conveys the products into the radiation cell, past the exposed radiation source along a defined path and at an appropriate speed, and out of the cell.

Electron Irradiation: the product is conveyed past a continuous or pulsed beam of high energy electrons (Beta radiation) which is scanned back and forth across the product pathway.

Responsibilities

1   Treatment by irradiation may be carried out by the pharmaceutical manufacturer or by an operator of a radiation facility under contract (a "contract manufacturer"), both of whom must hold an appropriate manufacturing authorisation.

2   The pharmaceutical manufacturer bears responsibility for the quality of the product including the attainment of the objective of irradiation. The contract operator of the radiation facility bears responsibility for ensuring that the dose of radiation required by the manufacturer is delivered to the irradiation container (i.e. the outermost container in which the products are irradiated).

3   The required dose including justified limits will be stated in the marketing authorisation for the product.

Dosimetry

4   Dosimetry is defined as the measurement of the absorbed dose by the use of dosimeters. Both understanding and correct use of the technique is essential for the validation, commissioning and control of the process.

5   The calibration of each batch of routine dosimeters should be traceable to a national or international standard. The period of validity of the calibration should be stated, justified and adhered to.

6   The same instrument should normally be used to establish the calibration curve of the routine dosimeters and to measure the change in their absorbance after irradiation. If a different instrument is used, the absolute absorbance of each instrument should be established.

7   Depending on the type of dosimeter used, due account should be taken of possible causes of inaccuracy including the change in moisture content, change in temperature, time elapsed between irradiation and measurement, and the dose rate.

8   The wavelength of the instrument used to measure the change in absorbance of dosimeters and the instrument used to measure their thickness should be subject to regular checks of calibration at intervals established on the basis of stability, purpose and usage.

Validation of the Process

9   Validation is the action of proving that the process, i.e. the delivery of the intended absorbed dose to the product, will achieve the expected results. The requirements for validation are given more fully in the note for guidance on "the use of ionising radiation in the manufacture of medicinal products."

10   Validation should include dose mapping to establish the distribution of absorbed dose within the irradiation container when packed with product in a defined configuration.

11   An irradiation process specification should include at least the following:

(a) details of the packaging of the product;
(b) the loading pattern(s) of product within the irradiation container. Particular care needs to be taken, when a mixture of products is allowed in the irradiation container, that there is no under-dosing of dense product

or shadowing of other products by dense product. Each mixed product arrangement must be specified and validated;

(c) the loading pattern of irradiation containers around the source (batch mode) or the pathway through the cell (continuous mode);

(d) maximum and minimum limits of absorbed dose to the product (and associated routine dosimetry);

(e) maximum and minimum limits of absorbed dose to the irradiation container and associated routine dosimetry to monitor this absorbed dose;

(f) other process parameters, including dose rate, maximum time of exposure, number of exposures, etc.

When irradiation is supplied under contract at least parts (d) and (e) of the irradiation process specification should form part of that contract.

Commissioning of the Plant

General

12   Commissioning is the exercise of obtaining and documenting evidence that the irradiation plant will perform consistently within predetermined limits when operated according to the process specification. In the context of this annex, predetermined limits are the maximum and minimum doses designed to be absorbed by the irradiation container. It must not be possible for variations to occur in the operation of the plant which give a dose to the container outside these limits without the knowledge of the operator.

13   Commissioning should include the following elements:

(a) design;
(b) dose mapping;
(c) documentation;
(d) requirement for re-commissioning.

Gamma irradiators

DESIGN

14   The absorbed dose received by a particular part of an irradiation container at any specific point in the irradiator depends primarily on the following factors:

(a) the activity and geometry of the source;
(b) the distance from source to container;
(c) the duration of irradiation controlled by the timer setting or conveyor speed;

(d) the composition and density of material, including other products, between the source and the particular part of the container.

15   The total absorbed dose will in addition depend on the path of containers through a continuous irradiator or the loading pattern in a batch irradiator, and on the number of exposure cycles.

16   For a continuous irradiator with a fixed path or a batch irradiator with a fixed loading pattern, and with a given source strength and type of product, the key plant parameter controlled by the operator is conveyor speed or timer setting.

DOSE MAPPING

17   For the dose mapping procedure, the irradiator should be filled with irradiation containers packed with dummy products or a representative product of uniform density. Dosimeters should be placed throughout a minimum of three loaded irradiation containers which are passed through the irradiator, surrounded by similar containers or dummy products. If the product is not uniformly packed, dosimeters should be placed in a larger number of containers.

18   The positioning of dosimeters will depend on the size of the irradiation container. For example, for containers up to $1 \times 1 \times 0.5$ m, a three-dimensional 20 cm grid throughout the container including the outside surfaces might be suitable. If the expected positions of the minimum and maximum dose are known from a previous irradiator performance characterisation, some dosimeters could be removed from regions of average dose and replaced to form a 10 cm grid in the regions of extreme dose.

19   The results of this procedure will give minimum and maximum absorbed doses in the product and on the container surface for a given set of plant parameters, product density and loading pattern.

20   Ideally, reference dosimeters should be used for the dose mapping exercise because of their greater precision. Routine dosimeters are permissible but it is advisable to place reference dosimeters beside them at the expected positions of minimum and maximum dose and at the routine monitoring position in each of the replicate irradiation containers. The observed values of dose will have an associated random uncertainty which can be estimated from the variations in replicate measurements.

21   The minimum observed dose, as measured by the routine dosimeters, necessary to ensure that all irradiation containers receive the minimum required dose will be set in the knowledge of the random variability of the routine dosimeters used.

22 Irradiator parameters should be kept constant, monitored and recorded during dose mapping. The records, together with the dosimetry results and all other records generated, should be retained.

Electron beam irradiators

23 The absorbed dose received by a particular portion of an irradiated product depends primarily on the following factors:

(a) the characteristics of the beam, which are: electron energy, average beam current, scan width and scan uniformity;
(b) the conveyor speed;
(c) the product composition and density;
(d) the composition, density and thickness of material between the output window and the particular portion of product;
(e) the output window to container distance.

24 Key parameters controlled by the operator are the characteristics of the beam and the conveyor speed.

25 For the dose-mapping procedure, dosimeters should be placed between layers of homogeneous absorber sheets making up a dummy product, or between layers of representative products of uniform density, such that at least ten measurements can be made within the maximum range of the electrons. Reference should also be made to sections 18–21.

26 Irradiator parameters should be kept constant, monitored and recorded during dose mapping. The records, together with the dosimetry results and all other records generated, should be retained.

Re-commissioning

27 Commissioning should be repeated if there is a change to the process or the irradiator which could affect the dose distribution to the irradiation container (e.g. change of source pencils). The extent to re-commissioning depends on the extent of the change in the irradiator or the load that has taken place. If in doubt, re-commission.

Premises

28 Premises should be designed and operated to segregate irradiated from non-irradiated containers to avoid their cross-contamination. Where materials are handled within closed irradiation containers, it may not be necessary

to segregate pharmaceutical from non-pharmaceutical materials, provided there is no risk of the former being contaminated by the latter.

Any possibility of contamination of the products by radionuclide from the source must be excluded.

Processing

29 Irradiation containers should be packed in accordance with the specified loading pattern(s) established during validation.

30 During the process, the radiation dose to the irradiation containers should be monitored using validated dosimetry procedures. The relationship between this dose and the dose absorbed by the product inside the container must have been established during process validation and plant commissioning.

31 Radiation indicators should be used as an aid to differentiating irradiated from non-irradiated containers. They should not be used as the sole means of differentiation or as an indication of satisfactory processing.

32 Processing of mixed loads of containers within the irradiation cell should only be done when it is known from commissioning trials or other evidence that the radiation dose received by individual containers remains within the limits specified.

33 When the required radiation dose is by design given during more than one exposure or passage through the plant, this should be with the agreement of the holder of the marketing authorisation and occur within a predetermined time period. Unplanned interruptions during irradiation should be notified to the holder of the marketing authorisation if this extends the irradiation process beyond a previously agreed period.

34 Non-irradiated products must be segregated from irradiated products at all times. Methods of doing this include the use of radiation indicators (item 31) and appropriate design of premises (item 28).

Gamma irradiators

35 For continuous processing modes, dosimeters should be placed so that at least two are exposed in the irradiation at all times.

36 For batch modes, at least two dosimeters should be exposed in positions related to the minimum dose position.

37 For continuous process modes, there should be a positive indication of the correct position of the source and an interlock between source position and

conveyor movement. Conveyor speed should be monitored continuously and recorded.

38   For batch process modes source movement and exposure times for each batch should be monitored and recorded.

39   For a given desired dose, the timer setting or conveyor speed requires adjustment for source decay and source additions. The period of validity of the setting or speed should be recorded and adhered to.

Electron beam irradiators

40   A dosimeter should be placed on every container.

41   There should be continuous recording of average beam current, electron energy, scan-width and conveyor speed. These variables, other than conveyor speed, need to be controlled within the defined limits established during commissioning since they are liable to instantaneous change.

Documentation

42   The numbers of containers received, irradiated and dispatched should be reconciled with each other and with the associated documentation. Any discrepancy should be reported and resolved.

43   The irradiation plant operator should certify in writing the range of doses received by each irradiated container within a batch or delivery.

44   Process and control records for each irradiation batch should be checked and signed by a nominated responsible person and retained. The method and place of retention should be agreed between the plant operator and the holder of the marketing authorisation.

45   The documentation associated with the validation and commissioning of the plant should be retained for one year after the expiry date or at least five years after the release of the last product processed by the plant, whichever is the longer.

Microbiological Monitoring

46   Microbiological monitoring is the responsibility of the pharmaceutical manufacturer. It may include environmental monitoring where product is manufactured and pre-irradiation monitoring of the product as specified in the marketing authorisation.

ANNEX 13 MANUFACTURE OF INVESTIGATIONAL MEDICINAL PRODUCTS

Principle

Investigational medicinal products should be produced in accordance with the principles and the detailed guidelines of Good Manufacturing Practice for Medicinal Products (The Rules Governing Medicinal Products in The European Community, Volume IV). Other guidelines published by the European Commission should be taken into account where relevant and as appropriate to the stage of development of the product. Procedures need to be flexible to provide for changes as knowledge of the process increases, and appropriate to the stage of development of the product.

In clinical trials there may be added risk to participating subjects compared to patients treated with marketed products. The application of GMP to the manufacture of investigational medicinal products is intended to ensure that trial subjects are not placed at risk, and that the results of clinical trials are unaffected by inadequate safety, quality or efficacy arising from unsatisfactory manufacture. Equally, it is intended to ensure that there is consistency between batches of the same investigational medicinal product used in the same or different clinical trials, and that changes during the development of an investigational medicinal product are adequately documented and justified.

The production of investigational medicinal products involves added complexity in comparison to marketed products by virtue of the lack of fixed routines, variety of clinical trial designs, consequent packaging designs, the need, often, for randomisation and blinding and increased risk of product cross-contamination and mix up. Furthermore, there may be incomplete knowledge of the potency and toxicity of the product and a lack of full process validation, or, marketed products may be used which have been re-packaged or modified in some way.

These challenges require personnel with a thorough understanding of, and training in, the application of GMP to investigational medicinal products. Co-operation is required with trial sponsors who undertake the ultimate responsibility for all aspects of the clinical trial including the quality of investigational medicinal products. The increased complexity in manufacturing operations requires a highly effective quality system.

The annex also includes guidance on ordering, shipping, and returning clinical supplies, which are at the interface with, and complementary to, guidelines on Good Clinical Practice.

Note: Products other than the test product, placebo or comparator may be supplied to subjects participating in a trial. Such products may be used as support or escape medication for preventative, diagnostic or therapeutic reasons and/or needed to ensure that adequate medical care is provided for the subject. They may also be used in accordance with the protocol to induce a physiological response. These products do not fall within the definition of investigational medicinal products and may be supplied by the sponsor, or the investigator. The sponsor should ensure that they are in accordance with the notification/request for authorisation to conduct the trial and that they are of appropriate quality for the purposes of the trial taking into account the source of the materials, whether or not they are the subject of a marketing authorisation and whether they have been repackaged. The advice and involvement of a Qualified Person is recommended in this task.

Glossary

Blinding

A procedure in which one or more parties to the trial are kept unaware of the treatment assignment(s). Single-blinding usually refers to the subject(s) being unaware, and double-blinding usually refers to the subject(s), investigator(s), monitor, and, in some cases, data analyst(s) being unaware of the treatment assignment(s). In relation to an investigational medicinal product, blinding shall mean the deliberate disguising of the identity of the product in accordance with the instructions of the sponsor. Unblinding shall mean the disclosure of the identity of blinded products.

Clinical trial

Any investigation in human subjects intended to discover or verify the clinical, pharmacological and/or other pharmacodynamic effects of an investigational product(s) and/or to identify any adverse reactions to an investigational product(s), and/or to study absorption, distribution, metabolism, and excretion of one or more investigational medicinal product(s) with the object of ascertaining its/their safety and/or efficacy.

Comparator product

An investigational or marketed product (i.e. active control), or placebo, used as a reference in a clinical trial.

Investigational medicinal product

A pharmaceutical form of an active substance or placebo being tested or used as a reference in a clinical trial, including a product with a marketing authorisation when used or assembled (formulated or packaged) in a way different from the authorised form, or when used for an unauthorised indication, or when used to gain further information about the authorised form.

Immediate packaging

The container or other form of packaging immediately in contact with the medicinal or investigational medicinal product.

Investigator

A person responsible for the conduct of the clinical trial at a trial site. If a trial is conducted by a team of individuals at a trial site, the investigator is the responsible leader of the team and may be called the principal investigator.

Manufacturer/importer of Investigational Medicinal Products

Any holder of the authorisation to manufacture/import referred to in Article 13.1 of Directive 2001/20/EC.

Order

Instruction to process, package and/or ship a certain number of units of investigational medicinal product(s).

Outer packaging

The packaging into which the immediate container is placed.

Product Specification File

A reference file containing, or referring to files containing, all the information necessary to draft the detailed written instructions on processing, packaging, quality control testing, batch release and shipping of an investigational medicinal product.

Randomisation

The process of assigning trial subjects to treatment or control groups using an element of chance to determine the assignments in order to reduce bias.

Randomisation Code

A listing in which the treatment assigned to each subject from the randomisation process is identified.

Shipping

The operation of packaging for shipment and sending of ordered medicinal products for clinical trials.

Sponsor

An individual, company, institution or organisation which takes responsibility for the initiation, management and/or financing of a clinical trial.

Quality Management

1   The Quality System, designed, set up and verified by the manufacturer or importer, should be described in written procedures available to the sponsor, taking into account the GMP principles and guidelines applicable to investigational medicinal products.

2   The product specifications and manufacturing instructions may be changed during development but full control and traceability of the changes should be maintained.

Personnel

3   All personnel involved with investigational medicinal products should be appropriately trained in the requirements specific to these types of product.

4   The Qualified Person should in particular be responsible for ensuring that there are systems in place that meet the requirements of this Annex and should therefore have a broad knowledge of pharmaceutical development and clinical trial processes. Guidance for the Qualified Person in connection with the certification of investigational medicinal products is given in paragraphs 38 to 41.

Premises and Equipment

5   The toxicity, potency and sensitising potential may not be fully understood for investigational medicinal products and this reinforces the need to minimise all risks of cross-contamination. The design of equipment and premises, inspection/ test methods and acceptance limits to be used after cleaning should reflect the nature of these risks. Consideration should be given to campaign working where appropriate. Account should be taken of the solubility of the product in decisions about the choice of cleaning solvent.

Documentation

Specifications and instructions

6   Specifications (for starting materials, primary packaging materials, intermediate, bulk products and finished products), manufacturing formulae and processing and packaging instructions should be as comprehensive as possible given the current state of knowledge. They should be periodically re-assessed during development and updated as necessary. Each new version should take into account the latest data, current technology used, regulatory and pharmacopoeial requirements, and should allow traceability to the previous document. Any changes should be carried out according to a written procedure, which should address any implications for product quality such as stability and bio-equivalence.

7 Rationales for changes should be recorded and the consequences of a change on product quality and on any on-going clinical trials should be investigated and documented.

Order

8 The order should request the processing and/or packaging of a certain number of units and/or their shipping and be given by or on behalf of the sponsor to the manufacturer. It should be in writing (though it may be transmitted by electronic means), and precise enough to avoid any ambiguity. It should be formally authorised and refer to the Product Specification File and the relevant clinical trial protocol as appropriate.

Product Specification File

9 The Product Specification File (see glossary) should be continually updated as development of the product proceeds, ensuring appropriate traceability to the previous versions. It should include, or refer to, the following documents:

- Specifications and analytical methods for starting materials, packaging materials, intermediate, bulk and finished product;
- Manufacturing methods;
- In-process testing and methods;
- Approved label copy;
- Relevant clinical trial protocols and randomisation codes, as appropriate;
- Relevant technical agreements with contract givers, as appropriate;
- Stability data;
- Storage and shipment conditions.

The above listing is not intended to be exclusive or exhaustive. The contents will vary depending on the product and stage of development. The information should form the basis for assessment of the suitability for certification and release of a particular batch by the Qualified Person and should therefore be accessible to him/her. Where different manufacturing steps are carried out at different locations under the responsibility of different Qualified Persons, it is acceptable to maintain separate files limited to information of relevance to the activities at the respective locations.

Manufacturing Formulae and Processing Instructions

10 For every manufacturing operation or supply there should be clear and adequate written instructions and written records. Where an operation is not repetitive it may not be necessary to produce Master Formulae and

Processing Instructions. Records are particularly important for the preparation of the final version of the documents to be used in routine manufacture once the marketing authorisation is granted.

11   The information in the Product Specification File should be used to produce the detailed written instructions on processing, packaging, quality control testing, storage conditions and shipping.

Packaging Instructions

12   Investigational medicinal products are normally packed in an individual way for each subject included in the clinical trial. The number of units to be packaged should be specified prior to the start of the packaging operations, including units necessary for carrying out quality control and any retention samples to be kept. Sufficient reconciliations should take place to ensure the correct quantity of each product required has been accounted for at each stage of processing.

Processing, testing and packaging batch records

13   Batch records should be kept in sufficient detail for the sequence of operations to be accurately determined. These records should contain any relevant remarks which justify the procedures used and any changes made, enhance knowledge of the product and develop the manufacturing operations.

14   Batch manufacturing records should be retained at least for the periods specified in Directive 91/356 as amended for investigational medicinal products.

Production

Packaging materials

15   Specifications and quality control checks should include measures to guard against unintentional unblinding due to changes in appearance between different batches of packaging materials.

Manufacturing operations

16   During development critical parameters should be identified and in-process controls primarily used to control the process. Provisional production parameters and in-process controls may be deduced from prior experience, including that gained from earlier development work. Careful consideration by key personnel is called for in order to formulate the necessary instructions and to adapt them continually to the experience gained

in production. Parameters identified and controlled should be justifiable based on knowledge available at the time.

17   Production processes for investigational medicinal products are not expected to be validated to the extent necessary for routine production but premises and equipment are expected to be validated. For sterile products, the validation of sterilising processes should be of the same standard as for products authorised for marketing.

Likewise, when required, virus inactivation/removal and that of other impurities of biological origin should be demonstrated, to assure the safety of biotechnologically derived products, by following the scientific principles and techniques defined in the available guidance in this area.

18   Validation of aseptic processes presents special problems when the batch size is small; in these cases the number of units filled may be the maximum number filled in production. If practicable, and otherwise consistent with simulating the process, a larger number of units should be filled with media to provide greater confidence in the results obtained. Filling and sealing is often a manual or semi-automated operation presenting great challenges to sterility so enhanced attention should be given to operator training, and validating the aseptic technique of individual operators.

Principles applicable to comparator product

19   If a product is modified, data should be available (e.g. stability, comparative dissolution, bioavailability) to demonstrate that these changes do not significantly alter the original quality characteristics of the product.

20   The expiry date stated for the comparator product in its original packaging might not be applicable to the product where it has been repackaged in a different container that may not offer equivalent protection, or be compatible with the product. A suitable use by date, taking into account the nature of the product, the characteristics of the container and the storage conditions to which the article may be subjected, should be determined by or on behalf of the sponsor. Such a date should be justified and must not be later than the expiry date of the original package. There should be compatibility of expiry dating and clinical trial duration.

Blinding operations

21   Where products are blinded, systems should be in place to ensure that the blind is achieved and maintained while allowing for identification of "blinded" products when necessary, including the batch numbers of the products before the blinding operation. Rapid identification of product should also be possible in an emergency.

Randomisation code

22   Procedures should describe the generation, security, distribution, handling and retention of any randomisation code used for packaging investigational products, and code-break mechanisms. Appropriate records should be maintained.

Packaging

23   During packaging of investigational medicinal products, it may be necessary to handle different products on the same packaging line at the same time. The risk of product mix-up must be minimised by using appropriate procedures and/or, specialised equipment as appropriate and relevant staff training.

24   Packaging and labelling of investigational medicinal products are likely to be more complex and more liable to errors (which are also harder to detect) than for marketed products, particularly when "blinded" products with similar appearance are used. Precautions against mis-labelling such as label reconciliation, line clearance, in-process control checks by appropriately trained staff should accordingly be intensified.

25   The packaging must ensure that the investigational medicinal product remains in good condition during transport and storage at intermediate destinations. Any opening or tampering of the outer packaging during transport should be readily discernible.

Labelling

26   Table 1 summarises the contents of articles 26-30 that follow. Labelling should comply with the requirements of Directive 91/356 as amended for Investigational Medicinal Products. The following information should be included on labels, unless its absence can be justified, e.g. use of a centralised electronic randomisation system:

(a) name, address and telephone number of the sponsor, contract research organisation or investigator (the main contact for information on the product, clinical trial and emergency unblinding);

(b) pharmaceutical dosage form, route of administration, quantity of dosage units, and in the case of open trials, the name/identifier and strength/potency;

(c) the batch and/or code number to identify the contents and packaging operation;

(d) a trial reference code allowing identification of the trial, site, investigator and sponsor if not given elsewhere;

(e) the trial subject identification number/treatment number and where relevant, the visit number;

(f) the name of the investigator (if not included in (a) or (d));

(g) directions for use (reference may be made to a leaflet or other explanatory document intended for the trial subject or person administering the product);

(h) "For clinical trial use only" or similar wording;

(i) the storage conditions;

(j) period of use (use-by date, expiry date or re-test date as applicable), in month/year format and in a manner that avoids any ambiguity;

(k) "keep out of reach of children" except when the product is for use in trials where the product is not taken home by subjects.

27 The address and telephone number of the main contact for information on the product, clinical trial and for emergency unblinding need not appear on the label where the subject has been given a leaflet or card which provides these details and has been instructed to keep this in their possession at all times.

28 Particulars should appear in the official language(s) of the country in which the investigational medicinal product is to be used. The particulars listed in Article 26 should appear on the immediate container and on the outer packaging (except for immediate containers in the cases described in Articles 29 and 30). The requirements with respect to the contents of the label on the immediate container and outer packaging are summarised in Table 1. Other languages may be included.

29 When the product is to be provided to the trial subject or the person administering the medication within an immediate container together with outer packaging that is intended to remain together, and the outer packaging carries the particulars listed in paragraph 26, the following information shall be included on the label of the immediate container (or any sealed dosing device that contains the immediate container):

(a) name of sponsor, contract research organisation or investigator;

(b) pharmaceutical dosage form, route of administration (may be excluded for oral solid dose forms), quantity of dosage units and in the case of open label trials, the name/identifier and strength/potency;

(c) batch and/or code number to identify the contents and packaging operation;

(d) a trial reference code allowing identification of the trial, site, investigator and sponsor if not given elsewhere;

(e) the trial subject identification number/treatment number and where relevant, the visit number.

30 If the immediate container takes the form of blister packs or small units such as ampoules on which the particulars required in paragraph 26

cannot be displayed, outer packaging should be provided bearing a label with those particulars. The immediate container should nevertheless contain the following:

(a) name of sponsor, contract research organisation or investigator;
(b) route of administration (may be excluded for oral solid dose forms) and in the case of open label trials, the name/identifier and strength/potency;
(c) batch and/or code number to identify the contents and packaging operation;
(d) a trial reference code allowing identification of the trial, site, investigator and sponsor if not given elsewhere;
(e) the trial subject identification number/treatment number and where relevant, the visit number.

31 Symbols or pictograms may be included to clarify certain information mentioned above. Additional information, warnings and/or handling instructions may be displayed.

32 For clinical trials with the characteristics identified in Article 14 of Directive 2001/20/EC, the following particulars should be added to the original container but should not obscure the original labelling:

(i) name of sponsor, contract research organisation or investigator;
(ii) trial reference code allowing identification of the trial site, investigator and trial subject.

33 If it becomes necessary to change the use-by date, an additional label should be affixed to the investigational medicinal product. This additional label should state the new use-by date and repeat the batch number. It may be superimposed on the old use-by date, but for quality control reasons, not on the original batch number. This operation should be performed at an appropriately authorised manufacturing site. However, when justified, it may be performed at the investigational site by or under the supervision of the clinical trial site pharmacist, or other health care professional in accordance with national regulations. Where this is not possible, it may be performed by the clinical trial monitor(s) who should be appropriately trained. The operation should be performed in accordance with GMP principles, specific and standard operating procedures and under contract, if applicable, and should be checked by a second person. This additional labelling should be properly documented in both the trial documentation and in the batch records.

Quality Control

34 As processes may not be standardised or fully validated, testing takes on more importance in ensuring that each batch meets its specification.

35   Quality control should be performed in accordance with the Product Specification File and in accordance with the information notified pursuant to Article 9(2) of Directive 2001/20/EC. Verification of the effectiveness of blinding should be performed and recorded.

36   Samples of each batch of investigational medicinal product, including blinded product should be retained for the periods specified in Directive 91/356 as amended for investigational medicinal products.

37   Consideration should be given to retaining samples from each packaging run/trial period until the clinical report has been prepared to enable confirmation of product identity in the event of, and as part of an investigation into inconsistent trial results.

Release of Batches

38   Release of investigational medicinal products (see paragraph 43) should not occur until after the Qualified Person has certified that the requirements of Article 13.3 of Directive 2001/20/EC have been met (see paragraph 39). The Qualified Person should take into account the elements listed in paragraph 40 as appropriate.

39   The duties of the Qualified Person in relation to investigational medicinal products are affected by the different circumstances that can arise and are referred to below. Table 2 summarises the elements that need to be considered for the most common circumstances:

(a)(i)   Product manufactured within EU but not subject to an EU marketing authorisation: the duties are laid down in Article 13.3(a) of Directive 2001/20/EC.

(a)(ii) Product sourced from the open market within EU in accordance with Article 80(b) of Directive 2001/83/EC and subject to an EU marketing authorisation, regardless of manufacturing origin: the duties are as described above, however, the scope of certification can be limited to assuring that the products are in accordance with the notification/request for authorisation to conduct the trial and any subsequent processing for the purpose of blinding, trial-specific packaging and labelling. The Product Specification File will be similarly restricted in scope (see paragraph 9).

(b)   Product imported directly from a third country: the duties are laid down in Article 13.3(b) of Directive 2001/20/EC. Where investigational medicinal products are imported from a third country and they are subject to arrangements concluded between the Community and that country, such as a Mutual Recognition Agreement (MRA), equivalent standards of Good Manufacturing Practice apply provided any such agreement is relevant to the product in question. In the absence of an MRA, the Qualified Person should determine that equivalent standards of Good Manufacturing Practice apply through knowledge of the quality system employed at the manufacturer. This knowledge is normally acquired through participation in audit of the manufacturer's quality systems. In either case, the Qualified Person may then certify on the basis of documentation supplied by the third country manufacturer (see paragraph 40).

(c)   For imported comparator products where adequate assurance cannot be obtained in order to certify that each batch has been manufactured to equivalent standards of Good Manufacturing Practice, the duty of the Qualified Person is defined in Article 13.3(c) of Directive 2001/20/EC.

40   Assessment of each batch for certification prior to release may include as appropriate:

- batch records, including control reports, in-process test reports and release reports demonstrating compliance with the product specification file, the order, protocol and randomisation code. These records should include all deviations or planned changes, and any consequent additional checks or tests, and should be completed and endorsed by the staff authorised to do so according to the quality system;
- production conditions;
- the validation status of facilities, processes and methods; examination of finished packs; where relevant, the results of any analyses or tests performed after importation;
- stability reports;
- the source and verification of conditions of storage and shipment;
- audit reports concerning the quality system of the manufacturer;
- documents certifying that the manufacturer is authorised to manufacture investigational medicinal products or comparators for export by the appropriate authorities in the country of export;
- where relevant, regulatory requirements for marketing authorisation, GMP standards applicable and any official verification of GMP compliance;
- all other factors of which the QP is aware that are relevant to the quality of the batch.

The relevance of the above elements is affected by the country of origin of the product, the manufacturer, and the marketed status of the product (with or without a marketing authorisation, in the EU or in a third country) and its phase of development.

The sponsor should ensure that the elements taken into account by the qualified person when certifying the batch are consistent with the information notified pursuant to Article 9(2) of Directive 2001/20/EC (see also paragraph 44).

41   Where investigational medicinal products are manufactured and packaged at different sites under the supervision of different Qualified Persons, the recommendations listed in Annex 16 to the GMP Guide should be followed as applicable.

42   Where, permitted in accordance with local regulations, packaging or labelling is carried out at the investigator site by, or under the supervision of a clinical trials pharmacist, or other health care professional as allowed in those regulations, the Qualified Person is not required to certify the activity in question. The sponsor is nevertheless responsible for ensuring that the activity is adequately documented and carried out in accordance with the principles of GMP and should seek the advice of the Qualified Person in this regard.

Shipping

43   Shipping of investigational products should be conducted according to instructions given by or on behalf of the sponsor in the shipping order.

44   Investigational medicinal products should remain under the control of the sponsor until after completion of a two-step release procedure: certification by the Qualified Person; and release following fulfilment of the requirements of Article 9 (Commencement of a clinical trial) of Directive 2001/20/EC. The sponsor should ensure that these are consistent with the details actually considered by the Qualified Person. Both releases should be recorded and retained in the relevant trial files held by or on behalf of the sponsor.

45   De-coding arrangements should be available to the appropriate responsible personnel before investigational medicinal products are shipped to the investigator site.

46   A detailed inventory of the shipments made by the manufacturer or importer should be maintained. It should particularly mention the addressees' identification.

47   Transfers of investigational medicinal products from one trial site to another should remain the exception. Such transfers should be covered by standard operating procedures. The product history while outside of the control of the manufacturer, through for example, trial monitoring reports and records of storage conditions at the original trial site should be reviewed as part of the assessment of the product's suitability for transfer and the advice of the Qualified person should be sought. The product should be returned to the manufacturer, or another authorised

manufacturer for re-labelling, if necessary, and certification by a Qualified Person. Records should be retained and full traceability ensured.

Complaints

48 The conclusions of any investigation carried out in relation to a complaint which could arise from the quality of the product should be discussed between the manufacturer or importer and the sponsor (if different). This should involve the Qualified Person and those responsible for the relevant clinical trial in order to assess any potential impact on the trial, product development and on subjects.

Recalls and Returns

Recalls

49 Procedures for retrieving investigational medicinal products and documenting this retrieval should be agreed by the sponsor, in collaboration with the manufacturer or importer where different. The investigator and monitor need to understand their obligations under the retrieval procedure.

50 The Sponsor should ensure that the supplier of any comparator or other medication to be used in a clinical trial has a system for communicating to the Sponsor the need to recall any product supplied.

Returns

51 Investigational medicinal products should be returned on agreed conditions defined by the sponsor, specified in approved written procedures.

52 Returned investigational medicinal products should be clearly identified and stored in an appropriately controlled, dedicated area. Inventory records of the returned medicinal products should be kept.

Destruction

53 The Sponsor is responsible for the destruction of unused and/or returned investigational medicinal products. Investigational medicinal products should therefore not be destroyed without prior written authorisation by the Sponsor.

54 The delivered, used and recovered quantities of product should be recorded, reconciled and verified by or on behalf of the Sponsor for each trial site and each trial period. Destruction of unused investigational medicinal products should be carried out for a given trial site or a given trial period only after

any discrepancies have been investigated and satisfactorily explained and the reconciliation has been accepted. Recording of destruction operations should be carried out in such a manner that all operations may be accounted for. The records should be kept by the Sponsor.

55   When destruction of investigational medicinal products takes place a dated certificate of, or receipt for destruction, should be provided to the Sponsor. These documents should clearly identify, or allow traceability to, the batches and/or patient numbers involved and the actual quantities destroyed.

Table 1   Summary of labelling details (§26 to 30)

(a) name, address and telephone number of the sponsor, contract research organisation or investigator (the main contact for information on the product, clinical trial and emergency unblinding)	GENERAL CASE For both the outer packaging and immediate container (§26)
(b) pharmaceutical dosage form, route of administration, quantity of dosage units, and in the case of open trials, the name/identifier and strength/potency;	
(c) the batch and/or code number to identify the contents and packaging operation;	Particulars a^1 to k
(d) a trial reference code allowing identification of the trial, site, investigator and sponsor if not given elsewhere;	
(e) the trial subject identification number/treatment number and where relevant, the visit number;	IMMEDIATE CONTAINER Where immediate container and outer packaging remain together throughout (§29)[5]
(f) the name of the investigator (if not included in (a) or (d));	
(g) directions for use (reference may be made to a leaflet or other explanatory document intended for the trial subject or person administering the product);	$a^2 b^3$ c d e
(h) "for clinical trial use only" or similar wording;	
(i) the storage conditions;	
(j) period of use (use-by date, expiry date or re-test date as applicable), in month/year format and in a manner that avoids any ambiguity;	IMMEDIATE CONTAINER Blisters or small packaging units (§30)[5]
(k) "keep out of reach of children" except when the product is for use in trials where the product is not taken home by subjects.	$a^2 b^{3,4}$ c d e

[1] The address and telephone number of the main contact for information on the product, clinical trial and for emergency unblinding need not appear on the label where the subject has been given a leaflet or card which provides these details and has been instructed to keep this in their possession at all times (§27).

[2] The address and telephone number of the main contact for information on the product, clinical trial and for emergency unblinding need not be included.

[3] Route of administration may be excluded for oral solid dose forms.

[4] The pharmaceutical dosage form and quantity of dosage units may be omitted.

[5] When the outer packaging carries the particulars listed in Article 26.

Table 2 Batch release of products

ELEMENTS TO BE TAKEN INTO ACCOUNT (3)	PRODUCT AVAILABLE IN THE EU		PRODUCT IMPORTED FROM THIRD COUNTRIES		
	Product manufactured in EU without MA	Product with MA and available on EU market	Product without any EU MA	Product with a EU MA	Comparator where documentation certifying that each batch has been manufactured in conditions at least equivalent to those laid down in Directive 91/356/EEC cannot be obtained
BEFORE CLINICAL TRIAL PROCESSING					
a) Shipping and storage conditions	Yes				
b) All relevant factors (1) showing that each batch has been manufactured and released in accordance with:					
Directive 91/356/EEC, or	Yes		(2)		
GMP standards at least equivalent to those laid down in Directive 91/356/EEC.	–		Yes		
c) Documentation showing that each batch has been released within the EU according to EU GMP requirements (see Directive 2001/83/EC, article 51), or documentation showing that the product is available on the EU market and has been procured in accordance with article 80(b) of Directive 2001/83/EC.		Yes			
d) Documentation showing that the product is available on the local market and documentation to establish confidence in the local regulatory requirements for marketing authorisation and release for local use.					Yes
e) Results of all analysis, tests and checks performed to assess the quality of the imported batch according to:					
the requirements of the MA (see Directive 2001/83/EC, article 51b), or			–	Yes	–
the Product Specification File, the Order, article 9.2 submission to the regulatory authorities.			Yes	–	Yes
Where these analyses and tests are not performed in the EU, this should be justified and the QP must certify that they have been carried out in accordance with GMP standards at least equivalent to those laid down in Directive 91/356/EEC.			Yes	Yes	Yes
AFTER CLINICAL TRIAL PROCESSING					
f) In addition to the assessment before clinical trial processing, all further relevant factors (1) showing that each batch has been processed for the purposes of blinding, trial-specific packaging, labelling and testing in accordance with:					
Directive 91/356/EEC, or	Yes		(2)		
GMP standards at least equivalent to those laid down in Directive 91/356/EEC.	–		Yes		

(1) These factors are summarised in paragraph 40.

(2) Where an MRA or similar arrangements are in place covering the products in question, equivalent standards of GMP apply.

(3) In all cases the information notified pursuant to Article 9(2) of Directive 2001/20/EC should be consistent with the elements actually taken into account by the QP who certifies the batch prior to release.

ANNEX 14 MANUFACTURE OF MEDICINAL[1] PRODUCTS DERIVED FROM HUMAN BLOOD OR PLASMA

Principle

In accordance with Directive 75/318/EEC[2], for biological medicinal products derived from human blood or plasma, starting materials include the source materials such as cells or fluids including blood or plasma. Medicinal products derived from human blood or plasma have certain special features arising from the biological nature of the source material. For example, disease-transmitting agents, especially viruses, may contaminate the source material. The safety of these products relies therefore on the control of source materials and their origin as well as on the subsequent manufacturing procedures, including virus removal and inactivation.

The general chapters of the guide to GMP apply to medicinal products derived from human blood or plasma, unless otherwise stated. Some of the Annexes may also apply, e.g. manufacture of sterile medicinal products, use of ionising radiation in the manufacture of medicinal products, manufacture of biological medicinal products and computerised systems. Since the quality of the final products is affected by all the steps in their manufacture, including the collection of blood or plasma, all operations should, therefore, be done in accordance with an appropriate system of Quality Assurance and current Good Manufacturing Practice.

By virtue of Directive 89/381/EEC, the necessary measures shall be taken to prevent the transmission of infectious diseases and the requirements and standards of the European Pharmacopoeia monographs regarding plasma for fractionation and medicinal products derived from human blood or plasma shall be applicable. These measures shall also comprise the Council Recommendation of 29 June 1998 "On the suitability of blood and plasma donors and the screening of donated blood in the European Community[3] (98/463/EC), the recommendations of the Council of Europe (see

---

[1] Council Directive 89/381/EEC of 14 June 1989 extending the scope of Directives 65/65/EEC and 75/319/EEC on the approximation of provisions laid down by law, regulation or administrative action relating to proprietary medicinal products and laying down special provisions for medicinal products derived from human blood or human plasma (OJ No L 181 of 28.6.1989).

[2] Council Directive 75/318/EEC, of 20 May 1975, on the approximation of the laws of Member States relating to analytical, pharmacotoxicological and clinical standards and protocols in respect of the testing of medicinal products (OJ No L 147 of 9.6.1975, p. 1) as last amended by Council Directive 93/39/EEC (OJ No L 214 of 24.8.1993, p. 22).

[3] O.J. L 20321.7.1998 p. 14.

"Guide to the Preparation, Use and Quality Assurance of Blood Components", Council of Europe Press) and the World Health Organization (see report by the WHO Expert Committee on Biological Standardisation, WHO Technical Report Series 840, 1994).

This annex should also be read in conjunction with the guidelines adopted by the CPMP, in particular "Note for guidance on plasma-derived medicinal products (CPMP/BWP/269/95 rev.2)", "Virus validation studies: the design, contribution and interpretation of studies validating the inactivation and removal of viruses" published in Volume 3A of the series "The Rules Governing Medicinal Products in the European Community") and "Contribution to part II of the structure of the dossier for applications for marketing authorisation-control of starting materials for the production of blood derivatives"(III/5272/94).

These documents are regularly revised and reference should be made to the latest revisions for current guidance.

The provisions of this annex apply to medicinal products derived from human blood and plasma. They do not cover blood components used in transfusion medicine, since these are presently not covered by EC directives. However many of these provisions may be applicable to such components and competent authorities may require compliance with them.

Glossary

Blood

Whole blood collected from a single donor and processed either for transfusion or further manufacturing

Blood components

Therapeutic components of blood (red cells, white cells, plasma, platelets), that can be prepared by centrifugation, filtration and freezing using conventional blood bank methodology

Medicinal product derived from blood or plasma

Same meaning as that given in Directive 89/381/EEC

Quality Management

1   Quality Assurance should cover all stages leading to the finished product, from collection (including donor selection, blood bags, anticoagulant solutions and test kits) to storage, transport, processing, quality control and delivery of the finished product, all in accordance with the texts referred to under Principle at the beginning of this Annex.

2   Blood or plasma used as a source material for the manufacture of medicinal products should be collected by establishments and be tested in laboratories which are subject to inspection and approved by a competent authority.

3   Procedures to determine the suitability of individuals to donate blood and plasma, used as a source material for the manufacture of medicinal products, and the results of the testing of their donations should be documented by the collection establishment and should be available to the manufacturer of the medicinal product.

4   Monitoring of the quality of medicinal products derived from human blood or plasma should be carried out in such a way that any deviations from the quality specifications can be detected.

5   Medicinal products derived from human blood or plasma which have been returned unused should normally not be re-issued; (see also point 5.65 of the main GMP Guide).

Premises and Equipment

6   The premises used for the collection of blood or plasma should be of suitable size, construction and location to facilitate their proper operation, cleaning and maintenance. Collection, processing and testing of blood and plasma should not be performed in the same area. There should be suitable donor interview facilities so that these interviews are carried out in private.

7   Manufacturing, collection and testing equipment should be designed, qualified and maintained to suit its intended purpose and should not present any hazard. Regular maintenance and calibration should be carried out and documented according to established procedures.

8   In the preparation of plasma-derived medicinal products, viral inactivation or removal procedures are used and steps should be taken to prevent cross-contamination of treated with untreated products; dedicated and distinct premises and equipment should be used for treated products.

Blood and Plasma Collection

9   A standard contract is required between the manufacturer of the medicinal product derived from human blood or plasma and the blood/plasma collection establishment or organisation responsible for collection. Guidance on the content of the standard contract is provided in "Contribution to part II of the structure of the dossier for applications for marketing

authorisation control of starting materials for the production of blood derivatives" (III/5272/94).

10   Each donor must be positively identified at reception and again before venepuncture; see also Council Recommendation of 29 June 1998 on the suitability of blood and plasma donors and the screening of donated blood in the European Community[4] (98/463/EC).

11   The method used to disinfect the skin of the donor should be clearly defined and shown to be effective. Adherence to that method should then be maintained.

12   Donation number labels must be re-checked independently to ensure that those on blood packs, sample tubes and donation records are identical.

13   Blood bag and apheresis systems should be inspected for damage or contamination before being used to collect blood or plasma. In order to ensure traceability, the batch number of blood bags and apheresis systems should be recorded.

Traceability and Post Collection Measures

14   While fully respecting confidentiality, there must be a system in place which enables the path taken by each donation to be traced, both forward from the donor and back from the finished medicinal product, including the customer (hospital or healthcare professional). It is normally the responsibility of this customer to identify the recipient.

15   Post-collection measures: A standard operating procedure describing the mutual information system between the blood/plasma collection establishment and the manufacturing/fractionation facility should be set up so that they can inform each other if, following donation:

- it is found that the donor did not meet the relevant donor health criteria;
- a subsequent donation from a donor previously found negative for viral markers is found positive for any of the viral markers;
- it is discovered that testing for viral markers has not been carried out according to agreed procedures;
- the donor has developed an infectious disease caused by an agent potentially transmissible by plasma-derived products (HBV, HCV, HAV and other non-A, non-B, non-C hepatitis viruses, HIV 1 and 2 and other agents in the light of current knowledge);
- the donor develops Creutzfeldt-Jakob disease (CJD or vCJD);

---

[4] O.J. L 20321.7.1998 p. 14.

- the recipient of blood or a blood component develops post-transfusion/infusion infection which implicates or can be traced back to the donor.

The procedures to be followed in the event of any of the above should be documented in the standard operating procedure. Look-back should consist of tracing back of previous donations for at least six months prior to the last negative donation. In the event of any of the above, a re-assessment of the batch documentation should always be carried out.

The need for withdrawal of the given batch should be carefully considered, taking into account criteria such as the transmissible agent involved, the size of the pool, the time period between donation and seroconversion, the nature of the product and its manufacturing method. Where there are indications that a donation contributing to a plasma pool was infected with HIV or hepatitis A, B or C, the case should be referred to the relevant competent authority(ies) responsible for the authorisation of the medicinal product and the company's view regarding continued manufacture from the implicated pool or of the possibility of withdrawal of the product(s) should be given. More specific guidance is given in the current version of the CPMP Note for Guidance on Plasma-derived Medicinal Products.

Production and Quality Control

16   Before any blood and plasma donations, or any product derived therefrom, are released for issue and/or fractionation, they should be tested, using a validated test method of suitable sensitivity and specificity, for the following markers of specific disease-transmitting agents:

- HBsAg;
- antibodies to HIV 1 and HIV 2;
- antibodies to HCV.

If a repeat-reactive result is found in any of these tests, the donation is not acceptable. (Additional tests may form part of national requirements)

17   The specified storage temperatures of blood, plasma and intermediate products when stored and during transportation from collection establishments to manufacturers, or between different manufacturing sites, should be checked and validated. The same applies to delivery of these products.

18   The first homogeneous plasma pool (e.g. after separation of the cryoprecipitate) should be tested using a validated test method, of suitable sensitivity and specificity, and found non-reactive for the following markers of specific disease-transmitting agents:

- HBsAg;
- antibodies to HIV 1 and HIV 2;
- antibodies to HCV.

Confirmed positive pools must be rejected.

19 Only batches derived from plasma pools tested and found non-reactive for HCV RNA by nucleic acid amplification technology (NAT), using a validated test method of suitable sensitivity and specificity, should be released.

20 Testing requirements for viruses, or other infectious agents, should be considered in the light of knowledge emerging as to infectious agents and the availability of appropriate test methods.

21 The labels on single units of plasma stored for pooling and fractionation must comply with the provisions of the European Pharmacopoeia monograph "Human Plasma for Fractionation" and bear at least the identification number of the donation, the name and address of the collection establishment or the references of the blood transfusion service responsible for preparation, the batch number of the container, the storage temperature, the total volume or weight of plasma, the type of anticoagulant used and the date of collection and/or separation.

22 In order to minimise the microbiological contamination of plasma for fractionation or the introduction of foreign material, the thawing and pooling should be performed at least in a grade D clean area, wearing the appropriate clothing and in addition face masks and gloves should be worn. Methods used for opening bags, pooling and thawing should be regularly monitored, e.g. by testing for bioburden. The cleanroom requirements for all other open manipulations should conform to the requirements of Annex 1 of the EU Guide to GMP.

23 Methods for clearly distinguishing between products or intermediates which have undergone a process of virus removal or inactivation, from those which have not, should be in place.

24 Validation of methods used for virus removal or virus inactivation should not be conducted in the production facilities in order not to put the routine manufacture at any risk of contamination with the viruses used for validation.

Retention of Samples

25 Where possible, samples of individual donations should be stored to facilitate any necessary look-back procedure. This would normally be the responsibility of the collection establishment. Samples of each pool of

plasma should be stored under suitable conditions for at least one year after the expiry date of the finished product with the longest shelf-life.

Disposal of Rejected Blood, Plasma or Intermediates

26   There should be a standard operating procedure for the safe and effective disposal of blood, plasma or intermediates.

ANNEX 15 QUALIFICATION AND VALIDATION

Principle

1   This Annex describes the principles of qualification and validation which are applicable to the manufacture of medicinal products. It is a requirement of GMP that manufacturers identify what validation work is needed to prove control of the critical aspects of their particular operations. Significant changes to the facilities, the equipment and the processes, which may affect the quality of the product, should be validated. A risk assessment approach should be used to determine the scope and extent of validation.

Planning for Validation

2   All validation activities should be planned. The key elements of a validation programme should be clearly defined and documented in a validation master plan (VMP) or equivalent documents.

3   The VMP should be a summary document which is brief, concise and clear.

4   The VMP should contain data on at least the following:

(a) validation policy;
(b) organisational structure of validation activities;
(c) summary of facilities, systems, equipment and processes to be validated;
(d) documentation format: the format to be used for protocols and reports;
(e) planning and scheduling;
(f) change control;
(g) reference to existing documents.

5   In case of large projects, it may be necessary to create separate validation master plans.

Documentation

6   A written protocol should be established that specifies how qualification and validation will be conducted. The protocol should be reviewed and approved. The protocol should specify critical steps and acceptance criteria.

7   A report that cross-references the qualification and/or validation protocol should be prepared, summarising the results obtained, commenting on any deviations observed, and drawing the necessary conclusions, including recommending changes necessary to correct deficiencies. Any changes to the

plan as defined in the protocol should be documented with appropriate justification.

8   After completion of a satisfactory qualification, a formal release for the next step in qualification and validation should be made as a written authorisation.

Qualification

Design qualification

9   The first element of the validation of new facilities, systems or equipment could be design qualification (DQ).

10   The compliance of the design with GMP should be demonstrated and documented.

Installation qualification

11   Installation qualification (IQ) should be performed on new or modified facilities, systems and equipment.

12   IQ should include, but not be limited to the following:

   (a) installation of equipment, piping, services and instrumentation checked to current engineering drawings and specifications;
   (b) collection and collation of supplier operating and working instructions and maintenance requirements;
   (c) calibration requirements;
   (d) verification of materials of construction.

Operational qualification

13   Operational qualification (OQ) should follow Installation qualification.

14   OQ should include, but not be limited to the following:

   (a) tests that have been developed from knowledge of processes, systems and equipment;
   (b) tests to include a condition or a set of conditions encompassing upper and lower operating limits, sometimes referred to as "worst case" conditions.

15   The completion of a successful Operational qualification should allow the finalisation of calibration, operating and cleaning procedures, operator training and preventative maintenance requirements. It should permit a formal "release" of the facilities, systems and equipment.

Performance qualification

16 Performance qualification (PQ) should follow successful completion of Installation qualification and Operational qualification.

17 PQ should include, but not be limited to the following:

(a) tests, using production materials, qualified substitutes or simulated product, that have been developed from knowledge of the process and the facilities, systems or equipment;

(b) tests to include a condition or set of conditions encompassing upper and lower operating limits.

18 Although PQ is described as a separate activity, it may in some cases be appropriate to perform it in conjunction with OQ.

Qualification of established (in-use) facilities, systems and equipment

19 Evidence should be available to support and verify the operating parameters and limits for the critical variables of the operating equipment. Additionally, the calibration, cleaning, preventative maintenance, operating procedures and operator training procedures and records should be documented.

Process Validation

General

20 The requirements and principles outlined in this chapter are applicable to the manufacture of pharmaceutical dosage forms. They cover the initial validation of new processes, subsequent validation of modified processes and re-validation.

21 Process validation should normally be completed prior to the distribution and sale of the medicinal product (prospective validation). In exceptional circumstances, where this is not possible, it may be necessary to validate processes during routine production (concurrent validation). Processes in use for some time should also be validated (retrospective validation).

22 Facilities, systems and equipment to be used should have been qualified and analytical testing methods should be validated. Staff taking part in the validation work should have been appropriately trained.

23 Facilities, systems, equipment and processes should be periodically evaluated to verify that they are still operating in a valid manner.

Prospective validation

24   Prospective validation should include, but not be limited to the following:

(a) short description of the process;
(b) summary of the critical processing steps to be investigated;
(c) list of the equipment/facilities to be used (including measuring/monitoring/recording equipment) together with its calibration status;
(d) finished product specifications for release;
(e) list of analytical methods, as appropriate;
(f) proposed in-process controls with acceptance criteria;
(g) additional testing to be carried out, with acceptance criteria and analytical validation, as appropriate;
(h) sampling plan;
(i) methods for recording and evaluating results;
(j) functions and responsibilities;
(k) proposed timetable.

25   Using this defined process (including specified components) a series of batches of the final product may be produced under routine conditions. In theory the number of process runs carried out and observations made should be sufficient to allow the normal extent of variation and trends to be established and to provide sufficient data for evaluation. It is generally considered acceptable that three consecutive batches/runs within the finally agreed parameters, would constitute a validation of the process.

26   Batches made for process validation should be the same size as the intended industrial scale batches.

27   If it is intended that validation batches be sold or supplied, the conditions under which they are produced should comply fully with the requirements of Good Manufacturing Practice, including the satisfactory outcome of the validation exercise, and with the marketing authorisation.

Concurrent validation

28   In exceptional circumstances it may be acceptable not to complete a validation programme before routine production starts.

29   The decision to carry out concurrent validation must be justified, documented and approved by authorised personnel.

30   Documentation requirements for concurrent validation are the same as specified for prospective validation.

Retrospective validation

31 Retrospective validation is only acceptable for well-established processes and will be inappropriate where there have been recent changes in the composition of the product, operating procedures or equipment.

32 Validation of such processes should be based on historical data. The steps involved require the preparation of a specific protocol and the reporting of the results of the data review, leading to a conclusion and a recommendation.

33 The source of data for this validation should include, but not be limited to batch processing and packaging records, process control charts, maintenance log books, records of personnel changes, process capability studies, finished product data, including trend cards and storage stability results.

34 Batches selected for retrospective validation should be representative of all batches made during the review period, including any batches that failed to meet specifications, and should be sufficient in number to demonstrate process consistency. Additional testing of retained samples may be needed to obtain the necessary amount or type of data to retrospectively validate the process.

35 For retrospective validation, generally data from ten to thirty consecutive batches should be examined to assess process consistency, but fewer batches may be examined if justified.

Cleaning Validation

36 Cleaning validation should be performed in order to confirm the effectiveness of a cleaning procedure. The rationale for selecting limits of carry over of product residues, cleaning agents and microbial contamination should be logically based on the materials involved. The limits should be achievable and verifiable.

37 Validated analytical methods having sensitivity to detect residues or contaminants should be used. The detection limit for each analytical method should be sufficiently sensitive to detect the established acceptable level of the residue or contaminant.

38 Normally only cleaning procedures for product contact surfaces of the equipment need to be validated. Consideration should be given to non-contact parts. The intervals between use and cleaning as well as cleaning

and reuse should be validated. Cleaning intervals and methods should be determined.

39 For cleaning procedures for products and processes which are similar, it is considered acceptable to select a representative range of similar products and processes. A single validation study utilising a "worst case" approach can be carried out which takes account of the critical issues.

40 Typically three consecutive applications of the cleaning procedure should be performed and shown to be successful in order to prove that the method is validated.

41 "Test until clean" is not considered an appropriate alternative to cleaning validation.

42 Products which simulate the physicochemical properties of the substances to be removed may exceptionally be used instead of the substances themselves, where such substances are either toxic or hazardous.

Change Control

43 Written procedures should be in place to describe the actions to be taken if a change is proposed to a starting material, product component, process equipment, process environment (or site), method of production or testing or any other change that may affect product quality or reproducibility of the process. Change control procedures should ensure that sufficient supporting data are generated to demonstrate that the revised process will result in a product of the desired quality, consistent with the approved specifications.

44 All changes that may affect product quality or reproducibility of the process should be formally requested, documented and accepted. The likely impact of the change of facilities, systems and equipment on the product should be evaluated, including risk analysis. The need for, and the extent of, re-qualification and re-validation should be determined.

Revalidation

45 Facilities, systems, equipment and processes, including cleaning, should be periodically evaluated to confirm that they remain valid. Where no significant changes have been made to the validated status, a review with evidence that facilities, systems, equipment and processes meet the prescribed requirements fulfils the need for revalidation.

Glossary

Definitions of terms relating to qualification and validation which are not given in the glossary of the current EC Guide to GMP, but which are used in this Annex, are given below.

Change control

A formal system by which qualified representatives of appropriate disciplines review proposed or actual changes that might affect the validated status of facilities, systems, equipment or processes. The intent is to determine the need for action that would ensure and document that the system is maintained in a validated state.

Cleaning validation

Cleaning validation is documented evidence that an approved cleaning procedure will provide equipment which is suitable for processing medicinal products.

Concurrent validation

Validation carried out during routine production of products intended for sale.

Design qualification (DQ)

The documented verification that the proposed design of the facilities, systems and equipment is suitable for the intended purpose.

Installation qualification (IQ)

The documented verification that the facilities, systems and equipment, as installed or modified, comply with the approved design and the manufacturer's recommendations.

Operational qualification (OQ)

The documented verification that the facilities, systems and equipment, as installed or modified, perform as intended throughout the anticipated operating ranges.

Performance qualification (PQ)

The documented verification that the facilities, systems and equipment, as connected together, can perform effectively and reproducibly, based on the approved process method and product specification.

Process validation

The documented evidence that the process, operated within established parameters, can perform effectively and reproducibly to produce a medicinal product meeting its predetermined specifications and quality attributes.

Prospective validation

Validation carried out before routine production of products intended for sale.

Retrospective validation

Validation of a process for a product which has been marketed based upon accumulated manufacturing, testing and control batch data.

Re-validation

A repeat of the process validation to provide an assurance that changes in the process/equipment introduced in accordance with change control procedures do not adversely affect process characteristics and product quality.

Risk analysis

Method to assess and characterise the critical parameters in the functionality of an equipment or process.

Simulated product

A material that closely approximates the physical and, where practical, the chemical characteristics (e.g. viscosity, particle size, pH, etc.) of the product under validation. In many cases, these characteristics may be satisfied by a placebo product batch.

System

A group of equipment with a common purpose.

Worst case

A condition or set of conditions encompassing upper and lower processing limits and circumstances, within standard operating procedures which pose the greatest chance of product or process failure when compared to ideal conditions. Such conditions do not necessarily induce product or process failure.

ANNEX 16 CERTIFICATION BY A QUALIFIED PERSON AND BATCH RELEASE

1 Scope

1.1 This annex to the Guide to Good Manufacturing Practice for Medicinal Products ("the Guide") gives guidance on the certification by a Qualified Person (Q.P.) and batch release within the European Community (EC) or European Economic Area (EEA) of medicinal products holding a marketing authorisation or made for export. The relevant legislative requirements are contained in Article 51 of Directive 2001/83/EC or Article 55 of Directive 2001/82/EC.

1.2 The annex covers in particular those cases where a batch has had different stages of production or testing conducted at different locations or by different manufacturers, and where an intermediate or bulk production batch is divided into more than one finished product batch. It also covers the release of batches which have been imported to the EC/EEA both when there is and is not a mutual recognition agreement between the Community and the third country. The guidance may also be applied to investigational medicinal products, subject to any difference in the legal provisions and more specific guidance in Annex 13 to the Guide.

1.3 This annex does not, of course, describe all possible arrangements which are legally acceptable. Neither does it address the official control authority batch release which may be specified for certain blood and immunological products in accordance with Article 11 point 5.4 and Articles 109[1] and 110 of Directive 2001/83/EC.

1.4 The basic arrangements for batch release for a product are defined by its Marketing Authorisation. Nothing in this annex should be taken as overriding those arrangements.

2 Principle

2.1 Each batch of finished product must be certified by a Q.P. within the EC/EEA before being released for sale or supply in the EC/EEA or for export.

---

[1] As amended by Directive 2002/98/EC of the European Parliament and of the Council of 27 January 2003 setting standards of quality and safety for the collection, testing, processing, storage and distribution of human blood and blood components and amending Directive 2001/83/EC (OJ L 33, 8.2.2003, p. 30).

2.2 The purpose of controlling batch release in this way is:

- to ensure that the batch has been manufactured and checked in accordance with the requirements of its marketing authorisation, the principles and guidelines of EC Good Manufacturing Practice or the good manufacturing practice of a third country recognised as equivalent under a mutual recognition agreement and any other relevant legal requirement before it is placed on the market, and
- in the event that a defect needs to be investigated or a batch recalled, to ensure that the Q.P. who certified the batch and the relevant records are readily identifiable.

3 Introduction

3.1 Manufacture, including quality control testing, of a batch of medicinal products takes place in stages which may be conducted at different sites and by different manufacturers. Each stage should be conducted in accordance with the relevant marketing authorisation, Good Manufacturing Practice and the laws of the Member State concerned and should be taken into account by the Q.P. who certifies the finished product batch before release to the market.

3.2 However in an industrial situation it is usually not possible for a single Q.P. to be closely involved with every stage of manufacture. The Q.P. who certifies a finished product batch may need therefore to rely in part on the advice and decisions of others. Before doing so he should ensure that this reliance is well founded, either from personal knowledge or from the confirmation by other Q.P.s within a quality system which he has accepted.

3.3 When some stages of manufacture occur in a third country it is still a requirement that production and testing are in accordance with the marketing authorisation, that the manufacturer is authorised according to the laws of the country concerned and that manufacture follows good manufacturing practices at least equivalent to those of the EC.

3.4 Certain words used in this annex have particular meanings attributed to them, as defined in the glossary [to Annex 16].

4 General

4.1 One batch of finished product may have different stages of manufacture, importation, testing and storage before release conducted at different sites. Each site should be approved under one or more manufacturing authorisations and should have at its disposal the services of at least one Q.P. However the correct manufacture of a particular batch of product, regardless of how many sites are involved, should be the overall concern of the Q.P. who certifies that finished product batch before release.

4.2 Different batches of a product may be manufactured or imported and released at different sites in the EC/EEA. For example a Community marketing authorisation may name batch release sites in more than one member state, and a national authorisation may also name more than one release site. In this situation the holder of the marketing authorisation and each site authorised to release batches of the product should be able to identify the site at which any particular batch has been released and the Q.P. who was responsible for certifying that batch.

4.3 The Q.P. who certifies a finished product batch before release may do so based on his personal knowledge of all the facilities and procedures employed, the expertise of the persons concerned and of the quality system within which they operate. Alternatively he may rely on the confirmation by one or more other Q.P.s of the compliance of intermediate stages of manufacture within a quality system which he has accepted.

This confirmation by other Q.P.s should be documented and should identify clearly the matters which have been confirmed. The systematic arrangements to achieve this should be defined in a written agreement.

4.4 The agreement mentioned above is required whenever a Q.P. wishes to rely on the confirmation by another Q.P. The agreement should be in general accordance with Chapter 7 of the Guide. The Q.P. who certifies the finished product batch should ensure the arrangements in the agreement are verified. The form of such an agreement should be appropriate to the relationship between the parties; for example a standard operating procedure within a company or a formal contract between different companies even if within the same group.

4.5 The agreement should include an obligation on the part of the provider of a bulk or intermediate product to notify the recipient(s) of any deviations, out-of-specification results, non-compliance with GMP, investigations, complaints or other matters which should be taken into account by the Q.P. who is responsible for certifying the finished product batch.

4.6 When a computerised system is used for recording certification and batch release, particular note should be taken of the guidance in Annex 11 to this Guide.

4.7 Certification of a finished product batch against a relevant marketing authorisation by a Q.P. in the EC/EEA need not be repeated on the same batch provided the batch has remained within the EC/EEA.

4.8 Whatever particular arrangements are made for certification and release of batches, it should always be possible to identify and recall without delay all products which could be rendered hazardous by a quality defect in the batch.

5 Batch Testing and Release of Products Manufactured in EC/EEA

5.1 *When all manufacture occurs at a single authorised site.*
When all production and control stages are carried out at a single site, the conduct of certain checks and controls may be delegated to others but the Q.P. at this site who certifies the finished product batch normally retains personal responsibility for these within a defined quality system. However he may, alternatively, take account of the confirmation of the intermediate stages by other Q.Ps on the site who are responsible for those stages.

5.2 *Different stages of manufacture are conducted at different sites within the same company.*
When different stages of the manufacture of a batch are carried out at different sites within the same company (which may or may not be covered by the same manufacturing authorisation) a Q.P. should be responsible for each stage. Certification of the finished product batch should be performed by a Q.P. of the manufacturing authorisation holder responsible for releasing the batch to the market, who may take personal responsibility for all stages or may take account of the confirmation of the earlier stages by the relevant Q.P.s responsible for those stages.

5.3 *Some intermediate stages of manufacture are contracted to a different company.*
One or more intermediate production and control stages may be contracted to a holder of a manufacturing authorisation in another company. A Q.P. of the contract giver may take account of the confirmation of the relevant stage by a Q.P. of the contract acceptor but is responsible for ensuring that this work is conducted within the terms of a written agreement. The finished product batch should be certified by a Q.P. of the manufacturing authorisation holder responsible for releasing the batch to the market.

5.4 *A bulk production batch is assembled at different sites into several finished product batches which are released under a single marketing authorisation. This could occur, for example, under a national marketing authorisation when the assembly sites are all within one member state or under a Community marketing authorisation when the sites are in more than one member state.*

5.4.1 One alternative is for a Q.P. of the manufacturing authorisation holder making the bulk production batch to certify all the finished product batches before release to the market. In doing so he may either take personal responsibility for all manufacturing stages or take account of the confirmation of assembly by the Q.P.s of the assembly sites.

5.4.2 Another alternative is for the certification of each finished product batch before release to the market to be performed by a Q.P of the manufacturer who has conducted the final assembly operation. In doing so he may either take personal responsibility for all manufacturing stages or take account of the confirmation of the bulk production batch by a Q.P. of the manufacturer of the bulk batch.

5.4.3 In all cases of assembly at different sites under a single marketing authorisation, there should be one person, normally a Q.P. of the manufacturer of the bulk production batch, who has an overall responsibility for all released finished product batches which are derived from one bulk production batch. The duty of this person is to be aware of any quality problems reported on any of the finished product batches and to co-ordinate any necessary action arising from a problem with the bulk batch. While the batch numbers of the bulk and finished product batches are not necessarily the same, there should be a documented link between the two numbers so that an audit trail can be established.

5.5 *A bulk production batch is assembled at different sites into several finished product batches which are released under different marketing authorisations. This could occur, for example, when a multi-national organisation holds national marketing authorisations for a product in several member states or when a generic manufacturer purchases bulk products and assembles and releases them for sale under his own marketing authorisation.*

5.5.1 A Q.P. of the manufacturer doing the assembly who certifies the finished product batch may either take personal responsibility for all manufacturing stages or may take account of the confirmation of the bulk production batch by a Q.P. of the bulk product manufacturer.

5.5.2 Any problem identified in any of the finished product batches which may have arisen in the bulk production batch should be communicated to the Q.P. responsible for confirming the bulk production batch, who should then take any necessary action in respect of all finished product batches produced from the suspected bulk production batch. This arrangement should be defined in a written agreement.

5.6 *A finished product batch is purchased and released to the market by a manufacturing authorisation holder in accordance with his own marketing authorisation. This could occur, for example, when a company supplying* *generic products holds a marketing authorisation for products made by another company, purchases finished products which have not been certified against his marketing authorisation and releases them under his own manufacturing authorisation in accordance with his own marketing authorisation.*

In this situation a Q.P. of the purchaser should certify the finished product batch before release. In doing so he may either take personal responsibility for all manufacturing stages or may take account of the confirmation of the batch by a Q.P. of the vendor manufacturer.

5.7   *The quality control laboratory and the production site are authorised under different manufacturing authorisations.*

A Q.P. certifying a finished product batch may either take personal responsibility for the laboratory testing or may take account of the confirmation by another Q.P. of the testing and results. The other laboratory and Q.P. need not be in the same member state as the manufacturing authorisation holder releasing the batch. In the absence of such confirmation the Q.P. should himself have personal knowledge of the laboratory and its procedures relevant to the finished product to be certified.

6   Batch Testing and Release of Products Imported from a Third Country

6.1   *General*

    6.1.1 Importation of finished products should be conducted by an importer as defined in the glossary to this annex.

    6.1.2 Each batch of imported finished product should be certified by a Q.P. of the importer before release for sale in the EC/EEA.

    6.1.3 Unless a mutual recognition agreement is in operation between the Community and the third country (see Section 7 [of Annex 16]), samples from each batch should be tested in the EC/EEA before certification of the finished product batch by a Q.P. Importation and testing need not necessarily be performed in the same member state.

    6.1.4 The guidance in this section should also be applied as appropriate to the importation of partially manufactured products.

6.2   *A complete batch or the first part of a batch of a medicinal product is imported.*

The batch or part batch should be certified by a Q.P of the importer before release. This Q.P. may take account of the confirmation of the checking, sampling or testing of the imported batch by a Q.P. of another manufacturing authorisation holder (i.e. within EC/EEA).

6.3   *Part of a finished product batch is imported after another part of the same batch has previously been imported to the same or a different site.*

6.3.1 A Q.P. of the importer receiving a subsequent part of the batch may take account of the testing and certification by a Q.P. of the first part of the batch. If this is done, the Q.P. should ensure, based on evidence, that the two parts do indeed come from the same batch, that the subsequent part has been transported under the same conditions as the first part and that the samples that were tested are representative of the whole batch.

6.3.2 The conditions in paragraph 6.3.1 is most likely to be met when the manufacturer in the third country and the importer(s) in the EC/EEA belong to the same organisation operating under a corporate system of quality assurance. If the Q.P. cannot ensure that the conditions in paragraph 6.3.1 are met, each part of the batch should be treated as a separate batch.

6.3.3 When different parts of the batch are released under the same marketing authorisation, one person, normally a Q.P. of the importer of the first part of a batch, should take overall responsibility for ensuring that records are kept of the importation of all parts of the batch and that the distribution of all parts of the batch is traceable within the EC/EEA. He should be made aware of any quality problems reported on any part of the batch and should co-ordinate any necessary action concerning these problems and their resolution.

This should be ensured by a written agreement between all the importers concerned.

6.4   *Location of sampling for testing in EC/EEA.*

6.4.1 Samples should be representative of the batch and be tested in the EC/EEA. In order to represent the batch it may be preferable to take some samples during processing in the third country. For example, samples for sterility testing may best be taken throughout the filling operation. However in order to represent the batch after storage and transportation some samples should also be taken after receipt of the batch in the EC/EEA.

6.4.2 When any samples are taken in a third country, they should either be shipped with and under the same conditions as the batch which they represent, or if sent separately it should be demonstrated that the samples are still representative of the batch, for example by defining and monitoring the conditions of storage and shipment. When the Q.P. wishes to rely on testing of samples taken in a third country, this should be justified on technical grounds.

7 Batch Testing and Release of Products Imported from a Third Country with which the EC has a Mutual Recognition Agreement (MRA)

7.1   Unless otherwise specified in the agreement, an MRA does not remove the requirement for a Q.P. within the EC/EEA to certify a batch before it is released for sale or supply within the EC/EEA. However, subject to details of the particular agreement, the Q.P. of the importer may rely on the manufacturer's confirmation that the batch has been made and tested in accordance with its marketing authorisation and the GMP of the third country and need not repeat the full testing. The Q.P. may certify the batch for release when he is satisfied with this confirmation and that the batch has been transported under the required conditions and has been received and stored in the EC/EEA by an importer as defined in Section 8 [Annex 16].

7.2   Other procedures, including those for receipt and certification of part batches at different times and/or at different sites, should be the same as in Section 6 [Annex 16].

8 Routine Duties of a Qualified Person

8.1   Before certifying a batch prior to release the Q.P. doing so should ensure, with reference to the guidance above, that at least the following requirements have been met:

(a) the batch and its manufacture comply with the provisions of the marketing authorisation (including the authorisation required for importation where relevant);

(b) manufacture has been carried out in accordance with Good Manufacturing Practice or, in the case of a batch imported from a third country, in accordance with good manufacturing practice standards at least equivalent to EC GMP;

(c) the principal manufacturing and testing processes have been validated; account has been taken of the actual production conditions and manufacturing records;

(d) any deviations or planned changes in production or quality control have been authorised by the persons responsible in accordance with a defined system. Any changes requiring variation to the marketing or manufacturing authorisation have been notified to and authorised by the relevant authority;

(e) all the necessary checks and tests have been performed, including any additional sampling, inspection, tests or checks initiated because of deviations or planned changes;

(**f**) all necessary production and quality control documentation has been completed and endorsed by the staff authorised to do so;

(**g**) all audits have been carried out as required by the quality assurance system;

(**h**) the QP should in addition take into account any other factors of which he is aware which are relevant to the quality of the batch.

A Q.P. may have additional duties in accordance with national legislation or administrative procedures.

8.2 A Q.P. who confirms the compliance of an intermediate stage of manufacture, as described in paragraph 4.3, has the same obligations as above in relation to that stage unless specified otherwise in the agreement between the Q.P.s.

8.3 A Q.P. should maintain his knowledge and experience up to date in the light of technical and scientific progress and changes in quality management relevant to the products which he is required to certify.

8.4 If a Q.P. is called upon to certify a batch of a product type with which he is unfamiliar, for example because the manufacturer for whom he works introduces a new product range or because he starts to work for a different manufacturer, he should first ensure that he has gained the relevant knowledge and experience necessary to fulfil this duty.

In accordance with national requirements the Q.P. may be required to notify the authorities of such a change and may be subject to renewed authorisation.

9   Glossary

Certain words and phrases in this annex are used with the particular meanings defined below. Reference should also be made to the Glossary in the main part of the Guide.

Bulk production batch

A batch of product, of a size described in the application for a marketing authorisation, either ready for assembly into final containers or in individual containers ready for assembly to final packs. (A bulk production batch may, for example, consist of a bulk quantity of liquid product, of solid dosage forms such as tablets or capsules, or of filled ampoules).

Certification of the finished product batch

The certification in a register or equivalent document by a Q.P., as defined in Article 51 of Directive 2001/83/EC and Article 55 of Directive 2001/82/EC, before a batch is released for sale or distribution.

Confirmation

A signed statement that a process or test has been conducted in accordance with GMP and the relevant marketing authorisation, as agreed in writing with the Q.P. responsible for certifying the finished product batch before release. *Confirm* and *confirmed* have equivalent meanings.

Finished product batch

With reference to the control of the finished product, a finished product batch is defined in Part 1 Module 3 point 3.2.2.5 of Directive 2001/83/EC[2] and in Part 2 Section F 1 of Directive 2001/82/EC. In the context of this annex the term in particular denotes the batch of product in its final pack for release to the market.

Importer

The holder of the authorisation required by Article 40.3 of Directive 2001/83/EC and Article 44.3 of Directive 2001/82/EC for importing medicinal products from third countries.

Mutual Recognition Agreement (MRA)

The "appropriate arrangement" between the Community and an exporting third country mentioned in Article 51(2) of Directive 2001/83/EC and Article 55(2) of Directive 2001/82/EC.

Qualified Person (Q.P.)

The person defined in Article 48 of Directive 2001/83/EC and Article 52 of Directive 2001/82/EC.

---

[2] Amended by Commission Directive 2003/63/EC of 25 June 2003 amending Directive 2001/83/EC of the European Parliament and of the Council on the Community code relating to medicinal products for human use (OJ L 159, 27.06.2003, p.46).

ANNEX 17 PARAMETRIC RELEASE

1   Principle

1.1   The definition of Parametric Release used in this Annex is based on that proposed by the European Organization for Quality: "A system of release that gives the assurance that the product is of the intended quality based on information collected during the manufacturing process and on the compliance with specific GMP requirements related to Parametric Release".

1.2   Parametric release should comply with the basic requirements of GMP, with applicable annexes and the following guidelines.

2   Parametric Release

2.1   It is recognised that a comprehensive set of in-process tests and controls may provide greater assurance of the finished product meeting specification than finished product testing.

2.2   Parametric release may be authorised for certain specific parameters as an alternative to routine testing of finished products. Authorisation for parametric release should be given, refused or withdrawn jointly by those responsible for assessing products together with the GMP inspectors.

3   Parametric Release for Sterile Products

3.1   This section is only concerned with that part of Parametric Release which deals with the routine release of finished products without carrying out a sterility test. Elimination of the sterility test is only valid on the basis of successful demonstration that predetermined, validated sterilising conditions have been achieved.

3.2   A sterility test only provides an opportunity to detect a major failure of the sterility assurance system due to statistical limitations of the method.

3.3   Parametric Release can be authorised if the data demonstrating correct processing of the batch provides sufficient assurance, on its own, that the process designed and validated to ensure the sterility of the product has been delivered.

3.4   At present Parametric release can only be approved for products terminally sterilized in their final container.

3.5   Sterilization methods according to European Pharmacopoeia requirements using steam, dry heat and ionising radiation may be considered for parametric release.

3.6   It is unlikely that a completely new product would be considered as suitable for Parametric Release because a period of satisfactory sterility test results will form part of the acceptance criteria. There may be cases when a new product is only a minor variation, from the sterility assurance point of view, and existing sterility test data from other products could be considered as relevant.

3.7   A risk analysis of the sterility assurance system focused on an evaluation of releasing non-sterilised products should be performed.

3.8   The manufacturer should have a history of good compliance with GMP.

3.9   The history of non-sterility of products and of results of sterility tests carried out on the product in question together with products processed through the same or a similar sterility assurance system should be taken into consideration when evaluating GMP compliance.

3.10   A qualified experienced sterility assurance engineer and a qualified microbiologist should normally be present on the site of production and sterilization.

3.11   The design and original validation of the product should ensure that integrity can be maintained under all relevant conditions.

3.12   The change control system should require review of change by sterility assurance personnel.

3.13   There should be a system to control microbiological contamination in the product before sterilisation.

3.14   There should be no possibility for mix ups between sterilised and non-sterilised products. Physical barriers or validated electronic systems may provide such assurance.

3.15   The sterilization records should be checked for compliance to specification by at least two independent systems. These systems may consist of two people or a validated computer system plus a person.

3.16   The following additional items should be confirmed prior to release of each batch of product.

- All planned maintenance and routine checks have been completed in the sterilizer used.
- All repairs and modifications have been approved by the sterility assurance engineer and microbiologist.
- All instrumentation was in calibration.
- The sterilizer had a current validation for the product load processed.

3.17 Once parametric release has been granted, decisions for release or rejection of a batch should be based on the approved specifications. Non-compliance with the specification for parametric release cannot be overruled by a pass of a sterility test.

4 Glossary

Parametric Release

A system of release that gives the assurance that the product is of the intended quality based on information collected during the manufacturing process and on the compliance with specific GMP requirements related to Parametric Release.

Sterility Assurance System

The sum total of the arrangements made to assure the sterility of products. For terminally sterilized products these typically include the following stages:

(a) Product design.
(b) Knowledge of and, if possible, control of the microbiological condition of starting materials and process aids (e.g. gases and lubricants).
(c) Control of the contamination of the process of manufacture to avoid the ingress of microorganisms and their multiplication in the product. This is usually accomplished by cleaning and sanitization of product contact surfaces, prevention of aerial contamination by handling in clean rooms, use of process control time limits and, if applicable, filtration stages.
(d) Prevention of mix up between sterile and non-sterile product streams.
(e) Maintenance of product integrity.
(f) The sterilization process.
(g) The totality of the Quality System that contains the Sterility Assurance System, e.g. change control, training, written procedures, release checks, planned preventative maintenance, failure mode analysis, prevention of human error, validation calibration, etc.

ANNEX 18 GOOD MANUFACTURING PRACTICE FOR ACTIVE PHARMACEUTICAL INGREDIENTS

Editor's note	Requirements for active substances used as starting materials from October 2005 are now covered in Part II.

ANNEX 19 REFERENCE AND RETENTION SAMPLES

Editor's note	Came into operation 1 June 2006.

1 Scope

1.1 This Annex to the Guide to Good Manufacturing Practice for Medicinal Products ("the GMP Guide") gives guidance on the taking and holding of reference samples of starting materials, packaging materials or finished products and retention samples of finished products.

1.2 Specific requirements for investigational medicinal products are given in Annex 13 to the Guide.

1.3 This annex also includes guidance on the taking of retention samples for parallel imported/ distributed medicinal products.

2 Principle

2.1 Samples are retained to fulfil two purposes; firstly to provide a sample for analytical testing and secondly to provide a specimen of the fully finished product. Samples may therefore fall into two categories:

Reference sample: a sample of a batch of starting material, packaging material or finished product which is stored for the purpose of being analysed should the need arise during the shelf life of the batch concerned. Where stability permits, reference samples from critical intermediate stages (e.g. those requiring analytical testing and release) or intermediates, that are transported outside of the manufacturer's control, should be kept.

Retention sample: a sample of a fully packaged unit from a batch of finished product. It is stored for identification purposes. For example, presentation, packaging, labelling, patient information leaflet, batch number, expiry date should the need arise during the shelf life of the batch concerned. There may be exceptional circumstances where this requirement can be met without retention of duplicate samples e.g. where small amounts of a batch are packaged for different markets or in the production of very expensive medicinal products.

For finished products, in many instances the reference and retention samples will be presented identically, i.e. as fully packaged units. In such circumstances, reference and retention samples may be regarded as inter-changeable.

2.2   It is necessary for the manufacturer, importer or site of batch release, as specified under Sections 7 and 8, to keep reference and/or retention samples from each batch of finished product and, for the manufacturer to keep a reference sample from a batch of starting material (subject to certain exceptions – see Section 3.2 below) and/or intermediate product. Each packaging site should keep reference samples of each batch of primary and printed packaging materials. Availability of printed materials as part of the reference and/or retention sample of the finished product can be accepted.

2.3   The reference and/or retention samples serve as a record of the batch of finished product or starting material and can be assessed in the event of, for example, a dosage form quality complaint, a query relating to compliance with the marketing authorisation, a labelling/packaging query or a pharmacovigilance report.

2.4   Records of traceability of samples should be maintained and be available for review by competent authorities.

3   Duration of Storage

3.1   Reference and retention samples from each batch of finished product should be retained for at least one year after the expiry date. The reference sample should be contained in its finished primary packaging or in packaging composed of the same material as the primary container in which the produce is marketed (for veterinary medicinal products other than immunologicals, see also Annex 4, paragraphs 8 & 9).

3.2   Unless a longer period is required under the law of the Member State of manufacture, samples of starting materials (other than solvents, gases or water used in the manufacturing process) shall be retained for at least two years after the release of product. That period may be shortened if the period of stability of the material, as indicated in the relevant specification, is shorter. Packaging materials should be retained for the duration of the shelf life of the finished product concerned.

4   Size of Reference and Retention Samples

4.1   The reference sample should be of sufficient size to permit the carrying out, on, at least, two occasions, of the full analytical controls on the batch in accordance with the Marketing Authorisation File which has been assessed and approved by the relevant Competent Authority/Authorities. Where it is necessary to do so, unopened packs should be used when carrying out each set of analytical controls. Any proposed exception to this should be justified to, and agreed with, the relevant competent authority.

4.2 Where applicable, national requirements relating to the size of reference samples and, if necessary, retention samples, should be followed.

4.3 Reference samples should be representative of the batch of starting material, intermediate product or finished product from which they are taken. Other samples may also be taken to monitor the most stressed part of a process (e.g. beginning or end of a process). Where a batch is packaged in two, or more, distinct packaging operations, at least one retention sample should be taken from each individual packaging operation. Any proposed exception to this should be justified to, and agreed with, the relevant competent authority.

4.4 It should be ensured that all necessary analytical materials and equipment are still available, or are readily obtainable, in order to carry out all tests given in the specification until one year after expiry of the last batch manufactured.

5 Storage Conditions

5.1 Storage of reference samples of finished products and active substances should be in accordance with the current version of the Note for Guidance on Declaration of Storage Conditions for Medicinal Products and Active Substances.

5.2 Storage conditions should be in accordance with the marketing authorisation (e.g. refrigerated storage where relevant).

6 Written Agreements

6.1 Where the marketing authorisation holder is not the same legal entity as the site(s) responsible for batch release within the EEA, the responsibility for taking and storage of reference/retention samples should be defined in a written agreement between the two parties in accordance with Chapter 7 of the EC Guide to Good Manufacturing Practice. This applies also where any manufacturing or batch release activity is carried out at a site other than that with overall responsibility for the batch on the EEA market and the arrangements between each different site for the taking and keeping of reference and retention samples should be defined in a written agreement.

6.2   The Qualified Person who certifies a batch for sale should ensure that all relevant reference and retention samples are accessible at all reasonable times. Where necessary, the arrangements for such access should be defined in a written agreement.

6.3   Where more than one site is involved in the manufacture of a finished product, the availability of written agreements is key to controlling the taking and location of reference and retention samples.

7   Reference Samples – General Points

7.1   Reference samples are for the purpose of analysis and, therefore, should be conveniently available to a laboratory with validated methodology. For starting materials used for medicinal products manufactured within the EEA, this is the original site of manufacture of the finished product. For finished products manufactured within the EEA, this is the original site of manufacture.

7.2   For finished products manufactured by a manufacturer in a country outside the EEA;

    7.2.1   where an operational Mutual Recognition Agreement (MRA) is in place, the reference sample may be taken and stored at the site of manufacture. This should be covered in a written agreement (as referred to in Section 6 above) between the importer/site of batch release and the manufacturer located outside the EEA.

    7.2.2   where an operational MRA is not in place, reference samples of the finished medicinal product should be taken and stored at an authorised manufacturer located within the EEA. These samples should be taken in accordance with written agreement(s) between all of the parties concerned. The samples should, preferably, be stored at the location where testing on importation has been performed.

    7.2.3   reference samples of starting materials and packaging materials should be kept at the original site at which they were used in the manufacture of the medicinal product.

8   Retention Samples – General Points

8.1   A retention sample should represent a batch of finished products as distributed in the EEA and may need to be examined in order to confirm non-technical attributes for compliance with the marketing authorisation or

EU legislation. Therefore, retention samples should in all cases be located within the EEA. These should preferably be stored at the site where the Qualified Person (Q.P.) certifying the finished product batch is located.

8.2   In accordance with Section 8.1 above, where an operational MRA is in place and reference samples are retained at a manufacturer located in a country outside the EEA (Section 7.2.2 above), separate retention samples should be kept within the EEA.

8.3   Retention samples should be stored at the premises of an authorised manufacturer in order to permit ready access by the Competent Authority.

8.4   Where more than one manufacturing site within the EEA is involved in the manufacture importation/packaging/testing/batch release, as appropriate of a product, the responsibility for taking and storage of retention samples should be defined in a written agreement(s) between the parties concerned.

9   Reference and Retention Samples for Parallel Imported/Parallel Distributed Products.

9.1   Where the secondary packaging is not opened, only the packaging material used needs to be retained, as there is no, or little, risk of product mix up.

9.2   Where the secondary packaging is opened, for example, to replace the carton or patient information leaflet, then one retention sample, per packaging operation, containing the product should be taken, as there is a risk of product mix-up during the assembly process. It is important to be able to identify quickly who is responsible in the event of a mix-up (original manufacturer or parallel import assembler), as it would affect the extent of any resulting recall.

10   Reference and Retention Samples in the Case of Closedown of a Manufacturer

10.1   Where a manufacturer closes down and the manufacturing authorisation is surrendered, revoked, or ceases to exist, it is probable that many unexpired batches of medicinal products manufactured by that manufacturer remain on the market. In order for those batches to remain on the market, the manufacturer should make detailed arrangements for transfer of reference and retention samples (and relevant GMP documentation) to an authorised storage site. The manufacturer should satisfy the Competent Authority that the arrangements for storage are satisfactory and that the samples can, if necessary, be readily accessed and analysed.

10.2　If the manufacturer is not in a position to make the necessary arrangements this may be delegated to another manufacturer. The Marketing Authorisation holder (MAH) is responsible for such delegation and for the provision of all necessary information to the Competent Authority. In addition, the MAH should, in relation to the suitability of the proposed arrangements for storage of reference and retention samples, consult with the competent authority of each Member State in which any unexpired batch has been placed on the market.

10.3　These requirements apply also in the event of the closedown of a manufacture located outside the EEA. In such instances, the importer has a particular responsibility to ensure that satisfactory arrangements are put in place and that the competent authority/authorities is/are consulted.

GLOSSARY OF TERMS USED IN THE EU GUIDE TO GMP

Note: *Definitions given below apply to the words as used in this guide. They may have different meanings in other contexts.*

AIR-LOCK

An enclosed space with two or more doors, and which is interposed between two or more rooms, e.g. of differing class of cleanliness, for the purpose of controlling the air-flow between those rooms when they need to be entered. An air-lock is designed for and used by either people or goods.

BATCH (OR LOT)

A defined quantity of starting material, packaging material or product processed in one process or series of processes so that it could be expected to be homogeneous.

Note: *To complete certain stages of manufacture, it may be necessary to divide a batch into a number of sub-batches, which are later brought together to form a final homogeneous batch. In the case of continuous manufacture, the batch must correspond to a defined fraction of the production, characterised by its intended homogeneity.*

For control of the finished product, the following definition has been given in Annex 1 of Directive 2001/83/EC as amended by Directive 2003/63/EC (see http://ec.europa.eu/enterprise/pharmaceuticals/eudralex/homev1.htm): "For the control of the finished product, a batch of a proprietary medicinal product comprises all the units of a pharmaceutical form which are made from the same initial mass of material and have undergone a single series of manufacturing operations or a single sterilisation operation or, in the case of a continuous production process, all the units manufactured in a given period of time."

BATCH NUMBER (OR LOT NUMBER)

A distinctive combination of numbers and/or letters which specifically identifies a batch.

BIOGENERATOR

A contained system, such as a fermenter, into which biological agents are introduced along with other materials so as to effect their multiplication or their production of other substances by reaction with the other materials. Biogenerators are generally fitted with devices for regulation, control, connection, material addition and material withdrawal.

BIOLOGICAL AGENTS

Micro-organisms, including genetically engineered micro-organisms, cell cultures and endoparasites, whether pathogenic or not.

BULK PRODUCT

Any product which has completed all processing stages up to, but not including, final packaging.

CALIBRATION

The set of operations which establish, under specified conditions, the relationship between values indicated by a measuring instrument or measuring system, or values represented by a material measure, and the corresponding known values of a reference standard.

CELL BANK

Cell bank system: A cell bank system is a system whereby successive batches of a product are manufactured by culture in cells derived from the same master cell bank. A number of containers from the master cell bank are used to prepare a working cell bank. The cell bank system is validated for a passage level or number of population doublings beyond that achieved during routine production.

Master cell bank: A culture of [fully characterised] cells distributed into containers in a single operation, processed together in such a manner as to ensure uniformity and stored in such a manner as to ensure stability. A master cell bank is usually stored at −70°C or lower.

Working cell bank: A culture of cells derived from the master cell bank and intended for use in the preparation of production cell cultures. The working cell bank is usually stored at −70°C or lower.

CELL CULTURE

The result from the in-vitro growth of cells isolated from multicellular organisms.

CLEAN AREA

An area with defined environmental control of particulate and microbial contamination, constructed and used in such a way as to reduce the introduction, generation and retention of contaminants within the area.

Note: *The different degrees of environmental control are defined in the Supplementary Guidelines for the Manufacture of sterile medicinal products.*

CLEAN/CONTAINED AREA

An area constructed and operated in such a manner that will achieve the aims of both a clean area and a contained area at the same time.

CONTAINMENT

The action of confining a biological agent or other entity within a defined space.

Primary containment: A system of containment which prevents the escape of a biological agent into the immediate working environment. It involves the use of closed containers or safety biological cabinets along with secure operating procedures.

Secondary containment: A system of containment which prevents the escape of a biological agent into the external environment or into other working areas. It involves the use of rooms with specially designed air handling, the existence of airlocks and/or sterilisers for the exit of materials and secure operating procedures. In many cases it may add to the effectiveness of primary containment.

CONTAINED AREA

An area constructed and operated in such a manner (and equipped with appropriate air handling and filtration) so as to prevent contamination of the external environment by biological agents from within the area.

CONTROLLED AREA

An area constructed and operated in such a manner that some attempt is made to control the introduction of potential contamination (an air supply approximating to grade D may be appropriate), and the consequences of accidental release of living organisms. The level of control exercised should reflect the nature of the organism employed in the process. At a minimum, the area should be maintained at a pressure negative to the immediate external environment and allow for the efficient removal of small quantities of airborne contaminants.

COMPUTERISED SYSTEM

A system including the input of data, electronic processing and the output of information to be used either for reporting or automatic control.

CROSS-CONTAMINATION

Contamination of a material or of a product with another material or product.

CRUDE PLANT (VEGETABLE DRUG)

Fresh or dried medicinal plant or parts thereof.

CRYOGENIC VESSEL

A container designed to contain liquefied gas at extremely low temperature.

CYLINDER

A container designed to contain gas at a high pressure.

EXOTIC ORGANISM

A biological agent where either the corresponding disease does not exist in a given country or geographical area, or where the disease is the subject of prophylactic measures or an eradication programme undertaken in the given country or geographical area.

FINISHED PRODUCT

A medicinal product which has undergone all stages of production, including packaging in its final container.

HERBAL MEDICINAL PRODUCT

Medicinal product containing, as active ingredients, exclusively plant material and/or vegetable drug preparations.

INFECTED

Contaminated with extraneous biological agents and therefore capable of spreading infection.

IN-PROCESS CONTROL

Checks performed during production in order to monitor and if necessary to adjust the process to ensure that the product conforms its specification. The control of the environment or equipment may also be regarded as a part of in-process control.

INTERMEDIATE PRODUCT

Partly processed material which must undergo further manufacturing steps before it becomes a bulk product.

LIQUIFIABLE GASES

Those which, at the normal filling temperature and pressure, remain as a liquid in the cylinder.

MANIFOLD

Equipment or apparatus designed to enable one or more gas containers to be filled simultaneously from the same source.

MANUFACTURE

All operations of purchase of materials and products, Production, Quality Control, release, storage, distribution of medicinal products and the related controls.

MANUFACTURER

Holder of a Manufacturing Authorisation as described in Article 40 of Directive 2001/83/EC.

MEDICINAL PLANT

Plant the whole or part of which is used for medicinal purpose.

MEDICINAL PRODUCT

Any substance or combination of substances presented for treating or preventing disease in human beings or animals. Any substance or combination of substances which may be administered to human beings or animals with a view to making a medical diagnosis or to restoring, correcting or modifying physiological functions in human beings or in animals is likewise considered a medicinal product.

PACKAGING

All operations, including filling and labelling, which a bulk product has to undergo in order to become a finished product.

Note: *Note Sterile filling would not normally be regarded as part of packaging, the bulk product being the filled, but not finally packaged, primary containers.*

PACKAGING MATERIAL

Any material employed in the packaging of a medicinal product, excluding any outer packaging used for transportation or shipment. Packaging materials are referred to as primary or secondary according to whether or not they are intended to be in direct contact with the product.

PROCEDURES

Description of the operations to be carried out, the precautions to be taken and measures to be applied directly or indirectly related to the manufacture of a medicinal product.

PRODUCTION

All operations involved in the preparation of a medicinal product, from receipt of materials, through processing and packaging, to its completion as a finished product.

QUALIFICATION

Action of proving that any equipment works correctly and actually leads to the expected results. The word *validation* is sometimes widened to incorporate the concept of qualification.

QUALITY CONTROL

See Section II, Chapter 1.

QUARANTINE

The status of starting or packaging materials, intermediate, bulk or finished products isolated physically or by other effective means whilst awaiting a decision on their release or refusal.

RADIOPHARMACEUTICAL

"Radiopharmaceutical" shall mean any medicinal product which, when ready for use, contains one or more radionuclides (radioactive isotopes) included for a medicinal purpose (Article 1(6) of Directive 2001/83/EC).

RECONCILIATION

A comparison, making due allowance for normal variation, between the amount of product or materials theoretically and actually produced or used.

RECORD

See Section II, Chapter 4.

RECOVERY

The introduction of all or part of previous batches of the required quality into another batch at a defined stage of manufacture.

REPROCESSING

The reworking of all or part of a batch of product of an unacceptable quality from a defined stage of production so that its quality may be rendered acceptable by one or more additional operations.

RETURN

Sending back to the manufacturer or distributor of a medicinal product which may or may not present a quality defect.

SEED LOT

Seed lot system: A seed lot system is a system according to which successive batches of a product are derived from the same master seed lot at a given passage level. For routine production, a working seed lot is prepared from the master seed lot. The final product is derived from the working seed lot and has not undergone more passages from the master seed lot than the vaccine shown in clinical studies to be satisfactory with respect to safety and efficacy. The origin and the passage history of the master seed lot and the working seed lot are recorded.

Master seed lot: A culture of a micro-organism distributed from a single bulk into containers in a single operation in such a manner as to ensure uniformity, to prevent contamination and to ensure stability. A master seed lot in liquid form is usually stored at or below $-70°$C. A freeze-dried master seed lot is stored at a temperature known to ensure stability.

Working seed lot: A culture of a micro-organism derived from the master seed lot and intended for use in production. Working seed lots are distributed into containers and stored as described above for master seed lots.

SPECIFICATION

See Section II, Chapter 4.

STARTING MATERIAL

Any substance used in the production of a medicinal product, but excluding packaging materials.

STERILITY

Sterility is the absence of living organisms. The conditions of the sterility test are given in the European Pharmacopoeia.

SYSTEM

Is used in the sense of a regulated pattern of interacting activities and techniques which are united to form an organised whole.

VALIDATION

Action of proving, in accordance with the principles of Good Manufacturing Practice, that any procedure, process, equipment, material, activity or system actually leads to the expected results (see also qualification).

PART II: Basic Requirements for Active Substances Used as Starting Materials

Contents of Part II

Contents continue

II

1 Introduction

This guideline was published in November 2000 as Annex 18 to the GMP Guide reflecting the EU's agreement to ICH Q7A and has been used by manufacturers and GMP inspectorates on a voluntary basis. Article 46 (f) of Directive 2001/83/EC and Article 50 (f) of Directive 2001/82/EC; as amended by Directives 2004/27/EC and 2004/28/EC, respectively, place new obligations on manufacturing authorisation holders to use only active substances that have been manufactured in accordance with Good Manufacturing Practice for starting materials. The directives go on to say that the principles of Good Manufacturing Practice for active substances are to be adopted as detailed guidelines. Member States have agreed that the text of former Annex 18 should form the basis of the detailed guidelines to create Part II of the GMP Guide.

1.1 Objective

These guidelines are intended to provide guidance regarding Good Manufacturing Practice (GMP) for the manufacture of active substances under an appropriate system for managing quality. It is also intended to help ensure that active substances meet the requirements for quality and purity that they purport or are represented to possess.

In these guidelines "manufacturing" includes all operations of receipt of materials, production, packaging, repackaging, labelling, relabelling, quality control, release, storage and distribution of active substances and the related controls. The term "should" indicates recommendations that are expected to apply unless shown to be inapplicable, modified in any relevant annexes to the GMP Guide, or replaced by an alternative demonstrated to provide at least an equivalent level of quality assurance.

The GMP Guide as a whole does not cover safety aspects for the personnel engaged in manufacture, nor aspects of protection of the environment. These controls are inherent responsibilities of the manufacturer and are governed by other parts of the legislation.

These guidelines are not intended to define registration requirements or modify pharmacopoeial requirements and do not affect the ability of the responsible competent authority to establish specific registration requirements regarding active substances within the context of marketing/manufacturing authorisations. All commitments in registration documents must be met.

1.2 Scope

These guidelines apply to the manufacture of active substances for medicinal products for both human and veterinary use. They apply to the manufacture of sterile active substances only up to the point immediately prior to the active substance being rendered sterile. The sterilisation and aseptic processing of sterile active substances are not covered, but should be performed in accordance with the principles and guidelines of GMP as laid down in Directive 2003/94/EC and interpreted in the GMP Guide including its Annex 1.

In the case of ectoparasiticides for veterinary use, other standards than these guidelines, that ensure that the material is of appropriate quality, may be used.

These guidelines exclude whole blood and plasma, as Directive 2002/98/EC and the technical requirements supporting that directive lay down the detailed requirements for the collection and testing of blood; however, it does include active substances that are produced using blood or plasma as raw materials.

Finally, these guidelines do not apply to bulk-packaged medicinal products. They apply to all other active starting materials subject to any derogations described in the annexes to the GMP Guide, in particular Annexes 2–7 where supplementary guidance for certain types of active substance may be found. The annexes will consequently undergo a review but in the meantime and only until this review is complete, manufacturers may choose to continue to use Part I of the basic requirements and the relevant annexes for products covered by those annexes, or may already apply Part II.

Section 19 contains guidance that only applies to the manufacture of active substances used in the production of investigational medicinal products although it should be noted that its application in this case, although recommended, is not required by Community legislation.

An "Active Substance Starting Material" is a raw material, intermediate or an active substance that is used in the production of an active substance and that is incorporated as a significant structural fragment into the structure of the active substance. An Active Substance Starting Material can be an article of commerce, a material purchased from one or more suppliers under contract or commercial agreement, or produced in-house. Active Substance Starting Materials normally have defined chemical properties and structure.

The manufacturer should designate and document the rationale for the point at which production of the active substance begins. For synthetic processes, this is known as the point at which "Active Substance Starting Materials" are entered into the process.

For other processes (e.g. fermentation, extraction, purification, etc.), this rationale should be established on a case-by-case basis. Table 1 gives guidance on the point at which the Active Substance Starting Material is normally introduced into the process.

From this point on, appropriate GMP as defined in these guidelines should be applied to these intermediate and/or active substance

Table 1 Application of this Guide to API Manufacturing

Type of Manufacturing	Application of this Guide to steps (shown in grey) used in this type of manufacturing				
Chemical Manufacturing	Production of the API Starting Material	Introduction of the API Starting Material into process	Production of Intermediate(s)	Isolation and purification	Physical processing, and packaging
API derived from animal sources	Collection of organ, fluid, or tissue	Cutting, mixing, and/or initial processing	Introduction of the API Starting Material into process	Isolation and purification	Physical processing, and packaging
API extracted from plant sources	Collection of plant	Cutting and initial extraction(s)	Introduction of the API Starting Material into process	Isolation and purification	Physical processing, and packaging
Herbal extracts used as API	Collection of plants	Cutting and initial extraction		Further extraction	Physical processing, and packaging
API consisting of comminuted or powdered herbs	Collection of plants and/or cultivation and harvesting	Cutting/ comminuting			Physical processing, and packaging
Biotechnology: fermentation/ cell culture	Establishment of master cell bank and working cell bank	Maintenance of working cell bank	Cell culture and/or fermentation	Isolation and purification	Physical processing, and packaging
"Classical" Fermentation to produce an API	Establishment of cell bank	Maintenance of the cell bank	Introduction of the cells into fermentation	Isolation and purification	Physical processing, and packaging

Increasing GMP requirements →

manufacturing steps. This would include the validation of critical process steps determined to impact the quality of the active substance. However, it should be noted that the fact that a manufacturer chooses to validate a process step does not necessarily define that step as critical.

The guidance in this document would normally be applied to the steps shown in grey in Table 1. It does not imply that all steps shown should be completed. The stringency of GMP in active substance manufacturing should increase as the process proceeds from early steps to final steps, purification, and packaging. Physical processing of active substances, such as granulation, coating or physical manipulation of particle size (e.g. milling, micronising), should be conducted at least to the standards of these guidelines. These guidelines do not apply to steps prior to the first introduction of the defined "Active Substance Starting Material."

In the remainder of this guideline the term Active Pharmaceutical Ingredient (API) is used repeatedly and should be considered interchangeable with the term "Active Substance". The glossary in Section 20 of Part II should only be applied in the context of Part II. Some of the same terms are already defined in Part I of the GMP guide and these, therefore, should only be applied in the context of Part I.

2 Quality Management

2.1 Principles

2.10 Quality should be the responsibility of all persons involved in manufacturing.

2.11 Each manufacturer should establish, document, and implement an effective system for managing quality that involves the active participation of management and appropriate manufacturing personnel.

2.12 The system for managing quality should encompass the organisational structure, procedures, processes and resources, as well as activities necessary to ensure confidence that the API will meet its intended specifications for quality and purity. All quality related activities should be defined and documented.

2.13 There should be a quality unit(s) that is independent of production and that fulfils both quality assurance (QA) and quality control (QC) responsibilities. This can be in the form of separate QA and QC units or a single individual or group, depending upon the size and structure of the organization.

2.14 The persons authorised to release intermediates and APIs should be specified.

2.15   All quality related activities should be recorded at the time they are performed.

2.16   Any deviation from established procedures should be documented and explained. Critical deviations should be investigated, and the investigation and its conclusions should be documented.

2.17   No materials should be released or used before the satisfactory completion of evaluation by the quality unit(s) unless there are appropriate systems in place to allow for such use (e.g. release under quarantine as described in Section 10.20 or the use of raw materials or intermediates pending completion of evaluation).

2.18   Procedures should exist for notifying responsible management in a timely manner of regulatory inspections, serious GMP deficiencies, product defects and related actions (e.g. quality related complaints, recalls, regulatory actions, etc.).

2.2   Responsibilities of the Quality Unit(s)

2.20   The quality unit(s) should be involved in all quality-related matters.

2.21   The quality unit(s) should review and approve all appropriate quality-related documents.

2.22   The main responsibilities of the independent quality unit(s) should not be delegated. These responsibilities should be described in writing and should include but not necessarily be limited to:

(1)   releasing or rejecting all APIs. Releasing or rejecting intermediates for use outside the control of the manufacturing company;
(2)   establishing a system to release or reject raw materials, intermediates, packaging and labelling materials;
(3)   reviewing completed batch production and laboratory control records of critical process steps before release of the API for distribution;
(4)   making sure that critical deviations are investigated and resolved;
(5)   approving all specifications and master production instructions;
(6)   approving all procedures impacting the quality of intermediates or APIs;
(7)   making sure that internal audits (self-inspections) are performed;
(8)   approving intermediate and API contract manufacturers;
(9)   approving changes that potentially impact intermediate or API quality;
(10)   reviewing and approving validation protocols and reports;
(11)   making sure that quality related complaints are investigated and resolved;

(12) making sure that effective systems are used for maintaining and calibrating critical equipment;

(13) making sure that materials are appropriately tested and the results are reported;

(14) making sure that there is stability data to support retest or expiry dates and storage conditions on APIs and/or intermediates where appropriate; and

(15) performing product quality reviews (as defined in Section 2.5).

2.3   Responsibility for Production Activities

The responsibility for production activities should be described in writing, and should include but not necessarily be limited to:

(1)   preparing, reviewing, approving and distributing the instructions for the production of intermediates or APIs according to written procedures;

(2)   producing APIs and, when appropriate, intermediates according to pre-approved instructions;

(3)   reviewing all production batch records and ensuring that these are completed and signed;

(4)   making sure that all production deviations are reported and evaluated and that critical deviations are investigated and the conclusions are recorded;

(5)   making sure that production facilities are clean and when appropriate disinfected;

(6)   making sure that the necessary calibrations are performed and records kept;

(7)   making sure that the premises and equipment are maintained and records kept;

(8)   making sure that validation protocols and reports are reviewed and approved;

(9)   evaluating proposed changes in product, process or equipment; and

(10) making sure that new and, when appropriate, modified facilities and equipment are qualified.

2.4   Internal Audits (Self Inspection)

2.40   In order to verify compliance with the principles of GMP for APIs, regular internal audits should be performed in accordance with an approved schedule.

2.41   Audit findings and corrective actions should be documented and brought to the attention of responsible management of the firm. Agreed corrective actions should be completed in a timely and effective manner.

2.5   Product Quality Review

2.50   Regular quality reviews of APIs should be conducted with the objective of verifying the consistency of the process. Such reviews should normally be conducted and documented annually and should include at least:

- a review of critical in-process control and critical API test results;
- a review of all batches that failed to meet established specification(s);
- a review of all critical deviations or non-conformances and related investigations;
- a review of any changes carried out to the processes or analytical methods;
- a review of results of the stability monitoring programme;
- a review of all quality-related returns, complaints and recalls; and
- a review of adequacy of corrective actions.

2.51   The results of this review should be evaluated and an assessment made of whether corrective action or any revalidation should be undertaken. Reasons for such corrective action should be documented. Agreed corrective actions should be completed in a timely and effective manner.

3   Personnel

3.1   Personnel Qualifications

3.10   There should be an adequate number of personnel qualified by appropriate education, training and/or experience to perform and supervise the manufacture of intermediates and APIs.

3.11   The responsibilities of all personnel engaged in the manufacture of intermediates and APIs should be specified in writing.

3.12   Training should be regularly conducted by qualified individuals and should cover, at a minimum, the particular operations that the employee performs and GMP as it relates to the employee's functions. Records of training should be maintained. Training should be periodically assessed.

3.2   Personnel Hygiene

3.20   Personnel should practice good sanitation and health habits.

3.21   Personnel should wear clean clothing suitable for the manufacturing activity with which they are involved and this clothing should be changed when appropriate. Additional protective apparel, such as head, face, hand, and arm coverings, should be worn when necessary, to protect intermediates and APIs from contamination.

3.22   Personnel should avoid direct contact with intermediates or APIs.

3.23   Smoking, eating, drinking, chewing and the storage of food should be restricted to certain designated areas separate from the manufacturing areas.

3.24   Personnel suffering from an infectious disease or having open lesions on the exposed surface of the body should not engage in activities that could result in compromising the quality of APIs. Any person shown at any time (either by medical examination or supervisory observation) to have an apparent illness or open lesions should be excluded from activities where the health condition could adversely affect the quality of the APIs until the condition is corrected or qualified medical personnel determine that the person's inclusion would not jeopardize the safety or quality of the APIs.

3.3 Consultants

3.30   Consultants advising on the manufacture and control of intermediates or APIs should have sufficient education, training, and experience, or any combination thereof, to advise on the subject for which they are retained.

3.31   Records should be maintained stating the name, address, qualifications, and type of service provided by these consultants.

4 Buildings and Facilities

4.1 Design and Construction

4.10   Buildings and facilities used in the manufacture of intermediates and APIs should be located, designed, and constructed to facilitate cleaning, maintenance, and operations as appropriate to the type and stage of manufacture. Facilities should also be designed to minimize potential contamination. Where microbiological specifications have been established for the intermediate or API, facilities should also be designed to limit exposure to objectionable microbiological contaminants as appropriate.

4.11   Buildings and facilities should have adequate space for the orderly placement of equipment and materials to prevent mix-ups and contamination.

4.12   Where the equipment itself (e.g., closed or contained systems) provides adequate protection of the material, such equipment can be located outdoors.

4.13   The flow of materials and personnel through the building or facilities should be designed to prevent mix-ups or contamination.

4.14   There should be defined areas or other control systems for the following activities:

- Receipt, identification, sampling, and quarantine of incoming materials, pending release or rejection;
- Quarantine before release or rejection of intermediates and APIs;
- Sampling of intermediates and APIs;
- Holding rejected materials before further disposition (e.g., return, reprocessing or destruction)
- Storage of released materials;
- Production operations;
- Packaging and labelling operations; and
- Laboratory operations.

4.15   Adequate, clean washing and toilet facilities should be provided for personnel. These washing facilities should be equipped with hot and cold water as appropriate, soap or detergent, air driers or single service towels. The washing and toilet facilities should be separate from, but easily accessible to, manufacturing areas. Adequate facilities for showering and/or changing clothes should be provided, when appropriate.

4.16   Laboratory areas/operations should normally be separated from production areas. Some laboratory areas, in particular those used for in-process controls, can be located in production areas, provided the operations of the production process do not adversely affect the accuracy of the laboratory measurements, and the laboratory and its operations do not adversely affect the production process or intermediate or API.

4.2   Utilities

4.20   All utilities that could impact on product quality (e.g. steam, gases, compressed air, and heating, ventilation and air conditioning) should be qualified and appropriately monitored and action should be taken when limits are exceeded. Drawings for these utility systems should be available.

4.21   Adequate ventilation, air filtration and exhaust systems should be provided, where appropriate. These systems should be designed and constructed to minimise risks of contamination and cross-contamination and should include equipment for control of air pressure, micro-organisms (if appropriate), dust, humidity, and temperature, as appropriate to the stage of manufacture. Particular attention should be given to areas where APIs are exposed to the environment.

4.22   If air is re-circulated to production areas, appropriate measures should be taken to control risks of contamination and cross-contamination.

4.23 Permanently installed pipework should be appropriately identified. This can be accomplished by identifying individual lines, documentation, computer control systems, or alternative means. Pipework should be located to avoid risks of contamination of the intermediate or API.

4.24 Drains should be of adequate size and should be provided with an air break or a suitable device to prevent back-siphonage, when appropriate.

4.3 Water

4.30 Water used in the manufacture of APIs should be demonstrated to be suitable for its intended use.

4.31 Unless otherwise justified, process water should, at a minimum, meet World Health Organization (WHO) guidelines for drinking (potable) water quality.

4.32 If drinking (potable) water is insufficient to assure API quality, and tighter chemical and/or microbiological water quality specifications are called for, appropriate specifications for physical/chemical attributes, total microbial counts, objectionable organisms and/or endotoxins should be established.

4.33 Where water used in the process is treated by the manufacturer to achieve a defined quality, the treatment process should be validated and monitored with appropriate action limits.

4.34 Where the manufacturer of a non-sterile API either intends or claims that it is suitable for use in further processing to produce a sterile drug (medicinal) product, water used in the final isolation and purification steps should be monitored and controlled for total microbial counts, objectionable organisms, and endotoxins.

4.4 Containment

4.40 Dedicated production areas, which can include facilities, air handling equipment and/or process equipment, should be employed in the production of highly sensitizing materials, such as penicillins or cephalosporins.

4.41 Dedicated production areas should also be considered when material of an infectious nature or high pharmacological activity or toxicity is involved (e.g., certain steroids or cytotoxic anti-cancer agents) unless validated inactivation and/or cleaning procedures are established and maintained.

4.42 Appropriate measures should be established and implemented to prevent cross-contamination from personnel, materials, etc. moving from one dedicated area to another.

4.43   Any production activities (including weighing, milling, or packaging) of highly toxic non-pharmaceutical materials such as herbicides and pesticides should not be conducted using the buildings and/or equipment being used for the production of APIs. Handling and storage of these highly toxic non-pharmaceutical materials should be separate from APIs.

4.5   Lighting

4.50   Adequate lighting should be provided in all areas to facilitate cleaning, maintenance, and proper operations.

4.6   Sewage and Refuse

4.60   Sewage, refuse, and other waste (e.g., solids, liquids, or gaseous by-products from manufacturing) in and from buildings and the immediate surrounding area should be disposed of in a safe, timely, and sanitary manner. Containers and/or pipes for waste material should be clearly identified.

4.7   Sanitation and Maintenance

4.70   Buildings used in the manufacture of intermediates and APIs should be properly maintained and repaired and kept in a clean condition.

4.71   Written procedures should be established assigning responsibility for sanitation and describing the cleaning schedules, methods, equipment, and materials to be used in cleaning buildings and facilities.

4.72   When necessary, written procedures should also be established for the use of suitable rodenticides, insecticides, fungicides, fumigating agents, and cleaning and sanitizing agents to prevent the contamination of equipment, raw materials, packaging/labelling materials, intermediates, and APIs.

5   Process Equipment

5.1   Design and Construction

5.10   Equipment used in the manufacture of intermediates and APIs should be of appropriate design and adequate size, and suitably located for its intended use, cleaning, sanitization (where appropriate), and maintenance.

5.11   Equipment should be constructed so that surfaces that contact raw materials, intermediates, or APIs do not alter the quality of the intermediates and APIs beyond the official or other established specifications.

5.12 Production equipment should only be used within its qualified operating range.

5.13 Major equipment (e.g., reactors, storage containers) and permanently installed processing lines used during the production of an intermediate or API should be appropriately identified.

5.14 Any substances associated with the operation of equipment, such as lubricants, heating fluids or coolants, should not contact intermediates or APIs so as to alter their quality beyond the official or other established specifications. Any deviations from this should be evaluated to ensure that there are no detrimental effects upon the fitness for purpose of the material. Wherever possible, food grade lubricants and oils should be used.

5.15 Closed or contained equipment should be used whenever appropriate. Where open equipment is used, or equipment is opened, appropriate precautions should be taken to minimize the risk of contamination.

5.16 A set of current drawings should be maintained for equipment and critical installations (e.g., instrumentation and utility systems).

5.2   Equipment Maintenance and Cleaning

5.20 Schedules and procedures (including assignment of responsibility) should be established for the preventative maintenance of equipment.

5.21 Written procedures should be established for cleaning of equipment and its subsequent release for use in the manufacture of intermediates and APIs. Cleaning procedures should contain sufficient details to enable operators to clean each type of equipment in a reproducible and effective manner. These procedures should include:

- Assignment of responsibility for cleaning of equipment;
- Cleaning schedules, including, where appropriate, sanitizing schedules;
- A complete description of the methods and materials, including dilution of cleaning agents used to clean equipment;
- When appropriate, instructions for disassembling and reassembling each article of equipment to ensure proper cleaning;
- Instructions for the removal or obliteration of previous batch identification;
- Instructions for the protection of clean equipment from contamination prior to use;
- Inspection of equipment for cleanliness immediately before use, if practical; and
- Establishing the maximum time that may elapse between the completion of processing and equipment cleaning, when appropriate.

5.22 Equipment and utensils should be cleaned, stored, and, where appropriate, sanitized or sterilized to prevent contamination or carry-over of a material that would alter the quality of the intermediate or API beyond the official or other established specifications.

5.23 Where equipment is assigned to continuous production or campaign production of successive batches of the same intermediate or API, equipment should be cleaned at appropriate intervals to prevent build-up and carry-over of contaminants (e.g. degradants or objectionable levels of micro-organisms).

5.24 Non-dedicated equipment should be cleaned between production of different materials to prevent cross-contamination.

5.25 Acceptance criteria for residues and the choice of cleaning procedures and cleaning agents should be defined and justified.

5.26 Equipment should be identified as to its contents and its cleanliness status by appropriate means.

5.3 Calibration

5.30 Control, weighing, measuring, monitoring and test equipment that is critical for assuring the quality of intermediates or APIs should be calibrated according to written procedures and an established schedule.

5.31 Equipment calibrations should be performed using standards traceable to certified standards, if existing.

5.32 Records of these calibrations should be maintained.

5.33 The current calibration status of critical equipment should be known and verifiable.

5.34 Instruments that do not meet calibration criteria should not be used.

5.35 Deviations from approved standards of calibration on critical instruments should be investigated to determine if these could have had an impact on the quality of the intermediate(s) or API(s) manufactured using this equipment since the last successful calibration.

5.4 Computerized Systems

5.40 GMP related computerized systems should be validated. The depth and scope of validation depends on the diversity, complexity and criticality of the computerized application.

5.41 Appropriate installation qualification and operational qualification should demonstrate the suitability of computer hardware and software to perform assigned tasks.

5.42 Commercially available software that has been qualified does not require the same level of testing. If an existing system was not validated at time of installation, a retrospective validation could be conducted if appropriate documentation is available.

5.43 Computerized systems should have sufficient controls to prevent unauthorized access or changes to data. There should be controls to prevent omissions in data (e.g. system turned off and data not captured). There should be a record of any data change made, the previous entry, who made the change, and when the change was made.

5.44 Written procedures should be available for the operation and maintenance of computerized systems.

5.45 Where critical data are being entered manually, there should be an additional check on the accuracy of the entry. This can be done by a second operator or by the system itself.

5.46 Incidents related to computerized systems that could affect the quality of intermediates or APIs or the reliability of records or test results should be recorded and investigated.

5.47 Changes to the computerized system should be made according to a change procedure and should be formally authorized, documented and tested. Records should be kept of all changes, including modifications and enhancements made to the hardware, software and any other critical component of the system. These records should demonstrate that the system is maintained in a validated state.

5.48 If system breakdowns or failures would result in the permanent loss of records, a back-up system should be provided. A means of ensuring data protection should be established for all computerized systems.

5.49 Data can be recorded by a second means in addition to the computer system.

6 Documentation and Records

6.1 Documentation System and Specifications

6.10 All documents related to the manufacture of intermediates or APIs should be prepared, reviewed, approved and distributed according to written procedures. Such documents can be in paper or electronic form.

6.11 The issuance, revision, superseding and withdrawal of all documents should be controlled with maintenance of revision histories.

6.12 A procedure should be established for retaining all appropriate documents (e.g., development history reports, scale-up reports, technical transfer reports, process validation reports, training records, production records, control records, and distribution records). The retention periods for these documents should be specified.

6.13 All production, control, and distribution records should be retained for at least 1 year after the expiry date of the batch. For APIs with retest dates, records should be retained for at least 3 years after the batch is completely distributed.

6.14 When entries are made in records, these should be made indelibly in spaces provided for such entries, directly after performing the activities, and should identify the person making the entry. Corrections to entries should be dated and signed and leave the original entry still readable.

6.15 During the retention period, originals or copies of records should be readily available at the establishment where the activities described in such records occurred. Records that can be promptly retrieved from another location by electronic or other means are acceptable.

6.16 Specifications, instructions, procedures, and records can be retained either as originals or as true copies such as photocopies, microfilm, microfiche, or other accurate reproductions of the original records. Where reduction techniques such as microfilming or electronic records are used, suitable retrieval equipment and a means to produce a hard copy should be readily available.

6.17 Specifications should be established and documented for raw materials, intermediates where necessary, APIs, and labelling and packaging materials. In addition, specifications may be appropriate for certain other materials, such as process aids, gaskets, or other materials used during the production of intermediates or APIs that could critically impact on quality. Acceptance criteria should be established and documented for in-process controls.

6.18 If electronic signatures are used on documents, they should be authenticated and secure.

6.2 Equipment Cleaning and Use Record

6.20 Records of major equipment use, cleaning, sanitization and/or sterilization and maintenance should show the date, time (if appropriate), product, and batch number of each batch processed in the equipment, and the person who performed the cleaning and maintenance.

6.21 If equipment is dedicated to manufacturing one intermediate or API, then individual equipment records are not necessary if batches of the intermediate or API follow in traceable sequence. In cases where dedicated equipment is employed, the records of cleaning, maintenance, and use can be part of the batch record or maintained separately.

6.3 Records of Raw Materials, Intermediates, API Labelling and Packaging Materials

6.30 Records should be maintained including:

- The name of the manufacturer, identity and quantity of each shipment of each batch of raw materials, intermediates or labelling and packaging materials for APIs; the name of the supplier; the supplier's control number(s), if known, or other identification number; the number allocated on receipt; and the date of receipt;
- The results of any test or examination performed and the conclusions derived from this;
- Records tracing the use of materials;
- Documentation of the examination and review of API labelling and packaging materials for conformity with established specifications; and
- The final decision regarding rejected raw materials, intermediates or API labelling and packaging materials.

6.31 Master (approved) labels should be maintained for comparison to issued labels.

6.4 Master Production Instructions (Master Production and Control Records)

6.40 To ensure uniformity from batch to batch, master production instructions for each intermediate and API should be prepared, dated, and signed by one person and independently checked, dated, and signed by a person in the quality unit(s).

6.41 Master production instructions should include:

- The name of the intermediate or API being manufactured and an identifying document reference code, if applicable;
- A complete list of raw materials and intermediates designated by names or codes sufficiently specific to identify any special quality characteristics;
- An accurate statement of the quantity or ratio of each raw material or intermediate to be used, including the unit of measure. Where the quantity is not fixed, the calculation for each batch size or rate of production

should be included. Variations to quantities should be included where they are justified;

- The production location and major production equipment to be used;
- Detailed production instructions, including the:
  - sequences to be followed;
  - ranges of process parameters to be used;
  - sampling instructions and in-process controls with their acceptance criteria, where appropriate;
  - time limits for completion of individual processing steps and/or the total process, where appropriate; and
  - expected yield ranges at appropriate phases of processing or time;

- Where appropriate, special notations and precautions to be followed, or cross references to these; and
- The instructions for storage of the intermediate or API to assure its suitability for use, including the labelling and packaging materials and special storage conditions with time limits, where appropriate.

6.5 Batch Production Records (Batch Production and Control Records)

6.50 Batch production records should be prepared for each intermediate and API and should include complete information relating to the production and control of each batch. The batch production record should be checked before issuance to assure that it is the correct version and a legible accurate reproduction of the appropriate master production instruction. If the batch production record is produced from a separate part of the master document, that document should include a reference to the current master production instruction being used.

6.51 These records should be numbered with a unique batch or identification number, dated and signed when issued. In continuous production, the product code together with the date and time can serve as the unique identifier until the final number is allocated.

6.52 Documentation of completion of each significant step in the batch production records (batch production and control records) should include:

- Dates and, when appropriate, times;
- Identity of major equipment (e.g., reactors, driers, mills, etc.) used;
- Specific identification of each batch, including weights, measures, and batch numbers of raw materials, intermediates, or any reprocessed materials used during manufacturing;
- Actual results recorded for critical process parameters;
- Any sampling performed;

- Signatures of the persons performing and directly supervising or checking each critical step in the operation;
- In-process and laboratory test results;
- Actual yield at appropriate phases or times;
- Description of packaging and label for intermediate or API;
- Representative label of API or intermediate if made commercially available;
- Any deviation noted, its evaluation, investigation conducted (if appropriate) or reference to that investigation if stored separately; and
- Results of release testing.

6.53   Written procedures should be established and followed for investigating critical deviations or the failure of a batch of intermediate or API to meet specifications. The investigation should extend to other batches that may have been associated with the specific failure or deviation.

6.6   Laboratory Control Records

6.60   Laboratory control records should include complete data derived from all tests conducted to ensure compliance with established specifications and standards, including examinations and assays, as follows:

- A description of samples received for testing, including the material name or source, batch number or other distinctive code, date sample was taken, and, where appropriate, the quantity and date the sample was received for testing;
- A statement of or reference to each test method used;
- A statement of the weight or measure of sample used for each test as described by the method; data on or cross-reference to the preparation and testing of reference standards, reagents and standard solutions;
- A complete record of all raw data generated during each test, in addition to graphs, charts, and spectra from laboratory instrumentation, properly identified to show the specific material and batch tested;
- A record of all calculations performed in connection with the test, including, for example, units of measure, conversion factors, and equivalency factors;
- A statement of the test results and how they compare with established acceptance criteria;
- The signature of the person who performed each test and the date(s) the tests were performed; and
- The date and signature of a second person showing that the original records have been reviewed for accuracy, completeness, and compliance with established standards.

6.61   Complete records should also be maintained for:

- Any modifications to an established analytical method,
- Periodic calibration of laboratory instruments, apparatus, gauges, and recording devices;
- All stability testing performed on APIs; and
- Out-of-specification (OOS) investigations.

6.7   Batch Production Record Review

6.70   Written procedures should be established and followed for the review and approval of batch production and laboratory control records, including packaging and labelling, to determine compliance of the intermediate or API with established specifications before a batch is released or distributed.

6.71   Batch production and laboratory control records of critical process steps should be reviewed and approved by the quality unit(s) before an API batch is released or distributed. Production and laboratory control records of non-critical process steps can be reviewed by qualified production personnel or other units following procedures approved by the quality unit(s).

6.72   All deviation, investigation, and OOS reports should be reviewed as part of the batch record review before the batch is released.

6.73   The quality unit(s) can delegate to the production unit the responsibility and authority for release of intermediates, except for those shipped outside the control of the manufacturing company.

7   Materials Management

7.1   General Controls

7.10   There should be written procedures describing the receipt, identification, quarantine, storage, handling, sampling, testing, and approval or rejection of materials.

7.11   Manufacturers of intermediates and/or APIs should have a system for evaluating the suppliers of critical materials.

7.12   Materials should be purchased against an agreed specification, from a supplier or suppliers approved by the quality unit(s).

7.13   If the supplier of a critical material is not the manufacturer of that material, the name and address of that manufacturer should be known by the intermediate and/or API manufacturer.

7.14   Changing the source of supply of critical raw materials should be treated according to Section 13, Change Control.

7.2   Receipt and Quarantine

7.20   Upon receipt and before acceptance, each container or grouping of containers of materials should be examined visually for correct labelling (including correlation between the name used by the supplier and the in-house name, if these are different), container damage, broken seals and evidence of tampering or contamination. Materials should be held under quarantine until they have been sampled, examined or tested as appropriate, and released for use.

7.21   Before incoming materials are mixed with existing stocks (e.g., solvents or stocks in silos), they should be identified as correct, tested, if appropriate, and released. Procedures should be available to prevent discharging incoming materials wrongly into the existing stock.

7.22   If bulk deliveries are made in non-dedicated tankers, there should be assurance of no cross-contamination from the tanker. Means of providing this assurance could include one or more of the following:

- certificate of cleaning
- testing for trace impurities
- audit of the supplier.

7.23   Large storage containers, and their attendant manifolds, filling and discharge lines should be appropriately identified.

7.24   Each container or grouping of containers (batches) of materials should be assigned and identified with a distinctive code, batch, or receipt number. This number should be used in recording the disposition of each batch. A system should be in place to identify the status of each batch.

7.3   Sampling and Testing of Incoming Production Materials

7.30   At least one test to verify the identity of each batch of material should be conducted, with the exception of the materials described below in Section 7.32. A supplier's Certificate of Analysis can be used in place of performing other tests, provided that the manufacturer has a system in place to evaluate suppliers.

7.31   Supplier approval should include an evaluation that provides adequate evidence (e.g., past quality history) that the manufacturer can consistently provide material meeting specifications. Full analyses should be conducted on at least three batches before reducing in-house testing. However, as a minimum, a full analysis should be performed at appropriate intervals and compared with the Certificates of Analysis. Reliability of Certificates of Analysis should be checked at regular intervals.

7.32   Processing aids, hazardous or highly toxic raw materials, other special materials, or materials transferred to another unit within the company's control do not need to be tested if the manufacturer's Certificate of Analysis is obtained, showing that these raw materials conform to established specifications. Visual examination of containers, labels, and recording of batch numbers should help in establishing the identity of these materials. The lack of on-site testing for these materials should be justified and documented.

7.33   Samples should be representative of the batch of material from which they are taken. Sampling methods should specify the number of containers to be sampled, which part of the container to sample, and the amount of material to be taken from each container. The number of containers to sample and the sample size should be based upon a sampling plan that takes into consideration the criticality of the material, material variability, past quality history of the supplier, and the quantity needed for analysis.

7.34   Sampling should be conducted at defined locations and by procedures designed to prevent contamination of the material sampled and contamination of other materials.

7.35   Containers from which samples are withdrawn should be opened carefully and subsequently re-closed. They should be marked to indicate that a sample has been taken.

7.4 Storage

7.40   Materials should be handled and stored in a manner to prevent degradation, contamination, and cross-contamination.

7.41   Materials stored in fibre drums, bags, or boxes should be stored off the floor and, when appropriate, suitably spaced to permit cleaning and inspection.

7.42   Materials should be stored under conditions and for a period that have no adverse affect on their quality, and should normally be controlled so that the oldest stock is used first.

7.43   Certain materials in suitable containers can be stored outdoors, provided identifying labels remain legible and containers are appropriately cleaned before opening and use.

7.44   Rejected materials should be identified and controlled under a quarantine system designed to prevent their unauthorised use in manufacturing.

7.5 Re-evaluation

7.50   Materials should be re-evaluated as appropriate to determine their suitability for use (e.g. after prolonged storage or exposure to heat or humidity).

8   Production and In-Process Controls

8.1   Production Operations

8.10   Raw materials for intermediate and API manufacturing should be weighed or measured under appropriate conditions that do not affect their suitability for use. Weighing and measuring devices should be of suitable accuracy for the intended use.

8.11   If a material is subdivided for later use in production operations, the container receiving the material should be suitable and should be so identified that the following information is available:

- Material name and/or item code;
- Receiving or control number;
- Weight or measure of material in the new container; and
- Re-evaluation or retest date if appropriate.

8.12   Critical weighing, measuring, or subdividing operations should be witnessed or subjected to an equivalent control. Prior to use, production personnel should verify that the materials are those specified in the batch record for the intended intermediate or API.

8.13   Other critical activities should be witnessed or subjected to an equivalent control.

8.14   Actual yields should be compared with expected yields at designated steps in the production process. Expected yields with appropriate ranges should be established based on previous laboratory, pilot scale, or manufacturing data. Deviations in yield associated with critical process steps should be investigated to determine their impact or potential impact on the resulting quality of affected batches.

8.15   Any deviation should be documented and explained. Any critical deviation should be investigated.

8.16   The processing status of major units of equipment should be indicated either on the individual units of equipment or by appropriate documentation, computer control systems, or alternative means.

8.17   Materials to be reprocessed or reworked should be appropriately controlled to prevent unauthorized use.

8.2   Time Limits

8.20   If time limits are specified in the master production instruction (see Section 6.41), these time limits should be met to ensure the quality of intermediates and APIs. Deviations should be documented and evaluated. Time limits may be inappropriate when processing to a target value (e.g., pH adjustment, hydrogenation, drying to predetermined specification) because completion of reactions or processing steps are determined by in-process sampling and testing.

8.21 Intermediates held for further processing should be stored under appropriate conditions to ensure their suitability for use.

8.3 In-process Sampling and Controls

8.30 Written procedures should be established to monitor the progress and control the performance of processing steps that cause variability in the quality characteristics of intermediates and APIs. In-process controls and their acceptance criteria should be defined based on the information gained during the development stage or historical data.

8.31 The acceptance criteria and type and extent of testing can depend on the nature of the intermediate or API being manufactured, the reaction or process step being conducted, and the degree to which the process introduces variability in the product's quality. Less stringent in-process controls may be appropriate in early processing steps, whereas tighter controls may be appropriate for later processing steps (e.g., isolation and purification steps).

8.32 Critical in-process controls (and critical process monitoring), including the control points and methods, should be stated in writing and approved by the quality unit(s).

8.33 In-process controls can be performed by qualified production department personnel and the process adjusted without prior quality unit(s) approval if the adjustments are made within pre-established limits approved by the quality unit(s). All tests and results should be fully documented as part of the batch record.

8.34 Written procedures should describe the sampling methods for in-process materials, intermediates, and APIs. Sampling plans and procedures should be based on scientifically sound sampling practices.

8.35 In-process sampling should be conducted using procedures designed to prevent contamination of the sampled material and other intermediates or APIs. Procedures should be established to ensure the integrity of samples after collection.

8.36 Out-of-specification (OOS) investigations are not normally needed for in-process tests that are performed for the purpose of monitoring and/or adjusting the process.

8.4   Blending Batches of Intermediates or APIs

8.40   For the purpose of this document, blending is defined as the process of combining materials within the same specification to produce a homogeneous intermediate or API. In-process mixing of fractions from single batches (e.g., collecting several centrifuge loads from a single crystallization batch) or combining fractions from several batches for further processing is considered to be part of the production process and is not considered to be blending.

8.41   Out-of-specification batches should not be blended with other batches for the purpose of meeting specifications. Each batch incorporated into the blend should have been manufactured using an established process and should have been individually tested and found to meet appropriate specifications prior to blending.

8.42   Acceptable blending operations include but are not limited to:

- Blending of small batches to increase batch size
- Blending of tailings (i.e., relatively small quantities of isolated material) from batches of the same intermediate or API to form a single batch.

8.43   Blending processes should be adequately controlled and documented and the blended batch should be tested for conformance to established specifications where appropriate.

8.44   The batch record of the blending process should allow traceability back to the individual batches that make up the blend.

8.45   Where physical attributes of the API are critical (e.g., APIs intended for use in solid oral dosage forms or suspensions), blending operations should be validated to show homogeneity of the combined batch. Validation should include testing of critical attributes (e.g., particle size distribution, bulk density, and tap density) that may be affected by the blending process.

8.46   If the blending could adversely affect stability, stability testing of the final blended batches should be performed.

8.47   The expiry or retest date of the blended batch should be based on the manufacturing date of the oldest tailings or batch in the blend.

8.5   Contamination Control

8.50   Residual materials can be carried over into successive batches of the same intermediate or API if there is adequate control. Examples include residue adhering to the wall of a micronizer, residual layer of damp crystals remaining in a centrifuge bowl after discharge, and incomplete discharge of fluids or crystals from a processing vessel upon transfer of the material to the next step in the process. Such carryover should not result in the carry-over of degradants or microbial contamination that may adversely alter the established API impurity profile.

8.51   Production operations should be conducted in a manner that will prevent contamination of intermediates or APIs by other materials.

8.52   Precautions to avoid contamination should be taken when APIs are handled after purification.

9   Packaging and Identification Labelling of APIs and Intermediates

9.1   General

9.10   There should be written procedures describing the receipt, identification, quarantine, sampling, examination and/or testing and release, and handling of packaging and labelling materials.

9.11   Packaging and labelling materials should conform to established specifications. Those that do not comply with such specifications should be rejected to prevent their use in operations for which they are unsuitable.

9.12   Records should be maintained for each shipment of labels and packaging materials showing receipt, examination, or testing, and whether accepted or rejected.

9.2   Packaging Materials

9.20   Containers should provide adequate protection against deterioration or contamination of the intermediate or API that may occur during transportation and recommended storage.

9.21   Containers should be clean and, where indicated by the nature of the intermediate or API, sanitized to ensure that they are suitable for their intended use. These containers should not be reactive, additive, or absorptive so as to alter the quality of the intermediate or API beyond the specified limits.

9.22   If containers are re-used, they should be cleaned in accordance with documented procedures and all previous labels should be removed or defaced.

9.3   Label Issuance and Control

9.30   Access to the label storage areas should be limited to authorised personnel.

9.31   Procedures should be used to reconcile the quantities of labels issued, used and returned and to evaluate discrepancies found between the number of containers labelled and the number of labels issued. Such discrepancies should be investigated, and the investigation should be approved by the quality unit(s).

9.32   All excess labels bearing batch numbers or other batch-related printing should be destroyed. Returned labels should be maintained and stored in a manner that prevents mix-ups and provides proper identification.

9.33   Obsolete and out-dated labels should be destroyed.

9.34   Printing devices used to print labels for packaging operations should be controlled to ensure that all imprinting conforms to the print specified in the batch production record.

9.35   Printed labels issued for a batch should be carefully examined for proper identity and conformity to specifications in the master production record. The results of this examination should be documented.

9.36   A printed label representative of those used should be included in the batch production record.

9.4   Packaging and Labelling Operations

9.40   There should be documented procedures designed to ensure that correct packaging materials and labels are used.

9.41   Labelling operations should be designed to prevent mix-ups. There should be physical or spatial separation from operations involving other intermediates or APIs.

9.42   Labels used on containers of intermediates or APIs should indicate the name or identifying code, the batch number of the product, and storage conditions, when such information is critical to assure the quality of intermediate or API.

9.43   If the intermediate or API is intended to be transferred outside the control of the manufacturer's material management system, the name and address of the manufacturer, quantity of contents, and special transport conditions and any special legal requirements should also be included on the label. For intermediates or APIs with an expiry date, the expiry date should be indicated on the label and Certificate of Analysis. For intermediates or APIs with a retest date, the retest date should be indicated on the label and/or Certificate of Analysis.

9.44   Packaging and labelling facilities should be inspected immediately before use to ensure that all materials not needed for the next packaging operation have been removed. This examination should be documented in the batch production records, the facility log, or other documentation system.

9.45 Packaged and labelled intermediates or APIs should be examined to ensure that containers and packages in the batch have the correct label. This examination should be part of the packaging operation. Results of these examinations should be recorded in the batch production or control records.

9.46 Intermediate or API containers that are transported outside of the manufacturer's control should be sealed in a manner such that, if the seal is breached or missing, the recipient will be alerted to the possibility that the contents may have been altered.

10 Storage and Distribution

10.1 Warehousing Procedures

10.10 Facilities should be available for the storage of all materials under appropriate conditions (e.g. controlled temperature and humidity when necessary). Records should be maintained of these conditions if they are critical for the maintenance of material characteristics.

10.11 Unless there is an alternative system to prevent the unintentional or unauthorised use of quarantined, rejected, returned, or recalled materials, separate storage areas should be assigned for their temporary storage until the decision as to their future use has been taken.

10.2 Distribution Procedures

10.20 APIs and intermediates should only be released for distribution to third parties after they have been released by the quality unit(s). APIs and intermediates can be transferred under quarantine to another unit under the company's control when authorized by the quality unit(s) and if appropriate controls and documentation are in place.

10.21 APIs and intermediates should be transported in a manner that does not adversely affect their quality.

10.22 Special transport or storage conditions for an API or intermediate should be stated on the label.

10.23 The manufacturer should ensure that the contract acceptor (contractor) for transportation of the API or intermediate knows and follows the appropriate transport and storage conditions.

10.24 A system should be in place by which the distribution of each batch of intermediate and/or API can be readily determined to permit its recall.

11   Laboratory Controls

11.1   General Controls

11.10   The independent quality unit(s) should have at its disposal adequate laboratory facilities.

11.11   There should be documented procedures describing sampling, testing, approval or rejection of materials, and recording and storage of laboratory data. Laboratory records should be maintained in accordance with Section 6.6.

11.12   All specifications, sampling plans, and test procedures should be scientifically sound and appropriate to ensure that raw materials, intermediates, APIs, and labels and packaging materials conform to established standards of quality and/or purity. Specifications and test procedures should be consistent with those included in the registration/filing. There can be specifications in addition to those in the registration/filing. Specifications, sampling plans, and test procedures, including changes to them, should be drafted by the appropriate organizational unit and reviewed and approved by the quality unit(s).

11.13   Appropriate specifications should be established for APIs in accordance with accepted standards and consistent with the manufacturing process. The specifications should include a control of the impurities (e.g. organic impurities, inorganic impurities, and residual solvents). If the API has a specification for microbiological purity, appropriate action limits for total microbial counts and objectionable organisms should be established and met. If the API has a specification for endotoxins, appropriate action limits should be established and met.

11.14   Laboratory controls should be followed and documented at the time of performance. Any departures from the above described procedures should be documented and explained.

11.15   Any out-of-specification result obtained should be investigated and documented according to a procedure. This procedure should require analysis of the data, assessment of whether a significant problem exists, allocation of the tasks for corrective actions, and conclusions. Any re-sampling and/or retesting after OOS results should be performed according to a documented procedure.

11.16   Reagents and standard solutions should be prepared and labelled following written procedures. "Use by" dates should be applied as appropriate for analytical reagents or standard solutions.

11.17 Primary reference standards should be obtained as appropriate for the manufacture of APIs. The source of each primary reference standard should be documented. Records should be maintained of each primary reference standard's storage and use in accordance with the supplier's recommendations. Primary reference standards obtained from an officially recognised source are normally used without testing if stored under conditions consistent with the supplier's recommendations.

11.18 Where a primary reference standard is not available from an officially recognized source, an "in-house primary standard" should be established. Appropriate testing should be performed to establish fully the identity and purity of the primary reference standard. Appropriate documentation of this testing should be maintained.

11.19 Secondary reference standards should be appropriately prepared, identified, tested, approved, and stored. The suitability of each batch of secondary reference standard should be determined prior to first use by comparing against a primary reference standard. Each batch of secondary reference standard should be periodically requalified in accordance with a written protocol.

11.2 Testing of Intermediates and APIs

11.20 For each batch of intermediate and API, appropriate laboratory tests should be conducted to determine conformance to specifications.

11.21 An impurity profile describing the identified and unidentified impurities present in a typical batch produced by a specific controlled production process should normally be established for each API. The impurity profile should include the identity or some qualitative analytical designation (e.g. retention time), the range of each impurity observed, and classification of each identified impurity (e.g. inorganic, organic, solvent). The impurity profile is normally dependent upon the production process and origin of the API. Impurity profiles are normally not necessary for APIs from herbal or animal tissue origin. Biotechnology considerations are covered in ICH Guideline Q6B.

11.22 The impurity profile should be compared at appropriate intervals against the impurity profile in the regulatory submission or compared against historical data in order to detect changes to the API resulting from modifications in raw materials, equipment operating parameters, or the production process.

11.23 Appropriate microbiological tests should be conducted on each batch of intermediate and API where microbial quality is specified.

11.3 Validation of Analytical Procedures

See Section 12.

11.4 Certificates of Analysis

11.40 Authentic Certificates of Analysis should be issued for each batch of intermediate or API on request.

11.41 Information on the name of the intermediate or API including where appropriate its grade, the batch number, and the date of release should be provided on the Certificate of Analysis. For intermediates or APIs with an expiry date, the expiry date should be provided on the label and Certificate of Analysis. For intermediates or APIs with a retest date, the retest date should be indicated on the label and/or Certificate of Analysis.

11.42 The Certificate should list each test performed in accordance with compendial or customer requirements, including the acceptance limits, and the numerical results obtained (if test results are numerical).

11.43 Certificates should be dated and signed by authorised personnel of the quality unit(s) and should show the name, address and telephone number of the original manufacturer. Where the analysis has been carried out by a repacker or reprocessor, the Certificate of Analysis should show the name, address and telephone number of the repacker/ reprocessor and a reference to the name of the original manufacturer.

11.44 If new Certificates are issued by or on behalf of repackers/ reprocessors, agents or brokers, these Certificates should show the name, address and telephone number of the laboratory that performed the analysis. They should also contain a reference to the name and address of the original manufacturer and to the original batch Certificate, a copy of which should be attached.

11.5 Stability Monitoring of APIs

11.50 A documented, on-going testing program should be designed to monitor the stability characteristics of APIs, and the results should be used to confirm appropriate storage conditions and retest or expiry dates.

11.51 The test procedures used in stability testing should be validated and be stability indicating.

11.52 Stability samples should be stored in containers that simulate the market container. For example, if the API is marketed in bags within fibre drums, stability samples can be packaged in bags of the same material and in smaller-scale drums of similar or identical material composition to the market drums.

11.53   Normally the first three commercial production batches should be placed on the stability monitoring program to confirm the retest or expiry date. However, where data from previous studies show that the API is expected to remain stable for at least two years, fewer than three batches can be used.

11.54   Thereafter, at least one batch per year of API manufactured (unless none is produced that year) should be added to the stability monitoring program and tested at least annually to confirm the stability.

11.55   For APIs with short shelf-lives, testing should be done more frequently. For example, for those biotechnological/biologic and other APIs with shelf-lives of one year or less, stability samples should be obtained and should be tested monthly for the first three months, and at three month intervals after that. When data exist that confirm that the stability of the API is not compromised, elimination of specific test intervals (e.g. 9-month testing) can be considered.

11.56   Where appropriate, the stability storage conditions should be consistent with the ICH guidelines on stability.

11.6   Expiry and Retest Dating

11.60   When an intermediate is intended to be transferred outside the control of the manufacturer's material management system and an expiry or retest date is assigned, supporting stability information should be available (e.g. published data, test results).

11.61   An API expiry or retest date should be based on an evaluation of data derived from stability studies. Common practice is to use a retest date, not an expiration date.

11.62   Preliminary API expiry or retest dates can be based on pilot scale batches if (1) the pilot batches employ a method of manufacture and procedure that simulates the final process to be used on a commercial manufacturing scale; and (2) the quality of the API represents the material to be made on a commercial scale.

11.63   A representative sample should be taken for the purpose of performing a retest.

11.7   Reserve/Retention Samples

11.70   The packaging and holding of reserve samples is for the purpose of potential future evaluation of the quality of batches of API and not for future stability testing purposes.

11.71   Appropriately identified reserve samples of each API batch should be retained for one year after the expiry date of the batch assigned by the manufacturer, or for three years after distribution of the batch, whichever is the longer. For APIs with retest dates, similar reserve samples should be retained for three years after the batch is completely distributed by the manufacturer.

11.72   The reserve sample should be stored in the same packaging system in which the API is stored or in one that is equivalent to or more protective than the marketed packaging system. Sufficient quantities should be retained to conduct at least two full compendial analyses or, when there is no pharmacopoeial monograph, two full specification analyses.

12   Validation

12.1   Validation Policy

12.10   The company's overall policy, intentions, and approach to validation, including the validation of production processes, cleaning procedures, analytical methods, in-process control test procedures, computerized systems, and persons responsible for design, review, approval and documentation of each validation phase, should be documented.

12.11   The critical parameters/attributes should normally be identified during the development stage or from historical data, and the ranges necessary for the reproducible operation should be defined. This should include:

- Defining the API in terms of its critical product attributes;
- Identifying process parameters that could affect the critical quality attributes of the API;
- Determining the range for each critical process parameter expected to be used during routine manufacturing and process control.

12.12   Validation should extend to those operations determined to be critical to the quality and purity of the API.

12.2   Validation Documentation

12.20   A written validation protocol should be established that specifies how validation of a particular process will be conducted. The protocol should be reviewed and approved by the quality unit(s) and other designated units.

12.21   The validation protocol should specify critical process steps and acceptance criteria as well as the type of validation to be conducted (e.g. retrospective, prospective, concurrent) and the number of process runs.

12.22   A validation report that cross-references the validation protocol should be prepared, summarising the results obtained, commenting on any deviations observed, and drawing the appropriate conclusions, including recommending changes to correct deficiencies.

12.23   Any variations from the validation protocol should be documented with appropriate justification.

12.3   Qualification

12.30   Before starting process validation activities, appropriate qualification of critical equipment and ancillary systems should be completed. Qualification is usually carried out by conducting the following activities, individually or combined:

- Design Qualification (DQ): documented verification that the proposed design of the facilities, equipment, or systems is suitable for the intended purpose;
- Installation Qualification (IQ): documented verification that the equipment or systems, as installed or modified, comply with the approved design, the manufacturer's recommendations and/or user requirements;
- Operational Qualification (OQ): documented verification that the equipment or systems, as installed or modified, perform as intended throughout the anticipated operating ranges;
- Performance Qualification (PQ): documented verification that the equipment and ancillary systems, as connected together, can perform effectively and reproducibly based on the approved process method and specifications.

12.4   Approaches to Process Validation

12.40   Process Validation (PV) is the documented evidence that the process, operated within established parameters, can perform effectively and reproducibly to produce an intermediate or API meeting its predetermined specifications and quality attributes.

12.41   There are three approaches to validation. Prospective validation is the preferred approach, but there are exceptions where the other approaches can be used. These approaches and their applicability are listed below.

12.42   Prospective validation should normally be performed for all API processes as defined in Section 12.12. Prospective validation performed on an API process should be completed before the commercial distribution of the final drug product manufactured from that API.

12.43   Concurrent validation can be conducted when data from replicate production runs are unavailable because only a limited number of API batches have been produced, API batches are produced infrequently, or API batches are produced by a validated process that has been modified. Prior to the completion of concurrent validation, batches can be released and used in final drug product for commercial distribution based on thorough monitoring and testing of the API batches.

12.44   An exception can be made for retrospective validation for well established processes that have been used without significant changes to API quality due to changes in raw materials, equipment, systems, facilities, or the production process. This validation approach may be used where:

(1) Critical quality attributes and critical process parameters have been identified;
(2) Appropriate in-process acceptance criteria and controls have been established;
(3) There have not been significant process/product failures attributable to causes other than operator error or equipment failures unrelated to equipment suitability; and
(4) Impurity profiles have been established for the existing API.

12.45   Batches selected for retrospective validation should be representative of all batches made during the review period, including any batches that failed to meet specifications, and should be sufficient in number to demonstrate process consistency. Retained samples can be tested to obtain data to retrospectively validate the process.

12.5   Process Validation Program

12.50   The number of process runs for validation should depend on the complexity of the process or the magnitude of the process change being considered. For prospective and concurrent validation, three consecutive successful production batches should be used as a guide, but there may be situations where additional process runs are warranted to prove consistency of the process (e.g., complex API processes or API processes with prolonged completion times). For retrospective validation, generally data from ten to thirty consecutive batches should be examined to assess process consistency, but fewer batches can be examined if justified.

12.51   Critical process parameters should be controlled and monitored during process validation studies. Process parameters unrelated to quality, such as variables controlled to minimize energy consumption or equipment use, need not be included in the process validation.

12.52   Process validation should confirm that the impurity profile for each API is within the limits specified. The impurity profile should be comparable to or better than historical data and, where applicable, the profile determined during process development or for batches used for pivotal clinical and toxicological studies.

12.6   Periodic Review of Validated Systems

12.60   Systems and processes should be periodically evaluated to verify that they are still operating in a valid manner. Where no significant changes have been made to the system or process, and a quality review confirms that the system or process is consistently producing material meeting its specifications, there is normally no need for revalidation.

12.7   Cleaning Validation

12.70   Cleaning procedures should normally be validated. In general, cleaning validation should be directed to situations or process steps where contamination or carryover of materials poses the greatest risk to API quality. For example, in early production it may be unnecessary to validate equipment cleaning procedures where residues are removed by subsequent purification steps.

12.71   Validation of cleaning procedures should reflect actual equipment usage patterns. If various APIs or intermediates are manufactured in the same equipment and the equipment is cleaned by the same process, a representative intermediate or API can be selected for cleaning validation. This selection should be based on the solubility and difficulty of cleaning and the calculation of residue limits based on potency, toxicity, and stability.

12.72   The cleaning validation protocol should describe the equipment to be cleaned, procedures, materials, acceptable cleaning levels, parameters to be monitored and controlled, and analytical methods. The protocol should also indicate the type of samples to be obtained and how they are collected and labelled.

12.73   Sampling should include swabbing, rinsing, or alternative methods (e.g., direct extraction), as appropriate, to detect both insoluble and soluble residues. The sampling methods used should be capable of quantitatively measuring levels of residues remaining on the equipment surfaces after cleaning. Swab sampling may be impractical when product contact surfaces are not easily accessible due to equipment design and/or process limitations (e.g., inner surfaces of hoses, transfer pipes, reactor tanks with small ports or handling toxic materials, and small intricate equipment such as micronizers and microfluidizers).

12.74 Validated analytical methods having sensitivity to detect residues or contaminants should be used. The detection limit for each analytical method should be sufficiently sensitive to detect the established acceptable level of the residue or contaminant. The method's attainable recovery level should be established. Residue limits should be practical, achievable, verifiable and based on the most deleterious residue. Limits can be established based on the minimum known pharmacological, toxicological, or physiological activity of the API or its most deleterious component.

12.75 Equipment cleaning/sanitization studies should address microbiological and endotoxin contamination for those processes where there is a need to reduce total microbiological count or endotoxins in the API, or other processes where such contamination could be of concern (e.g., non-sterile APIs used to manufacture sterile products).

12.76 Cleaning procedures should be monitored at appropriate intervals after validation to ensure that these procedures are effective when used during routine production. Equipment cleanliness can be monitored by analytical testing and visual examination, where feasible. Visual inspection can allow detection of gross contamination concentrated in small areas that could otherwise go undetected by sampling and/or analysis.

12.8 Validation of Analytical Methods

12.80 Analytical methods should be validated unless the method employed is included in the relevant pharmacopoeia or other recognised standard reference. The suitability of all testing methods used should nonetheless be verified under actual conditions of use and documented.

12.81 Methods should be validated to include consideration of characteristics included within the ICH guidelines on validation of analytical methods. The degree of analytical validation performed should reflect the purpose of the analysis and the stage of the API production process.

12.82 Appropriate qualification of analytical equipment should be considered before starting validation of analytical methods.

12.83 Complete records should be maintained of any modification of a validated analytical method. Such records should include the reason for the modification and appropriate data to verify that the modification produces results that are as accurate and reliable as the established method.

13   Change Control

13.10   A formal change control system should be established to evaluate all changes that may affect the production and control of the intermediate or API.

13.11   Written procedures should provide for the identification, documentation, appropriate review, and approval of changes in raw materials, specifications, analytical methods, facilities, support systems, equipment (including computer hardware), processing steps, labelling and packaging materials, and computer software.

13.12   Any proposals for GMP relevant changes should be drafted, reviewed, and approved by the appropriate organisational units, and reviewed and approved by the quality unit(s).

13.13   The potential impact of the proposed change on the quality of the intermediate or API should be evaluated. A classification procedure may help in determining the level of testing, validation, and documentation needed to justify changes to a validated process. Changes can be classified (e.g. as minor or major) depending on the nature and extent of the changes, and the effects these changes may impart on the process. Scientific judgement should determine what additional testing and validation studies are appropriate to justify a change in a validated process.

13.14   When implementing approved changes, measures should be taken to ensure that all documents affected by the changes are revised.

13.15   After the change has been implemented, there should be an evaluation of the first batches produced or tested under the change.

13.16   The potential for critical changes to affect established retest or expiry dates should be evaluated. If necessary, samples of the intermediate or API produced by the modified process can be placed on an accelerated stability program and/or can be added to the stability monitoring program.

13.17   Current dosage form manufacturers should be notified of changes from established production and process control procedures that can impact the quality of the API.

14   Rejection and Re-Use of Materials

14.1   Rejection

14.10   Intermediates and APIs failing to meet established specifications should be identified as such and quarantined. These intermediates or APIs can be reprocessed or reworked as described below. The final disposition of rejected materials should be recorded.

14.2 Reprocessing

14.20 Introducing an intermediate or API, including one that does not conform to standards or specifications, back into the process and reprocessing by repeating a crystallization step or other appropriate chemical or physical manipulation steps (e.g., distillation, filtration, chromatography, milling) that are part of the established manufacturing process is generally considered acceptable. However, if such reprocessing is used for a majority of batches, such reprocessing should be included as part of the standard manufacturing process.

14.21 Continuation of a process step after an in-process control test has shown that the step is incomplete is considered to be part of the normal process. This is not considered to be reprocessing.

14.22 Introducing unreacted material back into a process and repeating a chemical reaction is considered to be reprocessing unless it is part of the established process. Such reprocessing should be preceded by careful evaluation to ensure that the quality of the intermediate or API is not adversely impacted due to the potential formation of by-products and over-reacted materials.

14.3 Reworking

14.30 Before a decision is taken to rework batches that do not conform to established standards or specifications, an investigation into the reason for nonconformance should be performed.

14.31 Batches that have been reworked should be subjected to appropriate evaluation, testing, stability testing if warranted, and documentation to show that the reworked product is of equivalent quality to that produced by the original process. Concurrent validation is often the appropriate validation approach for rework procedures. This allows a protocol to define the rework procedure, how it will be carried out, and the expected results. If there is only one batch to be reworked, then a report can be written and the batch released once it is found to be acceptable.

14.32 Procedures should provide for comparing the impurity profile of each reworked batch against batches manufactured by the established process. Where routine analytical methods are inadequate to characterize the reworked batch, additional methods should be used.

14.4   Recovery of Materials and Solvents

14.40   Recovery (e.g. from mother liquor or filtrates) of reactants, intermediates, or the API is considered acceptable, provided that approved procedures exist for the recovery and the recovered materials meet specifications suitable for their intended use.

14.41   Solvents can be recovered and reused in the same processes or in different processes, provided that the recovery procedures are controlled and monitored to ensure that solvents meet appropriate standards before reuse or co-mingling with other approved materials.

14.42   Fresh and recovered solvents and reagents can be combined if adequate testing has shown their suitability for all manufacturing processes in which they may be used.

14.43   The use of recovered solvents, mother liquors, and other recovered materials should be adequately documented.

14.5   Returns

14.50   Returned intermediates or APIs should be identified as such and quarantined.

14.51   If the conditions under which returned intermediates or APIs have been stored or shipped before or during their return or the condition of their containers casts doubt on their quality, the returned intermediates or APIs should be reprocessed, reworked, or destroyed, as appropriate.

14.52   Records of returned intermediates or APIs should be maintained. For each return, documentation should include:

- Name and address of the consignee
- Intermediate or API, batch number, and quantity returned
- Reason for return
- Use or disposal of the returned intermediate or API.

15   Complaints and Recalls

15.10   All quality related complaints, whether received orally or in writing, should be recorded and investigated according to a written procedure.

15.11   Complaint records should include:

- Name and address of complainant;
- Name (and, where appropriate, title) and phone number of person submitting the complaint;

- Complaint nature (including name and batch number of the API);
- Date complaint is received;
- Action initially taken (including dates and identity of person taking the action);
- Any follow-up action taken;
- Response provided to the originator of complaint (including date response sent); and
- Final decision on intermediate or API batch or lot.

15.12   Records of complaints should be retained in order to evaluate trends, product related frequencies, and severity with a view to taking additional, and if appropriate, immediate corrective action.

15.13   There should be a written procedure that defines the circumstances under which a recall of an intermediate or API should be considered.

15.14   The recall procedure should designate who should be involved in evaluating the information, how a recall should be initiated, who should be informed about the recall, and how the recalled material should be treated.

15.15   In the event of a serious or potentially life-threatening situation, local, national, and/or international authorities should be informed and their advice sought.

16   Contract Manufacturers (including Laboratories)

16.10   All contract manufacturers (including laboratories) should comply with the GMP defined in this Guide. Special consideration should be given to the prevention of cross-contamination and to maintaining traceability.

16.11   Contract manufacturers (including laboratories) should be evaluated by the contract giver to ensure GMP compliance of the specific operations occurring at the contract sites.

16.12   There should be a written and approved contract or formal agreement between the contract giver and the contract acceptor that defines in detail the GMP responsibilities, including the quality measures, of each party.

16.13   The contract should permit the contract giver to audit the contract acceptor's facilities for compliance with GMP.

16.14   Where subcontracting is allowed, the contract acceptor should not pass to a third party any of the work entrusted to him under the contract without the contract giver's prior evaluation and approval of the arrangements.

16.15   Manufacturing and laboratory records should be kept at the site where the activity occurs and be readily available.

16.16　Changes in the process, equipment, test methods, specifications, or other contractual requirements should not be made unless the contract giver is informed and approves the changes.

17　Agents, Brokers, Traders, Distributors, Repackers, and Relabellers

17.1　Applicability

17.10　This section applies to any party other than the original manufacturer who may trade and/or take possession, repack, relabel, manipulate, distribute or store an API or intermediate.

17.11　All agents, brokers, traders, distributors, repackers, and relabellers should comply with GMP as defined in this Guide.

17.2　Traceability of Distributed APIs and Intermediates

17.20　Agents, brokers, traders, distributors, repackers, or relabellers should maintain complete traceability of APIs and intermediates that they distribute. Documents that should be retained and available include:

- Identity of original manufacturer;
- Address of original manufacturer;
- Purchase orders;
- Bills of lading (transportation documentation);
- Receipt documents;
- Name or designation of API or intermediate;
- Manufacturer's batch number;
- Transportation and distribution records;
- All authentic Certificates of Analysis, including those of the original manufacturer;
- Retest or expiry date.

17.3　Quality Management

17.30　Agents, brokers, traders, distributors, repackers, or relabellers should establish, document and implement an effective system of managing quality, as specified in Section 2.

17.4　Repackaging, Relabelling and Holding of APIs and Intermediates

17.40　Repackaging, relabelling and holding of APIs and intermediates should be performed under appropriate GMP controls, as stipulated in this

Guide, to avoid mix-ups and loss of API or intermediate identity or purity.

17.41 Repackaging should be conducted under appropriate environmental conditions to avoid contamination and cross-contamination.

17.5 Stability

17.50 Stability studies to justify assigned expiration or retest dates should be conducted if the API or intermediate is repackaged in a different type of container than that used by the API or intermediate manufacturer.

17.6 Transfer of Information

17.60 Agents, brokers, distributors, repackers, or relabellers should transfer all quality or regulatory information received from an API or intermediate manufacturer to the customer, and from the customer to the API or intermediate manufacturer.

17.61 The agent, broker, trader, distributor, repacker, or relabeller who supplies the API or intermediate to the customer should provide the name of the original API or intermediate manufacturer and the batch number(s) supplied.

17.62 The agent should also provide the identity of the original API or intermediate manufacturer to regulatory authorities upon request. The original manufacturer can respond to the regulatory authority directly or through its authorized agents, depending on the legal relationship between the authorized agents and the original API or intermediate manufacturer. (In this context "authorized" refers to authorized by the manufacturer.)

17.63 The specific guidance for Certificates of Analysis included in Section 11.4 should be met.

17.7 Handling of Complaints and Recalls

17.70 Agents, brokers, traders, distributors, repackers or relabellers should maintain records of complaints and recalls, as specified in Section 15, for all complaints and recalls that come to their attention.

17.71 If the situation warrants, the agents, brokers, traders, distributors, repackers, or relabellers should review the complaint with the original API or intermediate manufacturer in order to determine whether any further action, either with other customers who may have received this API or intermediate or with the regulatory authority, or both, should be initiated. The investigation into the cause for the complaint or recall should be conducted and documented by the appropriate party.

17.72   Where a complaint is referred to the original API or intermediate manufacturer, the record maintained by the agents, brokers, traders, distributors, repackers, or relabellers should include any response received from the original API or intermediate manufacturer (including date and information provided).

17.8   Handling of Returns

17.80   Returns should be handled as specified in Section 14.52. The agents, brokers, traders, distributors, repackers, or relabellers should maintain documentation of returned APIs and intermediates.

18   Specific Guidance for APIs Manufactured by Cell Culture/Fermentation

18.1   General

18.10   Section 18 is intended to address specific controls for APIs or intermediates manufactured by cell culture or fermentation using natural or recombinant organisms and that have not been covered adequately in the previous sections. It is not intended to be a stand-alone section. In general, the GMP principles in the other sections of this document apply. Note that the principles of fermentation for "classical" processes for production of small molecules and for processes using recombinant and non-recombinant organisms for production of proteins and/or polypeptides are the same, although the degree of control will differ. Where practical, this section will address these differences. In general, the degree of control for biotechnological processes used to produce proteins and polypeptides is greater than that for classical fermentation processes.

18.11   The term "biotechnological process" (biotech) refers to the use of cells or organisms that have been generated or modified by recombinant DNA, hybridoma or other technology to produce APIs. The APIs produced by biotechnological processes normally consist of high molecular weight substances, such as proteins and polypeptides, for which specific guidance is given in this section. Certain APIs of low molecular weight, such as antibiotics, amino acids, vitamins, and carbohydrates, can also be produced by recombinant DNA technology. The level of control for these types of API is similar to that employed for classical fermentation.

18.12   The term "classical fermentation" refers to processes that use microorganisms existing in nature and/or modified by conventional methods (e.g. irradiation or chemical mutagenesis) to produce APIs. APIs produced by "classical fermentation" are normally low molecular weight products such as antibiotics, amino acids, vitamins, and carbohydrates.

18.13 Production of APIs or intermediates from cell culture or fermentation involves biological processes such as cultivation of cells or extraction and purification of material from living organisms. Note that there may be additional process steps, such as physicochemical modification, that are part of the manufacturing process. The raw materials used (media, buffer components) may provide the potential for growth of microbiological contaminants. Depending on the source, method of preparation, and the intended use of the API or intermediate, control of bioburden, viral contamination, and/or endotoxins during manufacturing and monitoring of the process at appropriate stages may be necessary.

18.14 Appropriate controls should be established at all stages of manufacturing to assure intermediate and/or API quality. While this Guide starts at the cell culture/fermentation step, prior steps (e.g. cell banking) should be performed under appropriate process controls. This Guide covers cell culture/fermentation from the point at which a vial of the cell bank is retrieved for use in manufacturing.

18.15 Appropriate equipment and environmental controls should be used to minimize the risk of contamination. The acceptance criteria for quality of the environment and the frequency of monitoring should depend on the step in production and the production conditions (open, closed, or contained systems).

18.16 In general, process controls should take into account:

- Maintenance of the working cell bank (where appropriate);
- Proper inoculation and expansion of the culture;
- Control of the critical operating parameters during fermentation/cell culture;
- Monitoring of the process for cell growth, viability (for most cell culture processes) and productivity where appropriate;
- Harvest and purification procedures that remove cells, cellular debris and media components while protecting the intermediate or API from contamination (particularly of a microbiological nature) and from loss of quality;
- Monitoring of bioburden and, where needed, endotoxin levels at appropriate stages of production; and
- Viral safety concerns as described in ICH Guideline Q5A *Quality of Biotechnological Products: Viral Safety Evaluation of Biotechnology Products Derived from Cell Lines of Human or Animal Origin.*

18.17 Where appropriate, the removal of media components, host cell proteins, other process-related impurities, product-related impurities and contaminants should be demonstrated.

18.2   Cell Bank Maintenance and Record Keeping

18.20   Access to cell banks should be limited to authorized personnel.

18.21   Cell banks should be maintained under storage conditions designed to maintain viability and prevent contamination.

18.22   Records of the use of the vials from the cell banks and storage conditions should be maintained.

18.23   Where appropriate, cell banks should be periodically monitored to determine suitability for use.

18.24   See ICH Guideline Q5D *Quality of Biotechnological Products: Derivation and Characterization of Cell Substrates Used for Production of Biotechnological/Biological Products* for a more complete discussion of cell banking.

18.3   Cell Culture/Fermentation

18.30   Where aseptic addition of cell substrates, media, buffers, and gases is needed, closed or contained systems should be used where possible. If the inoculation of the initial vessel or subsequent transfers or additions (media, buffers) are performed in open vessels, there should be controls and procedures in place to minimize the risk of contamination.

18.31   Where the quality of the API can be affected by microbial contamination, manipulations using open vessels should be performed in a biosafety cabinet or similarly controlled environment.

18.32   Personnel should be appropriately gowned and take special precautions handling the cultures.

18.33   Critical operating parameters (for example temperature, pH, agitation rates, addition of gases, pressure) should be monitored to ensure consistency with the established process. Cell growth, viability (for most cell culture processes), and, where appropriate, productivity should also be monitored. Critical parameters will vary from one process to another, and for classical fermentation, certain parameters (cell viability, for example) may not need to be monitored.

18.34   Cell culture equipment should be cleaned and sterilized after use. As appropriate, fermentation equipment should be cleaned, and sanitized or sterilized.

18.35   Culture media should be sterilized before use when appropriate to protect the quality of the API.

18.36   There should be appropriate procedures in place to detect contamination and determine the course of action to be taken. This should include procedures to determine the impact of the contamination on the product and those to decontaminate the equipment and return it to a condition to be used in subsequent batches. Foreign organisms observed during fermentation processes should be identified as appropriate and the effect of their presence on product quality should be assessed, if necessary. The results of such assessments should be taken into consideration in the disposition of the material produced.

18.37   Records of contamination events should be maintained.

18.38   Shared (multi-product) equipment may warrant additional testing after cleaning between product campaigns, as appropriate, to minimize the risk of cross-contamination.

18.4   Harvesting, Isolation and Purification

18.40   Harvesting steps, either to remove cells or cellular components or to collect cellular components after disruption, should be performed in equipment and areas designed to minimize the risk of contamination.

18.41   Harvest and purification procedures that remove or inactivate the producing organism, cellular debris and media components (while minimizing degradation, contamination, and loss of quality) should be adequate to ensure that the intermediate or API is recovered with consistent quality.

18.42   All equipment should be properly cleaned and, as appropriate, sanitized after use. Multiple successive batching without cleaning can be used if intermediate or API quality is not compromised.

18.43   If open systems are used, purification should be performed under environmental conditions appropriate for the preservation of product quality.

18.44   Additional controls, such as the use of dedicated chromatography resins or additional testing, may be appropriate if equipment is to be used for multiple products.

18.5   Viral Removal/Inactivation Steps

18.50   See the ICH Guideline Q5A *Quality of Biotechnological Products: Viral Safety Evaluation of Biotechnology Products Derived from Cell Lines of Human or Animal Origin* for more specific information.

18.51   Viral removal and viral inactivation steps are critical processing steps for some processes and should be performed within their validated parameters.

18.52   Appropriate precautions should be taken to prevent potential viral contamination from pre-viral to post-viral removal/inactivation steps. Therefore, open processing should be performed in areas that are separate from other processing activities and have separate air handling units.

18.53 The same equipment is not normally used for different purification steps. However, if the same equipment is to be used, the equipment should be appropriately cleaned and sanitized before reuse. Appropriate precautions should be taken to prevent potential virus carry-over (e.g. through equipment or environment) from previous steps.

19   APIs for Use in Clinical Trials

19.1   General

19.10 Not all the controls in the previous sections of this Guide are appropriate for the manufacture of a new API for investigational use during its development. Section 19 provides specific guidance unique to these circumstances.

19.11 The controls used in the manufacture of APIs for use in clinical trials should be consistent with the stage of development of the drug product incorporating the API. Process and test procedures should be flexible to provide for changes as knowledge of the process increases and clinical testing of a drug product progresses from pre-clinical stages through clinical stages. Once drug development reaches the stage where the API is produced for use in drug products intended for clinical trials, manufacturers should ensure that APIs are manufactured in suitable facilities using appropriate production and control procedures to ensure the quality of the API.

19.2   Quality

19.20 Appropriate GMP concepts should be applied in the production of APIs for use in clinical trials with a suitable mechanism of approval of each batch.

19.21 A quality unit(s) independent from production should be established for the approval or rejection of each batch of API for use in clinical trials.

19.22 Some of the testing functions commonly performed by the quality unit(s) can be performed within other organizational units.

19.23 Quality measures should include a system for testing of raw materials, packaging materials, intermediates, and APIs.

19.24 Process and quality problems should be evaluated.

19.25 Labelling for APIs intended for use in clinical trials should be appropriately controlled and should identify the material as being for investigational use.

19.3 Equipment and Facilities

19.30 During all phases of clinical development, including the use of small-scale facilities or laboratories to manufacture batches of APIs for use in clinical trials, procedures should be in place to ensure that equipment is calibrated, clean and suitable for its intended use.

19.31 Procedures for the use of facilities should ensure that materials are handled in a manner that minimizes the risk of contamination and cross-contamination.

19.4 Control of Raw Materials

19.40 Raw materials used in production of APIs for use in clinical trials should be evaluated by testing, or received with a supplier's analysis and subjected to identity testing. When a material is considered hazardous, a supplier's analysis should suffice.

19.41 In some instances, the suitability of a raw material can be determined before use based on acceptability in small-scale reactions (i.e., use testing) rather than on analytical testing alone.

19.5 Production

19.50 The production of APIs for use in clinical trials should be documented in laboratory notebooks, batch records, or by other appropriate means. These documents should include information on the use of production materials, equipment, processing, and scientific observations.

19.51 Expected yields can be more variable and less defined than the expected yields used in commercial processes. Investigations into yield variations are not expected.

19.6 Validation

19.60 Process validation for the production of APIs for use in clinical trials is normally inappropriate, where a single API batch is produced or where process changes during API development make batch replication difficult or inexact. The combination of controls, calibration, and, where appropriate, equipment qualification assures API quality during this development phase.

19.61 Process validation should be conducted in accordance with Section 12 when batches are produced for commercial use, even when such batches are produced on a pilot or small scale.

19.7 Changes

19.70   Changes are expected during development, as knowledge is gained and the production is scaled up. Every change in the production, specifications, or test procedures should be adequately recorded.

19.8 Laboratory Controls

19.80   While analytical methods performed to evaluate a batch of API for clinical trials may not yet be validated, they should be scientifically sound.

19.81   A system for retaining reserve samples of all batches should be in place. This system should ensure that a sufficient quantity of each reserve sample is retained for an appropriate length of time after approval, termination, or discontinuation of an application.

19.82   Expiry and retest dating as defined in Section 11.6 applies to existing APIs used in clinical trials. For new APIs, Section 11.6 does not normally apply in early stages of clinical trials.

19.9 Documentation

19.90   A system should be in place to ensure that information gained during the development and the manufacture of APIs for use in clinical trials is documented and available.

19.91   The development and implementation of the analytical methods used to support the release of a batch of API for use in clinical trials should be appropriately documented.

19.92   A system for retaining production and control records and documents should be used. This system should ensure that records and documents are retained for an appropriate length of time after the approval, termination, or discontinuation of an application.

20 Glossary to Part II

Acceptance Criteria
Numerical limits, ranges, or other suitable measures for acceptance of test results.

Active Pharmaceutical Ingredient (API) (or drug substance)
Any substance or mixture of substances intended to be used in the manufacture of a drug (medicinal) product and that, when used in the production of

a drug, becomes an active ingredient of the drug product. Such substances are intended to furnish pharmacological activity or other direct effect in the diagnosis, cure, mitigation, treatment, or prevention of disease or to affect the structure and function of the body.

API Starting Material

A raw material, intermediate, or an API that is used in the production of an API and that is incorporated as a significant structural fragment into the structure of the API. An API starting material can be an article of commerce, a material purchased from one or more suppliers under contract or commercial agreement, or produced in-house. API starting materials are normally of defined chemical properties and structure.

Batch (or Lot)

A specific quantity of material produced in a process or series of processes so that it is expected to be homogeneous within specified limits. In the case of continuous production, a batch may correspond to a defined fraction of the production. The batch size can be defined either by a fixed quantity or by the amount produced in a fixed time interval.

Batch Number (or Lot Number)

A unique combination of numbers, letters, and/or symbols that identifies a batch (or lot) and from which the production and distribution history can be determined.

Bioburden

The level and type (e.g. objectionable or not) of micro-organisms that can be present in raw materials, API starting materials, intermediates or APIs. Bioburden should not be considered contamination unless the levels have been exceeded or defined objectionable organisms have been detected.

Calibration

The demonstration that a particular instrument or device produces results within specified limits by comparison with those produced by a reference or traceable standard over an appropriate range of measurements.

Computer System

A group of hardware components and associated software, designed and assembled to perform a specific function or group of functions.

Computerized System

A process or operation integrated with a computer system.

Contamination

The undesired introduction of impurities of a chemical or microbiological nature, or of foreign matter, into or onto a raw material, intermediate, or

API during production, sampling, packaging or repackaging, storage or transport.

Contract Manufacturer

A manufacturer performing some aspect of manufacturing on behalf of the original manufacturer.

Critical

Describes a process step, process condition, test requirement, or other relevant parameter or item that must be controlled within predetermined criteria to ensure that the API meets its specification.

Cross-Contamination

Contamination of a material or product with another material or product.

Deviation

Departure from an approved instruction or established standard.

Drug (Medicinal) Product

The dosage form in the final immediate packaging intended for marketing (Reference Q1A).

Drug Substance

See Active Pharmaceutical Ingredient.

Expiry Date (or Expiration date)

The date placed on the container/labels of an API designating the time during which the API is expected to remain within established shelf-life specifications if stored under defined conditions, and after which it should not be used.

Impurity

Any component present in the intermediate or API that is not the desired entity.

Impurity Profile

A description of the identified and unidentified impurities present in an API.

In-Process Control (or Process Control)

Checks performed during production in order to monitor and, if appropriate, to adjust the process and/or to ensure that the intermediate or API conforms to its specifications.

Intermediate

A material produced during steps of the processing of an API that undergoes further molecular change or purification before it becomes an API. Intermediates may or may not be isolated. (Note: this Guide only addresses those intermediates produced after the point that the company has defined as the point at which the production of the API begins.)

Lot

See Batch.

Lot Number

See Batch number.

Manufacture

All operations of receipt of materials, production, packaging, repackaging, labelling, relabelling, quality control, release, storage, and distribution of APIs and related controls.

Material

A general term used to denote raw materials (starting materials, reagents, solvents), process aids, intermediates, APIs and packaging and labelling materials.

Mother Liquor

The residual liquid which remains after the crystallization or isolation processes. A mother liquor may contain unreacted materials, intermediates, levels of the API and/or impurities. It may be used for further processing.

Packaging Material

Any material intended to protect an intermediate or API during storage and transport.

Procedure

A documented description of the operations to be performed, the precautions to be taken and measures to be applied directly or indirectly related to the manufacture of an intermediate or API.

Process Aids

Materials, excluding solvents, used as an aid in the manufacture of an intermediate or API that do not themselves participate in a chemical or biological reaction (e.g. filter aid, activated carbon, etc.).

Process Control

See In-Process Control.

Production

All operations involved in the preparation of an API from receipt of materials through processing and packaging of the API.

Qualification

Action of proving and documenting that equipment or ancillary systems are properly installed, work correctly, and actually lead to the expected results. Qualification is part of validation, but the individual qualification steps alone do not constitute process validation.

Quality Assurance (QA)

The sum total of the organised arrangements made with the object of ensuring that all APIs are of the quality required for their intended use and that quality systems are maintained.

Quality Control (QC)

Checking or testing that specifications are met.

Quality Unit(s)

An organizational unit independent of production which fulfills both Quality Assurance and Quality Control responsibilities. This can be in the form of separate QA and QC units or a single individual or group, depending upon the size and structure of the organization.

Quarantine

The status of materials isolated physically or by other effective means pending a decision on their subsequent approval or rejection.

Raw Material

A general term used to denote starting materials, reagents, and solvents intended for use in the production of intermediates or APIs.

Reference Standard, Primary

A substance that has been shown by an extensive set of analytical tests to be authentic material that should be of high purity. This standard can be: (1) obtained from an officially recognised source, or (2) prepared by independent synthesis, or (3) obtained from existing production material of high purity, or (4) prepared by further purification of existing production material.

Reference Standard, Secondary

A substance of established quality and purity, as shown by comparison to a primary reference standard, used as a reference standard for routine laboratory analysis.

Reprocessing

Introducing an intermediate or API, including one that does not conform to standards or specifications, back into the process and repeating a crystallization step or other appropriate chemical or physical manipulation steps (e.g., distillation, filtration, chromatography, milling) that are part of the established manufacturing process. Continuation of a process step after an in-process control test has shown that the step is incomplete is considered to be part of the normal process, and not reprocessing.

Retest Date

The date when a material should be re-examined to ensure that it is still suitable for use.

Reworking

Subjecting an intermediate or API that does not conform to standards or specifications to one or more processing steps that are different from the established manufacturing process to obtain acceptable quality intermediate or API (e.g., recrystallizing with a different solvent).

Signature (signed)

See definition for signed.

Signed (signature)

The record of the individual who performed a particular action or review. This record can be initials, full handwritten signature, personal seal, or authenticated and secure electronic signature.

Solvent

An inorganic or organic liquid used as a vehicle for the preparation of solutions or suspensions in the manufacture of an intermediate or API.

Specification

A list of tests, references to analytical procedures, and appropriate acceptance criteria that are numerical limits, ranges, or other criteria for the test described. It establishes the set of criteria to which a material should conform to be considered acceptable for its intended use. "Conformance to specification" means that the material, when tested according to the listed analytical procedures, will meet the listed acceptance criteria.

Validation

A documented program that provides a high degree of assurance that a specific process, method, or system will consistently produce a result meeting pre-determined acceptance criteria.

Validation Protocol

A written plan stating how validation will be conducted and defining acceptance criteria. For example, the protocol for a manufacturing process identifies processing equipment, critical process parameters/operating ranges, product characteristics, sampling, test data to be collected, number of validation runs, and acceptable test results.

Yield, Expected

The quantity of material or the percentage of theoretical yield anticipated at any appropriate phase of production based on previous laboratory, pilot scale, or manufacturing data.

Yield, Theoretical

The quantity that would be produced at any appropriate phase of production, based upon the quantity of material to be used, in the absence of any loss or error in actual production.

UK Guidance on Manufacture

Contents

Manufacturers' Obligations

The holder of a manufacturer's licence must comply with certain obligations in relation to the manufacture and assembly of relevant medicinal products. These obligations are set out in Regulation 2 of The Medicines for Human Use (Manufacturing, Wholesale Dealing and Miscellaneous Amendments) Regulations 2005 [SI 2005 No. 2789]. They require that the licence holder shall:

(a) comply with the principles of good manufacturing practice;

(b) only use active starting materials which have been manufactured or assembled in accordance with good manufacturing practice, unless they are for use in an exempt medicinal product;

(c) maintain such staff, premises, equipment and facilities necessary to conduct the manufacture and assembly of relevant medicinal products in accordance with the requirements of their manufacturer's licence and the marketing authorizations of the medicinal product being manufactured;

(d) maintain such staff, premises, equipment and facilities for the handling, control, storage and distribution of the relevant medicinal products manufactured or assembled in accordance with their manufacturer's licence as necessary to maintain the quality of those medicinal products;

(e) ensure that any arrangements made for the control, storage and distribution of the relevant medicinal products are adequate to maintain the quality of those products;

(f) not carry out any manufacture or assembly of medicinal products other than in accordance with their manufacturer's licence and at the premises specified in the licence;

(g) not use any premises for the handling, control, storage or distribution of relevant medicinal products other than those named on their manufacturer's licence which have been approved by the licensing authority for that purpose;

(h) inform the licensing authority before making any material alteration to the premises or facilities used under their manufacturer's licence, or in the operations for which they are used;

(i) inform the licensing authority of any proposed changes to any personnel named in their manufacturer's licence as responsible for quality control, including the person named as the qualified person;

(j) permit the licensing authority to carry out inspections, take samples or copies of documentation as necessary to enable the licensing authority to ascertain whether there are any grounds for suspending, revoking or terminating the manufacturer's licence or to verifying any statement contained in an application for a licence;

(k) ensure that any blood or blood component that they import into the United Kingdom and use as a starting material or raw material in the manufacture of a relevant medicinal product meets equivalent standards of quality and safety to those laid down in Commission Directive 2004/33/EC, implementing Directive 2002/98/EC of the European Parliament and of the Council as regards certain technical requirements for blood and blood components.

(l) ensure that he has at all times at his disposal the services of at least one qualified person who is responsible for carrying out, in relation to the medicinal products being manufactured or assembled, the duties specified in Article 51 of the Directive 2001/83/EC as amended. (See Section 8).

Where the manufacturer's licence holder distributes the relevant medicinal product manufactured or assembled in accordance with the manufacturer's licence he shall:

- comply with the principles of good distribution practice;
- ensure the appropriate and continued supply of the medicinal product that he manufactures or assembles;
- sell only, or offer for sale or supply, the medicinal product in accordance and conformity with a marketing authorization unless it is an exempt medicinal product or is distributed to another Member State where it can be legally used as an unlicensed relevant medicinal product in the Member State concerned;
- distribute only their medicinal products to a holder of a wholesale dealer's licence relating to those products; a holder of an authorization granted by the competent authority of another EEA State authorising the supply of those products by way of wholesale dealing; any person who may lawfully sell those products by retail or who may lawfully supply them in circumstances corresponding to retail sale; or any person who may lawfully administer those products;
- where the relevant medicinal product is supplied to a person for retail sale or supply, the manufacturer's licence holder must enclose with the product a document which makes it possible to ascertain the date on which the supply took place; the name and pharmaceutical form of the product supplied; the quantity of product supplied; and the names and addresses of the person or persons from whom the products were supplied.

The Standard Provisions are incorporated into all manufacturer's licences in the form set out in Schedule 1 of the "Manufacturing and Wholesale Dealing Regulations", that is, those provisions which may be included in all licences unless an individual licence provides variations to them. They require that the manufacturer's licence holder shall:

(a) place their quality control system referred to in Article 11(1) of Commission Directive 2003/94/EC under the authority of the head of the Quality Control (QC);

(b) provide information about the products being manufactured or assembled under their manufacturer's licence and about the operations being conducted in relation to such manufacture or assembly as may be requested by the licensing authority;

(c) inform the licensing authority of any proposed changes to be made to any personnel named in his licence, responsible for supervising the production operations; in charge of the animals from which are derived any substances used in the production of the medicinal products being manufactured or assembled; or responsible for the culture of any living tissues used in the manufacture of the medicinal products being manufactured or assembled;

(d) keep readily available for inspection by a person authorised by the licensing authority the batch documentation referred to in Article 9(1) of Commission Directive 2003/94/EC, and permit that person to take copies or make extracts from such documentation;

(e) keep readily available for examination by a person authorised by the Licensing Authority, samples of each batch of finished relevant medicinal product referred to in Article 11(4) of Commission Directive 2003/94/EC;

(f) withhold any batch of any medicinal product from sale or export so far as may be reasonably practicable for up to 6 weeks when informed that it does not comply with its licence specifications or with the provisions of the Act or of any regulations under the Act;

(g) ensure that any tests for determining conformity with the standards and specifications applying to any particular product used in the manufacture of a medicinal product shall, except so far as the conditions of the product specification for that product otherwise provide, be applied to samples taken from the medicinal product after all manufacturing processes have been completed, or at such earlier stage in the manufacture as may be approved by the licensing authority;

(h) where the manufacturer's licence relates to the assembly of any relevant medicinal product or class of product, and the licence holder supplies that relevant medicinal product at such a stage of assembly that does not fully comply with the provisions of the product specification that relate to labelling, the licence holder shall communicate the particulars of those provisions to the person to whom that product has been so supplied;

(i) where the manufacturer's licence relates to the assembly of a relevant medicinal product; and that medicinal product is not manufactured by the licence holder; and particulars as to the name and address of the manufacturer of, or of the person who imports, that relevant medicinal product have been given by the licence holder to the licensing authority, the licence holder shall forthwith notify the licensing authority in writing of any changes in such particulars;

(j) keep readily available for examination by a person authorised by the licensing authority durable records of the details of manufacture of any intermediate products held by him which are for use in the manufacture of biological medicinal products for human use and shall be in such form as to ensure that the manufacturer's licence holder has a comprehensive record of all matters that are relevant to an evaluation of the safety, quality and efficacy of any finished biological medicinal product for human use which he manufactures using those intermediate products. The records shall not be destroyed without the consent of the licensing authority until the records of the details of manufacture of any finished medicinal products which were or may be manufactured using those intermediate products may be destroyed in accordance with the requirements of these Regulations;

(k) arrange for animals which are used in the production of any medicinal products, to be housed in premises of such a nature, and be managed in such a manner, as to facilitate compliance with the provisions relating to them in the relevant marketing authorizations;

(l) take all reasonable precautions and exercise all due diligence to ensure that any information he provides to the licensing authority which is relevant to an evaluation of the safety, quality or efficacy of any medicinal product for human use which he manufactures or assembles; or any starting materials or intermediate products that he holds which are for use in the manufacture of relevant medicinal products, is not false or misleading in any material particular.

The manufacturer's licence holder may use a contract laboratory pursuant to Article 11(2) of Commission Directive 2003/94/EC if operated by a person approved by the licensing authority, i.e. if not on the manufacturer's licence a contract laboratory will not be acceptable[1].

For any changes to the information shown on a licence, prior approval from the licensing authority must be obtained.

Qualified Persons

General

All holders of a manufacturer's licence for licensed products, including for the purposes of import, are required to have available the services of a Qualified Person (QP), who must be named on the licence. When considering a nomination, the licensing authority (the MHRA) routinely takes into account the assessment of the nominee's eligibility made by the

---

[1] A contract laboratory is required to be named on the manufacturer's licence.

joint assessment panel of the Institute of Biology, the Royal Pharmaceutical Society of Great Britain and the Royal Society of Chemistry. Exceptionally, the MHRA will assess a nominee directly if he or she is not a member of any of these professional bodies.

Title IV of Directive 2001/83/EC as amended lays down the requirements for QPs in relation to products for human use. Article 51 defines the duties of the QP; Articles 49 and 50 define the requirements for eligibility under the permanent and transitional arrangements respectively, and Article 52 requires Member States to ensure that the duties of QPs are fulfilled, either through administrative measures or by making such persons subject to a professional code of conduct. Title IV of Directive 2001/82/EC as amended lays down equivalent requirements in relation to veterinary products. Guidance on the duties of QPs is given in the EU Guide to GMP and in particular in its Annex 16.

By inspection and other means the licensing authority routinely assesses whether or not QPs are fulfilling their duties. In making this assessment, reference is made to the *Code of Practice for Qualified Persons* produced jointly by the Institute of Biology, the Royal Pharmaceutical Society of Great Britain and the Royal Society of Chemistry in collaboration with the MHRA and the Veterinary Medicines Directorate. This reference is made whether or not the QP in question is a member of one or more of these bodies (see next section).

All QPs should be guided in fulfilling their duties by the Code of Practice, although the references in Sections 11.1 and 12.4 to the disciplinary machinery of the professional bodies, and in Section 11.6 to the advice which professional bodies can give, would not be relevant in the case of a QP who is not a member of one of these bodies. The European Industrial Pharmacists Group adopted a similar code[2] in 1995 for the guidance of its members.

Code of Practice for Qualified Persons in the Pharmaceutical Industry

1.0 Introduction

1.1 The concept of the Qualified Person (QP), first established in 1975, is a unique regulatory requirement that applies only within the European Union (EU). The only comparable situation exists within Member States of the European Economic Area (EEA) with whom the EU has reciprocal agreements.

---

[2] European Industrial Pharmacists Group (est. June 1966). Code of Practice for Qualified Persons. Available from the Industrial Pharmacists Group of the Royal Pharmaceutical Society of Great Britain.

1.2   Each holder of an Authorisation to Manufacture products for use in a Clinical Trial or products subject to Marketing Authorisations, within Member States of the EU, must name a person or persons who are eligible to act in the capacity of QP.

1.3   The requirement for QP covers both Human and Veterinary Medicinal Products including those intended for export.

1.4   Particular conditions for formal qualifications and practical experience for eligibility to act as a QP are specified in the relevant EU Council Directives (see 2 below). Ensuring compliance with these conditions is the responsibility of the Competent Authorities of the Member States.

1.5   The primary legal responsibility of the QP is to certify batches of Medicinal Product prior to use in a Clinical Trial (Human Medicinal Products only) or prior to release for sale and placing on the market (Human and Veterinary Medicinal Products). However, the wider technical, ethical and professional obligations in terms of patient Safety, Quality and Efficacy must also be considered. Hence this professional Code of Practice, which is designed to take account of these issues.

2.0   Regulatory Basis for the Qualified Person

For ease of reference the key regulatory documents concerning the QP are as follows:

(i)   Principles and Guidelines of Good Manufacturing Practice for Medicinal Products for Human Use: Directive 2003/94/EC **Article 7**.
(ii)   Principles and Guidelines of Good Manufacturing Practice for Veterinary Medicinal Products: Directive 91/412/EEC **Article 7**.
(iii) Good Clinical Practice in the Conduct of Clinical Trials on Medicinal Products for Human Use: Directive 2001/20/EC **Article 13**.
(iv) Community Code Relating to Veterinary Medicinal Products: Directive 2001/82/EC - Title IV - Manufacture and Imports **Articles 44–57**.
(v)   Community Code Relating to Medicinal Products for Human Use: Directive 2001/83/EC Title IV Manufacture and Importation **Articles 40–53**.
(vi) Good Manufacturing Practices: Eudralex Volume 4

Annex 13: Manufacture of Investigational Medicinal Products
Annex 16: Certification by a Qualified Person and Batch Release

3.0   Purpose of the Code

3.1   The legal functions of the Qualified Person (QP) are stated in Article 51 of Directive 2001/83/EC or Article 55 of Directive 2001/82/EC and reproduced in the preface to the UK Joint Professional Bodies' Study Guide 2000.

3.2   The aims and objectives of the Code of Practice are to provide operational guidelines for carrying out the functions of the Qualified Person within a professional code of conduct in accordance with Article 56 of Council Directive 2001/82/EC and/or Article 52 of Council Directive 2001/83/EC.

3.3   The Code is in the interests of Qualified Persons, their employers, patients and the Competent Authorities of the Member States.

4.0   Application of the Code

4.1   The Code is equally applicable to Qualified Persons who have achieved that status under the transitional arrangements, and under the permanent provisions.

4.2   Qualified Persons have a professional duty to decline to act as Qualified Persons in the release of product types for which they do not possess the relevant experience and knowledge.

4.3   It should be noted that Qualified Persons are eligible to certify batches of medicinal product as follows:

(i)   those who have achieved Qualified Person status under the permanent provisions are eligible to certify batches of human or veterinary medicinal products in any member state within the European Union (EU);

(ii)   those who have achieved Qualified Person status under the transitional arrangements for human medicines are eligible to certify batches of human or veterinary medicinal products, and such certification is restricted to acting in the United Kingdom (UK) although such products, once certified, can legally be sold or supplied throughout the EU;

(iii) those who have achieved Qualified Person status under the transitional arrangements for veterinary medicines are only eligible to certify batches of veterinary medicinal products, and such certification is restricted to acting in the UK although such products, once certified, can legally be sold or supplied throughout the EU.

4.4   The Code applies equally to Qualified Persons involved in human and/or veterinary medicines.

4.5   The Licensing Authority may refer to this Code in connection with disciplinary proceedings against a Qualified Person under Article 52 of Directive 2001/83/EC or Article 56 of Directive 2001/82/EC.

5.0   Terminology

5.1   The terminology used in this Code of Practice corresponds with that used in the current versions of the EC directives on Good Pharmaceutical

Manufacturing Practice (GMP) and the Guide to Good Pharmaceutical Manufacturing Practice.

5.2   Within the EU the terms Marketing Authorisation, Manufacturing Authorisation and Investigational Medicinal Products Authorisation are generally used and shall henceforth be referred to throughout this Code.

The UK licensing system currently uses the equivalent terms Product Licence (= Marketing Authorisation) and Manufacturer's Licence (= Manufacturing Authorisation).

6.0   General Principles

6.1   Pharmaceutical Manufacturers and the Competent Authorities of the Member States have a duty to ensure that patients are properly protected and that medicinal products meet appropriate requirements for safety, quality and efficacy.

6.2   The legal framework is provided by the European Directives and "The Rules Governing Medicinal Products in the European Union", which are implemented by individual Member States' national legislation.

6.3   An operational framework is provided in the current Volume 4 of the Rules Governing Medical Products in the European Union "Good Manufacturing Practices". In Chapter 1 of the Guidelines, Quality Management, it states that:

"The holder of a Manufacturing Authorisation must manufacture medicinal products so as to ensure that they are fit for their intended use, comply with the requirements of the Marketing Authorisation and do not place patients at risk due to inadequate safety, quality or efficacy. The attainment of this quality objective is the responsibility of senior management and requires the participation and commitment by staff in many different departments and at all levels within the company, the company's suppliers and the distributors.

To achieve the quality objective reliably there must be a comprehensively designed and correctly implemented system of Quality Assurance incorporating Good Manufacturing Practice and thus Quality Control. It should be fully documented and its effectiveness monitored. All parts of the Quality Assurance system should be adequately resourced with competent personnel, and suitable and sufficient premises, equipment and facilities. There are additional legal responsibilities for the holder of the Manufacturing Authorisation and for the Qualified Person(s).

The basic concepts of Quality Assurance, Good Manufacturing Practice and Quality Control are inter-related. They are described here in order to emphasise their relationships and their fundamental importance to the production and control of medicinal products."

6.4   Qualified Persons should be aware that whilst Quality Management applies to full-scale manufacture, it also extends to original product design, development, formulation and preparation of medicinal products for use in clinical trials. This includes the establishment of well-defined manufacturing processes, sampling programmes and analytical tests methods and appropriate specifications for ingredients, printed and unprinted packaging components and finished dosage forms.

7.0   Routine Duties of a Qualified Person

Qualified Persons have routine duties, some of which may be delegated (see later), in line with the above general principles. Before certifying a batch prior to release the Qualified Person doing so should always **ensure** that the following requirements have been met:

*"The meaning of the word **ensure** in this context is that the Qualified Person must be confident that various actions, which may not be under his/her direct control, have in fact been taken."* See also *Section 8.*

7.1   The Marketing Authorisation and Manufacturing Authorisation or Investigational Medicinal Products Authorisation requirements for the Medicinal Products have been met for the batch concerned.

7.2   The principles and guidelines of GMP as stated in Directive 2003/94/EC (Human) or Directive 91/412/EEC (Veterinary) and as interpreted in the EU Guide to GMP have been followed.

7.3   The principal manufacturing and testing processes have been validated.

7.4   All the necessary quality control checks and tests have been performed, and account taken of the manufacturing and packaging conditions including a review of batch records. *The EU Guide to GMP suggests that the Head of Production and the Head of Quality Control assume line management responsibilities for these activities.*

7.5   Any changes or deviations in manufacturing, packaging or quality control have been notified in accordance with a well-defined reporting system before any product batch is released. Such changes may need notification to and approval by the Competent Authorities of the Member States.

7.6   Any additional sampling, inspection, tests and checks have been carried out or initiated, as appropriate, to cover changes or deviations.

7.7   All necessary manufacturing, packaging and associated documentation has been completed and endorsed by suitably authorised staff trained in the concept of Quality Assurance and Good Manufacturing Practices.

7.8   Regular audits, self-inspections and spot checks are being carried out by experienced staff.

7.9   All relevant factors have been considered including any not specifically associated with the output batch directly under review (e.g. calibration and maintenance records, environmental monitoring).

7.10   The legal requirements regarding imported products have been fully met. *For products imported from outside the EU or EEA, the Qualified Person should ensure testing within the EU/EEA to the requirements of the Marketing Authorisation and any other tests to assure quality of the products, unless a mutual recognition agreement between the EU and the third country concerned allows the acceptance of manufacturer's batch certification in lieu.*

   The Qualified Person should also be satisfied that the medicinal products have been manufactured in accordance with GMP standards which are equivalent to those of the EU or EEA.

7.11   The Qualified Person should also recognise the need to consult other company experts in the various areas of the Study Guide to reinforce his/her knowledge on appropriate points when a doubtful situation arises *(e.g. stability, unusual analytical results, process or equipment changes, potential environmental or microbiological risks, re-labelling, abnormal yields, cross contamination risks etc.).*

7.12   To maintain a register (or equivalent document) as a record of product batches certified by the Qualified Person prior to batch release.

7.13   To retain reference samples of each product batch at the site of manufacture for a period of time in compliance with EU regulations and the Licensing Authority's requirements.

7.14   In considering how to perform the above duties, 7.1 to 7.13, the Qualified Person will have to take account of the nature and size of the operations being performed. For example, in a very small company with a limited range of products it may be possible that the Qualified Person can take direct responsibility for some or all of the tasks outlined above. In larger organisations, the Qualified Person will be dependent upon the knowledge and expertise of his/her colleagues in undertaking some or all of the tasks.

   However, it is of paramount importance that the Qualified Person takes steps, within a well planned Quality Management System, to assure himself or herself that the tasks allocated are in fact being performed satisfactorily. Hence the routine duties of the Qualified Person depend very much upon a team effort wherein the individuals concerned realise the position and responsibility of the Qualified Person and provide every support.

   What cannot be over emphasised in this context is the Qualified Person's commitment to meet regularly with professional colleagues in all functional groups and to understand their contribution and impact upon quality.

The certification of a batch prior to release must be performed by a Qualified Person.

8.0 Performance of Duties and Regulatory Compliance

8.1   Management, as a requirement of Quality Assurance, should clearly define the areas of work and the method of operating in the absence of the regular Qualified Person.

In the absence of one Qualified Person, the task of certifying batches can only be delegated to another Qualified Person nominated on the Manufacturing Authorisation and who is knowledgeable and experienced with regard to the medicinal products under review.

8.2   Whilst each Qualified Person has a personal and professional responsibility for being certain that the various checks and tests have been carried out, the detail of this work is described in the EU Guide to GMP as normally the responsibility of the Head of Production and the Head of Quality Control who must ensure that appropriately trained and experienced staff are available.

Ultimately the Qualified Person must be satisfied either directly or, more usually, by the proper operation of quality systems, which include appropriate approvals, audits, self inspections and spot checks that manufacturing, packaging and quality control testing have complied with relevant requirements.

Batch certification without such adequate steps may be regarded as professional misconduct.

8.3   It must be recognised that the Qualified Person depends upon many of his/her working colleagues for the achievement of quality and regulatory compliance in the manufacture of medicinal products. It is therefore of paramount importance that he or she achieves a good working relationship with other persons in positions of responsibility. These are likely to include those responsible for:

- processing and packing operations
- quality control laboratories
- validation
- application and maintenance of Manufacturing and Marketing Authorisations
- provision of engineering services
- procurement of starting and packaging materials
- storage, transport and distribution
- contract services.

8.4   It is recommended that the company and the Qualified Person take the necessary steps to appraise other functional groups, and the responsible people who belong to them, of the role of the Qualified Person within the company and how they should give proper support.

8.5   Ensuring compliance with the conditions of the Marketing Authorisation is a primary duty of the Qualified Person. It is, therefore, essential that the Qualified Person has access at all times to the dossiers upon which Marketing Authorisations have been granted, including any variations affecting such approval. The control of change needs to be rigorously monitored by the Qualified Person especially where there are implications for compliance, quality and patient safety. Particular attention needs to be paid to this when the manufacturer is making products for a Marketing Authorisation holder in a different company.

8.6   The Qualified Person should be present at the manufacturing site for a sufficient proportion of the working time in order to discharge the legal and professional obligations outlined in this Code and to ensure the proper operation of a Quality Management System including the control of any delegated duties.

8.7   Manufacturing Authorisations contain the names of the persons responsible for Production, Quality Control, and the name(s) of the Qualified Person(s). The duties of these members of staff must be clear in their respective job descriptions and they must have the authority required under the relevant EC directives.

9.0   Number and Location of Qualified Persons

9.1   The provisions in Article 52 of Council Directive 2001/82/EC and/or Article 48 of Council Directive 2001/83/EC and the principles outlined in the EU Guide to GMP for Medicinal Products only require a company or organisation to nominate one person on a Manufacturing Authorisation to carry out the duties of the Qualified Person provided that person is at the disposal of the company at all times and can carry out the required functions.

9.2   Some organisations may have a complex structure, or operate at several locations, or both, which would make it necessary, where justified, to nominate several Qualified Persons on its Manufacturing Authorisation.

10.0   Contracted Qualified Persons

10.1   In a number of cases, especially with smaller companies, a "Contracted Qualified Person" provides the service. In such cases the duties and responsibilities of a "Contracted Qualified Person" are the same as those Qualified Persons who are permanently employed by their company; the QP is not an employee of the company but provides his services under contract.

The term "Contracted Qualified Person" is not a formal title and is used only in the sense of a Qualified Person providing an independent service under contract to a company.

10.2 In addition to compliance with the provisions applicable to all Qualified Persons including all the routine duties outlined in this Code of Practice, Contracted Qualified Persons should observe the following:

- have a clear written contract which delineates the duties and responsibilities of the Qualified Person – as agreed between the company and the "Contracted Qualified Person". Both should sign and retain a copy of the contract;
- be readily available to the staff of the company for advice and discussion, and also be present during regulatory inspections and involved in communications with the inspectors;
- ensure that the company to whom the services are provided will allow free access to any people, information, documentation, premises, procedures etc. which are relevant to the decision-making processes when certifying batches for sale. In addition the company should inform the Qualified Person of any deviations which need to be considered in relation to batch certification. Such deviations should be provided to the Qualified Person promptly and in writing;
- ensure that sufficient spot checks, inspections, and audits of the company (whether in the EU or overseas) are carried out; in particular the "Contracted Qualified Person" should satisfy himself/herself that an effective pharmaceutical Quality Management System is being operated.

10.3 Particularly for smaller companies, the person acting as contracted QP may agree with the company to provide some of the necessary services such as, for example, staff training, internal audits and maintenance of authorisations, personally in addition to performing strictly QP duties.

10.4 If any doubt exists concerning the duties and responsibilities between the Qualified Person and the company who requires his/her services, it is recommended that he or she should contact their local Regulatory Inspector or their professional body for advice.

10.5 **This Code of Practice should be brought to the attention of the Chief Executive Officer of the company who wishes to have the services of a "Contracted Qualified Person".**

11.0 Contract Manufacture and/or Testing

11.1 Where products are manufactured and/or packed under contract there should be a clearly written technical agreement between the contract giver and the contract acceptor. Such an agreement should be reviewed and approved by the Qualified Person engaged by the contract giver and acceptor. The agreement should clearly delineate the areas and responsibilities of both Qualified Persons.

11.2   The contract acceptor, who normally will be required to hold a manufacturing authorisation, may accept full responsibility for batch certification provided that the Qualified Person has all the appropriate information (including access to relevant details in the Marketing Authorisation(s)) and authority to fulfil these duties. Nevertheless the decision concerning responsibility for batch certification remains a matter between contract giver and acceptor depending on the circumstances.

11.3   The provisions in 11.1 apply equally to the testing of samples under contract. The contract testing laboratory may not hold its own manufacturing authorisation but in this case must be authorised on the contract giver's authorisation.

12.0   Continuing Professional Development

12.1   Qualified Persons have a personal and professional duty to keep their knowledge and experience up to date (Annex 16, item 8.3, EU Guide to GMP, Volume 4 of "The Rules Governing Medicinal Products in the European Union"). It is expected that this would cover the current state of pharmaceutical quality management, regulatory aspects and GMP guideline standards, product manufacturing and control technology, and general work practices.

12.2   Records of Continuing Professional Development (CPD) should be kept to reflect this important longer-term aspect of the Qualified Person's continued performance of professional duties.

12.3   Attention is drawn to the individual Member State's statements on CPD, which underline the importance of this aspect of a Qualified Person's performance of duties. These statements appear as Appendix 1 to this Code, and they will also be of value to those Qualified Persons who are not members of any of the three professional bodies.

12.4   In the event of a Qualified Person making a major change in job responsibilities, for example from a company making only sterile dosage forms to one with a wider range of products including solid dose forms, the Qualified Person and the senior management of the company involved should recognise the need for additional education and training and take adequate steps to demonstrate that proper provision is made for this. Such extra training should be undertaken before the Qualified Person acts in a new situation.

13.0 Professional Conduct

13.1 Qualified Persons are subject to the overall jurisdiction of the Bye-laws, Charters and Regulations, Codes of Conduct, Disciplinary Regulations and any general guidelines of their own professional body, and should have access to them.

13.2 Qualified Persons have duties not only to their employer but also to the Competent Authorities of the Member States and its inspection service. They must ensure that appropriate senior company executives are made fully aware of any manufacturing and/or testing difficulties which may cast doubt on the certification of batches or post facto might require a product recall.

13.3 If there is any aspect of the Quality Assurance system which is not in accordance with the Directives and Guidelines for Good Manufacturing Practice then the Qualified Person has a duty to bring this to the attention of Senior Management and ensure that appropriate corrective measures are taken.

13.4 Qualified Persons should establish a good working relationship with Regulatory Inspectors and as far as possible provide information on request during site inspections.

NB. There may be situations outside of site inspections where the Qualified Person may wish to consult with the local Regulatory Inspector for advice or clarification in particular circumstances with which the Qualified Person is faced.

13.5 The following assumption is made by the professional bodies acting jointly when certifying the eligibility of a Qualified Person:

- in co-operation with their employers, Qualified Persons will undertake Continuing Professional Development to maintain and extend their technical and professional competence. (See also Section 12.0 above.)

13.6 The following assumptions are made, firstly by the professional bodies acting jointly when certifying the eligibility of a Qualified Person and, secondly, by the Competent Authority when accepting an eligible Qualified Person for nomination on a Manufacturing Authorisation:

- in cases where undue pressures to depart from professional obligations cannot be counterbalanced by reference to this and other relevant Codes of Practice, Qualified Persons, preferably having informed their employer first, should consult the appropriate professional body for confidential advice.
- management has a duty to provide Qualified Persons with appropriate resources and to ensure that Quality Management Systems and

communications are working effectively. Therefore, Qualified Persons also have a duty to make representations to management, if necessary in writing, whenever standards appear to be falling short of Good Manufacturing Practice(s). This duty should be reflected by appropriate wording in the Qualified Person's job description.

14.0   Disciplinary Procedures

14.1   Article 56 of Council Directive 2001/82/EC and Article 52 of Council Directive 2001/83/EC. read inter alia:

"Member States shall ensure that the duties of Qualified Persons...are fulfilled, either by means of appropriate administrative measures or by making such persons subject to a professional Code of Conduct.

Member States may provide for the temporary suspension of such a person upon the commencement of administrative or disciplinary procedures against him for failure to fulfil his obligations."

If it were found that a QP had certified in a register or equivalent document a product batch as fit for sale without ensuring that the relevant tests and checks had been carried out, this failure might be a matter for consideration by the appropriate professional body to which he/she might belong as a matter of professional misconduct.

14.2   The UK professional bodies have established disciplinary procedures to deal with cases of possible misconduct. One of the powers is to remove the name of an individual from the appropriate register or registers and they will act together as appropriate in the case of a Qualified Person who is a member of two or three of the Societies. In such cases, professional bodies will inform the Competent Authority.

14.3   The Member State Competent Authority is the body with the power to delete the Qualified Person's name from the Manufacturing Authorisation.

Appendix 1: UK Statements on CPD

INSTITUTE OF BIOLOGY

CONTINUING PROFESSIONAL DEVELOPMENT STATEMENT

In common with many other professional biologists, Qualified Persons work in a changing scientific, commercial and regulatory environment. This requires individuals to commit themselves to updating their knowledge and skills in order to maintain their competence to do the job. Increasingly, there is a demand from employees undertaking such development to have it recognised, and for employers to be able to demonstrate the competence of their employees to regulatory bodies, their customers and the general public. Continuing Professional Development (CPD) emphasises quality and confers a competitive edge.

The Institute of Biology has, therefore, placed a high priority on the development of a Continuing Professional Development scheme, to ensure that chartered biologists keep up to date and maintain their competence. The Institute is in the process of carrying out a pilot CPD scheme based on national occupational standards for professional biologists developed by the Science, Technology and Mathematics Council. The CPD scheme has been designed as a benefit and to support members in advancing self-education whilst also underpinning professional competence.

The scheme focuses on the demonstration of work place competence maintained by informal and formal activities, such as reading, conference attendance and short courses. The scheme initially is voluntary.

ROYAL PHARMACEUTICAL SOCIETY OF GREAT BRITAIN

CONTINUING PROFESSIONAL DEVELOPMENT STATEMENT

The Royal Pharmaceutical Society of Great Britain (RPSGB) seeks to safeguard and promote the interests of the public and the profession by identifying the fundamental role and accountability of pharmacists. Pharmacists must keep up to date with changes in pharmacy practice, the law relating to pharmacy and the knowledge and technology applicable to pharmacy, and to maintain competence and effectiveness as a practitioner.

The "key responsibilities of a pharmacist" are set out in the RPSGB's Code of Ethics.

The Code of Ethics states that practising pharmacists are expected to maintain records of their continuing professional development (CPD) and make the records available for review by the Society on request. CPD records should contain evidence that practising pharmacists:

(a) continually review the skills and knowledge required for their field(s) of practice, identify those skills or knowledge in need of development or improvement and audit their performance as part of the review;
(b) plan appropriate learning activities to address identified learning needs and implement their plans;
(c) evaluate what they have learned and effectively translate their learning into improved professional practice.

The RPSGB produces guidance on good practice for ensuring professional competence in Medicines, Ethics and Practice: A Guide for Pharmacists which is sent to all registered pharmacists on an annual basis. This includes guidance on identifying continuing professional development needs, deciding how to meet those needs, recording planning of and participation in CPD and evaluating the outcome of any CPD participation.

All pharmacists, including those eligible to act as Qualified Persons, are encouraged to document any identified training and development needs, how they have planned to meet them and what has actually been done in an attempt to meet them. Pharmacists are advised to retain training records and record CPD in an approved format for this purpose.

Continuing Professional Development is becoming increasingly important in all areas of practice and it is in the interests of all pharmacists to retain evidence/records of participation. Further information about the RPSGB CPD scheme can be found on the RPSGB website at: www.rpsgb.org.

ROYAL SOCIETY OF CHEMISTRY

CONTINUING PROFESSIONAL DEVELOPMENT STATEMENT

Continuing Professional Development (CPD) has been defined by the RSC as:

"the responsibility of individuals for the systematic maintenance, improvement and broadening of knowledge and skills to ensure continuing competence as a professional throughout their career."

In today's world, professionals are required to demonstrate that their knowledge and professional skills are being kept up to date. Advances in the chemical sciences and the increasing need to use a variety of skills particularly when working at the interfaces with different scientific areas requires members to develop and maintain a range of skills. This will ensure that they are able to meet the needs of evolving employment requirements.

CPD for RSC members on the Register of Eligible Qualified Persons is important because registrants should be able to demonstrate that their expertise is up to date to ensure that the Register has public credibility. The CPD scheme links to the competencies required for registration as an Eligible Qualified Person.

Members on the Register of Eligible Qualified Persons is important because registrants should be able to demonstrate that their expertise is up to date to ensure that the Register has public credibility. The CPD scheme links to the competencies required for registration as an Eligible Qualified Person.

Members on the Register of Eligible Qualified Persons are requested to submit a CPD return annually. Participation in the scheme is voluntary, but submission of an appropriate CPD return will be recognised in the Register.

Further information about the RSC CPD scheme can be found on the RSC website at www.rsc.org/members/cpd.

Import from Third Countries

For medicinal products imported into the EU from third countries (i.e. countries other than the EEA Member States), the provisions of Articles 51 and 55, respectively, of Directive 2001/83/EC as amended are required to be applied. This includes the full qualitative and quantitative analysis of at least all the active substances and all the other tests or checks necessary to ensure the quality of the medicinal products is in accordance with the requirements of the marketing authorisation. It is the Qualified Person of the importer who is responsible for ensuring that these requirements are met.

Mutual Recognition Agreements on Good Manufacturing Practice (GMP) and Manufacturing Authorisation

The European Community has Mutual Recognition Agreements (MRAs) with several third countries with which it has substantial trade. The pharmaceutical or GMP sectors of these MRAs provide benefit to exporters and importers of medicinal products in the EU trading with these countries.

The basis for an MRA concerning medicinal products is equivalence of the principles and guidelines of GMP, the inspection systems and, in most cases, the arrangements for authorising manufacturers between both parties. An MRA only becomes operational after a mutual agreement of equivalence. The benefits of an MRA when in operation include:

- authority for an importer to accept a manufacturer's batch certification of compliance with GMP, the relevant marketing authorisation and certificate of analysis. The Qualified Person (QP) of the importer in the EU may certify an imported batch on the basis of such a certificate in place of full testing within the EU, in accordance with Article 51.2 of Directive 2001/83/EC as amended. Importers and exporters who wish to benefit from a MRA should use this certificate. The format of the certificate is shown below;
- normal acceptance between competent authorities of inspection reports and certification of authorisation and GMP compliance of a manufacturer.

MRAs that include a medicinal products sector have been negotiated between the EC and the following countries:

- Australia
- Canada
- Japan
- New Zealand
- Switzerland.

The MRA between the EC and United States is not in operation. The transitional period ended November 2001 but no decision on a formal extension has been taken. The two-way alert systems remain in operation.

The operational status and scope of individual MRAs at any given time may be checked on the Commission's website or with the MHRA.

Content of the Fabricator's/Manufacturer's Batch Certificate for Drug/Medicinal Products Exported to Countries Under the Scope of a Mutual Recognition Agreement (MRA)

[Letterhead of exporting manufacturer]

1 Name of product.

Proprietary, brand or trade name in the importing country.

2 Importing country.
3 Marketing authorisation number.

The marketing authorisation number of the product in the importing country should be provided.

4 Strength/potency.

Identity (name) and amount per unit dose required for all active ingredients/constituents.

5 Dosage form (pharmaceutical form).
6 Package size (contents of container) and type (e.g. vials, bottles, blisters).
7 Lot/batch number.

As related to the product.

8 Date of fabrication/manufacture.

In accordance with national (local) requirements.

9 Expiry date.
10 Name and address of fabricator(s)/manufacturer(s) – manufacturing site(s).

All sites involved in the manufacture including packaging and Quality Control of the batch should be listed with name and address. The name and address must correspond to the information provided on the manufacturing authorisation/establishment licence.

11 Number of Manufacturing Authorisation/Licence or Certificate of GMP Compliance of a manufacturer/ fabricator.

The number should be given for each site listed under item 10.

12 Results of analysis.

Should include the authorised specifications, all results obtained and refer to the methods used (may refer to a separate certificate of analysis which must be dated, signed and attached).

13 Comments/remarks.

Any additional information that can be of value to the importer and/or inspector verifying the compliance of the batch certificate (e.g. specific storage or transportation conditions).

14 Certification statement.

This statement should cover the fabrication/manufacturing, including packaging and Quality Control. The following text should be used: "I hereby certify that the above information is authentic and accurate. This batch of product has been fabricated/manufactured, including packaging and Quality Control at the above mentioned site(s) in full compliance with the GMP requirements of the local Regulatory Authority and with the specifications in the marketing authorisation of the importing country. The batch processing, packaging and analysis records were reviewed and found to be in compliance with GMP".

15 Name and position/title of person authorising the batch release.

Including its company/site name and address, if more than one company is mentioned under item 10.

16 Signature of person authorising the batch release.
17 Date of signature.

UK Guidance on Certificates of Analysis

In certain circumstances a Certificate of Analysis from a third party may be used as part of a system to ensure the quality of materials. For such a certificate to be considered acceptable the following conditions should apply.

(a) The person responsible for Quality Control (QC) in the purchasing company must assure himself that the organisation issuing the certificate is competent to do so, whether that organisation is part of the supplying company or is independent of it (e.g. is a contract analytical service).

(b) The Certificate must:
   (i) Identify the organisation issuing it.

(ii) Be authorised by a person competent to do so, and state his qualifications and position. "Authorisation" may be by signature or acceptable electronic means (please refer to the guidance given for the similar situation when a Qualified Person (QP) releases a batch of finished products for sale, see paragraph 19 of Annex 11 to the EC Guide to GMP).

(iii) Name the material to which it refers and identify it by a batch number.

(iv) State that the material has been tested, by whom and when this was done.

(v) State the specification (e.g. EP) and methods against which, and by which, the tests were performed.

(vi) Give the test results obtained, or declare that the results obtained showed compliance with the stated specification.

Certificates which merely carry such statements as "a typical analysis is...", or state that the material is of a particular quality with no supporting evidence, are not acceptable.

Possession of a Certificate of Analysis does not eliminate the need to confirm the identity of the material supplied.

Possession of a Certificate of Analysis does not absolve the purchaser from ultimate responsibility for the correctness of the material to which it refers.

The above paragraphs, whilst particularly relevant to the certification of starting materials, also apply as appropriate to other materials and products.

Note that the Certificate of Analysis described above is not *the Manufacturer's Batch Certificate used within the context of a Mutual Recognition Agreement* (see Mutual Recognition Agreement section above).

GMP for Starting Materials

(To be read in conjunction with Part II of the EC Guide to GMP.)

From 30 October 2005, new Community requirements obliged manufacturing authorisation holders to use as starting materials only active substances that have been manufactured in accordance with GMP.

This includes both total and partial manufacture, as well as any repackaging or re-labelling activities carried out by a distributor or broker. Herb APIs used as active substances for traditional herbal medicinal products as defined in Directive 2004/24/EC will also be required to comply with the new requirements.

The amending legislation gives powers to the competent authorities in Member States to carry out inspections at the premises of manufacturers of such materials, the marketing authorisation (MA) holder and any laboratories employed by the MA holder. These inspections will be conducted by the competent authority, may be unannounced and may be carried out at the request of an API manufacturer, another Member State, the Commission, or the European Medicines Agency (EMEA). The competent authority will be empowered to inspect premises, take samples and examine documents.

The responsibility for confirming that the active substances in use have been manufactured in accordance with GMP rests with the holder of the manufacturing authorisation in the EU. The primary means by which EU regulatory authorities will supervise compliance with the requirement for active substances to be manufactured in accordance with GMP will be through review of audit reports during inspections of manufacturing authorisation holders.

Audits of API manufacturers should be performed by suitably trained auditors. During inspections the competence of auditors will be assessed and if not deemed appropriate this will be raised as an issue.

The new Community requirements do not require licensing of API manufacturers. However, a report will be provided to the manufacturer or MA holder who has undergone the inspection and, where relevant, a certificate of GMP compliance issued. Certificates will be entered on a central Community database, as will be any failures in compliance.

Manufacture and Importation of Unlicensed Medicines for Human Use

Introduction

UK medicines legislation provides certain exemptions for the supply and use of unlicensed medicine for human use. Two of the more important exemptions are outlined here: the manufacture and supply of unlicensed relevant medicinal products for individual patients ("specials") and the importation and supply of unlicensed relevant medicinal products for individual patients.

A "relevant medicinal product" is one to which the requirements of Directive 2001/83/EC as amended apply unless subject to an exemption in that Directive.

Manufacture and supply of unlicensed relevant medicinal products for individual patients ("specials")

The Medicines for Human Use (Marketing Authorisations Etc.) Regulations 1994 as amended [SI 1994 No. 3144] require that medicinal products are licensed before they are marketed in the UK. However some patients may have special clinical needs that cannot be met by licensed medicinal products. So that these special needs may be met, the law allows manufacture and supply of unlicensed medicinal products (commonly known as "specials"), subject to certain conditions.

The conditions, laid down in Schedule 1 of the Regulations, are that there is a bona fide unsolicited order, the product is formulated in accordance with the requirement of a doctor or dentist registered in the UK and the product is for use by one of their individual patients (on the basis of "special need") on the practitioner's direct personal responsibility. If a "special" is manufactured in the UK, the manufacturer must hold a manufacturer's (specials) licence issued by the MHRA. A "special" may not be advertised and may not be supplied if an equivalent licensed product is available which could meet the patient's needs. Essential records must be kept and serious adverse drug reactions reported to the MHRA. The MHRA Guidance Note 14 *The supply of unlicensed relevant medicinal products for individual patients* provides guidance to manufacturers about the conditions under which they may manufacture and supply "specials" and their legal obligations.

Importation and supply of unlicensed relevant medicinal products for individual patients

An unlicensed relevant medicinal product may only be imported in accordance with The Medicines for Human Use (Manufacturing, Wholesale Dealing and Miscellaneous Amendments) Regulations 2005 [SI 2005/2789]. An importer must hold the appropriate wholesale dealer's or manufacturer's (import) licence (for further information see the MHRA Guidance Notes 5 and 6: *Notes for applicants and holders of a manufacturer's/wholesale dealer's licence*) and must comply with the conditions of their licence. Wholesale dealers and importers from third countries licence conditions include the requirement that they must notify the MHRA on each occasion that they intend to import such a product. Importation may proceed unless the importer has been informed by the MHRA within 28 days that it objects to importation. The MHRA may object and prevent importation because it has concerns about the safety or quality of the product or because there is an equivalent licensed medicinal product available and it is not satisfied that there is a "special need" for the supply to an individual patient.

An imported unlicensed relevant medicinal product may only be supplied in accordance with Schedule 1 to The Medicines for Human Use (Marketing Authorisations Etc.) Regulations 1994 as amended [SI 1994 No. 3144]. Schedule 1 exempts, under defined conditions (discussed in the previous section on "specials") such a product when it is supplied to meet the "special need" of an individual patient. The MHRA Guidance Note 14 provides guidance to importers about the conditions under which they may import and supply unlicensed relevant medicinal products and their legal obligations.

The manufacturer or assembler of "specials" must also demonstrate compliance with the European Commission's *Notes for guidance on minimising the risk of transmitting animal spongiform encephalopathy agents via medicinal products* and future updates, in accordance with The Unlicensed Medicinal Products for Human Use (Transmissible Spongiform Encephalopathies) (Safety) Regulations 2003 [SI 2003/1680]. (See the MHRA's interim guidance: *Minimising the risk of Transmission of Transmissible Spongiform Encephalopathies via Unlicensed Medicinal Products for Human Use*, available from the MHRA's website www.mhra.gov.uk.)

Contact

For further information about notifications of intention to import, please contact:

The Unlicensed Imports Section, 17th floor, Market Towers, 1 Nine Elms Lane, London SW8 5NQ, UK.

Telephone: +44 (0)20 7084 2574
Fax: +44 (0)20 7084 2676
E-mail: info@mhra.gsi.gov.uk

LEGISLATION ON MANUFACTURE

EU Legislation on Manufacture

Contents

DIRECTIVE 2001/83/EC, AS AMENDED, TITLE IV, MANUFACTURE AND IMPORTATION

Directive 2001/83/EC of the European Parliament and of the Council of 6 November 2001 on the Community code relating to medicinal products for human use as amended by Directive 2004/27/EC

Title IV: Manufacture and Importation

> Editor's note
>
> Title IV of this directive is reproduced below. Reference should be made to the full Directive for the preamble, definitions and the general and final provisions.

Article 40

1   Member States shall take all appropriate measures to ensure that the manufacture of the medicinal products within their territory is subject to the holding of an authorization. This manufacturing authorization shall be required notwithstanding that the medicinal products manufactured are intended for export.

2   The authorization referred to in paragraph 1 shall be required for both total and partial manufacture, and for the various processes of dividing up, packaging or presentation. However, such authorization shall not be required for preparation, dividing up, changes in packaging or presentation where these processes are carried out, solely for retail supply, by pharmacists in dispensing pharmacies or by persons legally authorized in the Member States to carry out such processes.

3   Authorization referred to in paragraph 1 shall also be required for imports coming from third countries into a Member State; this Title and Article 118 shall have corresponding application to such imports as they have to manufacture.

4   The Member States shall forward to the Agency a copy of the authorisation referred to in paragraph 1. The Agency shall enter that information on the Community database referred to in Article 111(6).

Article 41

In order to obtain the manufacturing authorization, the applicant shall meet at least the following requirements:

(a) specify the medicinal products and pharmaceutical forms which are to be manufactured or imported and also the place where they are to be manufactured and/or controlled;

(b) have at his disposal, for the manufacture or import of the above, suitable and sufficient premises, technical equipment and control facilities complying with the legal requirements which the Member State concerned lays down as regards both manufacture and control and the storage of medicinal products, in accordance with Article 20;

(c) have at his disposal the services of at least one qualified person within the meaning of Article 48. The applicant shall provide particulars in support of the above in his application.

Article 42

1 The competent authority of the Member State shall issue the manufacturing authorization only after having made sure of the accuracy of the particulars supplied pursuant to Article 41, by means of an inquiry carried out by its agents.

2 In order to ensure that the requirements referred to in Article 41 are complied with, authorization may be made conditional on the carrying out of certain obligations imposed either when authorization is granted or at a later date.

3 The authorization shall apply only to the premises specified in the application and to the medicinal products and pharmaceutical forms specified in that same application.

Article 43

The Member States shall take all appropriate measures to ensure that the time taken for the procedure for granting the manufacturing authorization does not exceed 90 days from the day on which the competent authority receives the application.

Article 44

If the holder of the manufacturing authorization requests a change in any of the particulars referred to in points (a) and (b) of the first paragraph of Article 41, the time taken for the procedure relating to this request shall not exceed 30 days. In exceptional cases this period of time may be extended to 90 days.

Article 45

The competent authority of the Member State may require from the applicant further information concerning the particulars supplied pursuant to Article 41 and concerning the qualified person referred to in Article 48; where the competent authority concerned exercises this right, application of the time-limits referred to in Article 43 and 44 shall be suspended until the additional data required have been supplied.

Article 46

The holder of a manufacturing authorization shall at least be obliged:

(a) to have at his disposal the services of staff who comply with the legal requirements existing in the Member State concerned both as regards manufacture and controls;

(b) to dispose of the authorized medicinal products only in accordance with the legislation of the Member States concerned;

(c) to give prior notice to the competent authority of any changes he may wish to make to any of the particulars supplied pursuant to Article 41; the competent authority shall, in any event, be immediately informed if the qualified person referred to in Article 48 is replaced unexpectedly;

(d) to allow the agents of the competent authority of the Member State concerned access to his premises at any time;

(e) to enable the qualified person referred to in Article 48 to carry out his duties, for example by placing at his disposal all the necessary facilities;

(f) to comply with the principles and guidelines of good manufacturing practice for medicinal products and to use as starting materials only active substances, which have been manufactured in accordance with the detailed guidelines on good manufacturing practice for starting materials. This point shall also be applicable to certain excipients, the list of which as well as the specific conditions of application shall be established by a Directive adopted by the Commission in accordance with the procedure referred to in Article 121(2).

Article 46a

1   For the purposes of this Directive, manufacture of active substances used as starting materials shall include both total and partial manufacture or import of an active substance used as a starting material as defined in Part I, point 3.2.1.1 (b) Annex I, and the various processes of dividing up, packaging or presentation prior to its incorporation into a medicinal product, including repackaging or relabelling, such as are carried out by a distributor of starting materials.

2   Any amendments necessary to adapt paragraph 1 to new scientific and technical developments shall be laid down in accordance with the procedure referred to in Article 121(2).

Article 47

The principles and guidelines of good manufacturing practices for medicinal products referred to in Article 46(f) shall be adopted in the form of a directive, in accordance with the procedure referred to in Article 121(2). Detailed guidelines in line with those principles will be published by the Commission and revised necessary to take account of technical and scientific progress. The principles of good manufacturing practice for active substances used as starting materials referred to in point (f) of Article 46 shall be adopted in the form of detailed guidelines. The Commission shall also publish guidelines on the form and content of the authorisation referred to in Article 40(1), on the reports referred to in Article 111(3) and on the form and content of the certificate of good manufacturing practice referred to in Article 111(5).

Article 48

1   Member States shall take all appropriate measures to ensure that the holder of the manufacturing authorization has permanently and continuously at his disposal the services of at least one qualified person, in accordance with the conditions laid down in Article 49, responsible in particular for carrying out the duties specified in Article 51.

2   If he personally fulfils the conditions laid down in Article 49, the holder of the authorization may himself assume the responsibility referred to in paragraph 1.

Article 49

1   Member States shall ensure that the qualified person referred to in Article 48 fulfils the conditions of qualification set out in paragraphs 2 and 3.

2   A qualified person shall be in possession of a diploma, certificate or other evidence of formal qualifications awarded on completion of a university course of study, or a course recognized as equivalent by the Member State concerned, extending over a period of at least four years of theoretical and practical study in one of the following scientific disciplines: pharmacy, medicine, veterinary medicine, chemistry, pharmaceutical chemistry and technology, biology.

However, the minimum duration of the university course may be three and a half years where the course is followed by a period of theoretical and practical training of a minimum duration of one year and including a training period of at least six months in a pharmacy open to the public, corroborated by an examination at university level.

Where two university courses or two courses recognized by the State as equivalent co-exist in a Member State and where one of these extends over four years and the other over three years, the three-year course leading to a diploma, certificate or other evidence of formal qualifications awarded on completion of a university course or its recognized equivalent shall be considered to fulfil the condition of duration referred to in the second subparagraph in so far as the diplomas, certificates or other evidence of formal qualifications awarded on completion of both courses are recognized as equivalent by the State in question.

The course shall include theoretical and practical study bearing upon at least the following basic subjects:

- Experimental physics
- General and inorganic chemistry
- Organic chemistry
- Analytical chemistry
- Pharmaceutical chemistry, including analysis of medicinal products
- General and applied biochemistry (medical)
- Physiology
- Microbiology
- Pharmacology
- Pharmaceutical technology
- Toxicology
- Pharmacognosy (study of the composition and effects of the natural active substances of plant and animal origin).

Studies in these subjects should be so balanced as to enable the person concerned to fulfil the obligations specified in Article 51.

In so far as certain diplomas, certificates or other evidence of formal qualifications mentioned in the first subparagraph do not fulfil the criteria laid down in this paragraph, the competent authority of the Member State shall ensure that the person concerned provides evidence of adequate knowledge of the subjects involved.

3   The qualified person shall have acquired practical experience over at least two years, in one or more undertakings which are authorized to manufacture medicinal products, in the activities of qualitative analysis of medicinal products, of quantitative analysis of active substances and of the testing and checking necessary to ensure the quality of medicinal products.

The duration of practical experience may be reduced by one year where a university course lasts for at least five years and by a year and a half where the course lasts for at least six years.

Article 50

1 A person engaging in the activities of the person referred to in Article 48 from the time of the application of Directive 75/319/EEC, in a Member State without complying with the provisions of Article 49 shall be eligible to continue to engage in those activities within the Community.

2 The holder of a diploma, certificate or other evidence of formal qualifications awarded on completion of a university course or a course recognized as equivalent by the Member State concerned in a scientific discipline allowing him to engage in the activities of the person referred to in Article 48 in accordance with the laws of that State may – if he began his course prior to 21 May 1975 – be considered as qualified to carry out in that State the duties of the person referred to in Article 48 provided that he has previously engaged in the following activities for at least two years before 21 May 1985 following notification of this directive in one or more undertakings authorized to manufacture: production supervision and/or qualitative and quantitative analysis of active substances, and the necessary testing and checking under the direct authority of the person referred to in Article 48 to ensure the quality of the medicinal products.

If the person concerned has acquired the practical experience referred to in the first subparagraph before 21 May 1965, a further one year's practical experience in accordance with the conditions referred to in the first subparagraph will be required to be completed immediately before he engages in such activities.

Article 51

1 Member States shall take all appropriate measures to ensure that the qualified person referred to in Article 48, without prejudice to his relationship with the holder of the manufacturing authorization, is responsible, in the context of the procedures referred to in Article 52, for securing:

(a) in the case of medicinal products manufactured within the Member States concerned, that each batch of medicinal products has been manufactured and checked in compliance with the laws in force in that Member State and in accordance with the requirements of the marketing authorisation;

(b) in the case of medicinal products coming from third countries, irrespective of whether the product has been manufactured in the Community, that each production batch has undergone in a Member State a full qualitative analysis, a quantitative analysis of at least all the active substances and all the other tests or checks necessary to ensure the quality of medicinal products in accordance with the requirements of the marketing authorisation.

The batches of medicinal products which have undergone such controls in a Member State shall be exempt from the controls if they are marketed in another Member State, accompanied by the control reports signed by the qualified person.

2   In the case of medicinal products imported from a third country, where appropriate arrangements have been made by the Community with the exporting country to ensure that the manufacturer of the medicinal product applies standards of good manufacturing practice at least equivalent to those laid down by the Community, and to ensure that the controls referred to under point (b) of the first subparagraph of paragraph 1 have been carried out in the exporting country, the qualified person may be relieved of responsibility for carrying out those controls.

3   In all cases and particularly where the medicinal products are released for sale, the qualified person must certify in a register or equivalent document provided for that purpose, that each production batch satisfies the provisions of this Article; the said register or equivalent document must be kept up to date as operations are carried out and must remain at the disposal of the agents of the competent authority for the period specified in the provisions of the Member State concerned and in any event for at least five years.

Article 52

Member States shall ensure that the duties of qualified persons referred to in Article 48 are fulfilled, either by means of appropriate administrative measures or by making such persons subject to a professional code of conduct. Member States may provide for the temporary suspension of such a person upon the commencement of administrative or disciplinary procedures against him for failure to fulfil his obligations.

DIRECTIVE 2003/94/EC, LAYING DOWN THE PRINCIPLES AND GUIDELINES OF GOOD MANUFACTURING PRACTICE FOR HUMAN MEDICINES

Directive 2003/94/EC, laying down the principles and guidelines of good manufacturing practice in respect of medicinal products for human use and investigational medicinal products for human use

Editor's note   The Articles of this Directive are reproduced below. Reference should be made to the full Directive for the preambles.

Article 1

SCOPE

This Directive lays down the principles and guidelines of good manufacturing practice in respect of medicinal products for human use whose manufacture requires the authorisation referred to in Article 40 of Directive 2001/83/EC and in respect of investigational medicinal products for human use whose manufacture requires the authorisation referred to in Article 13 of Directive 2001/20/EC.

Article 2

DEFINITIONS

For the purposes of this Directive, the following definitions shall apply:

1 "medicinal product" means any product as defined in Article 1(2) of Directive 2001/83/EC;

2 "investigational medicinal product" means any product as defined in Article 2(d) of Directive 2001/20/EC;

3 "manufacturer" means any person engaged in activities for which the authorisation referred to in Article 40(1) and (3) of Directive 2001/83/EC or the authorisation referred to in Article 13(1) of Directive 2001/20/EC is required;

4 "qualified person" means the person referred to in Article 48 of Directive 2001/83/EC or in Article 13(2) of Directive 2001/20/EC;

5 "pharmaceutical quality assurance" means the total sum of the organised arrangements made with the object of ensuring that medicinal products or investigational medicinal products are of the quality required for their intended use;

6 "good manufacturing practice" means the part of quality assurance which ensures that products are consistently produced and controlled in accordance with the quality standards appropriate to their intended use;

7 "blinding" means the deliberate disguising of the identity of an invest- igational medicinal product in accordance with the instructions of the sponsor;

8 "unblinding" means the disclosure of the identity of a blinded product.

Article 3

INSPECTIONS

1 By means of the repeated inspections referred to in Article 111(1) of Directive 2001/83/EC and by means of the inspections referred to in Article 15(1)

of Directive 2001/20/EC, the Member States shall ensure that manufacturers respect the principles and guidelines of good manufacturing practice laid down by this Directive. Member States shall also take into account the compilation, published by the Commission, of Community procedures on inspections and exchange of information.

2   For the interpretation of the principles and guidelines of good manufacturing practice, the manufacturers and the competent authorities shall take into account the detailed guidelines referred to in the second paragraph of Article 47 of Directive 2001/83/EC, published by the Commission in the "Guide to good manufacturing practice for medicinal products and for investigational medicinal products".

Article 4

CONFORMITY WITH GOOD MANUFACTURING PRACTICE

1   The manufacturer shall ensure that manufacturing operations are carried out in accordance with good manufacturing practice and with the manufacturing authorisation. This provision shall also apply to medicinal products intended only for export.

2   For medicinal products and investigational medicinal products imported from third countries, the importer shall ensure that the products have been manufactured in accordance with standards which are at least equivalent to the good manufacturing practice standards laid down by the Community.

In addition, an importer of medicinal products shall ensure that such products have been manufactured by manufacturers duly authorised to do so. An importer of investigational medicinal products shall ensure that such products have been manufactured by a manufacturer notified to the competent authorities and accepted by them for that purpose.

Article 5

COMPLIANCE WITH MARKETING AUTHORISATION

1   The manufacturer shall ensure that all manufacturing operations for medicinal products subject to a marketing authorisation are carried out in accordance with the information provided in the application for marketing authorisation as accepted by the competent authorities.

In the case of investigational medicinal products, the manufacturer shall ensure that all manufacturing operations are carried out in accordance with the information provided by the sponsor pursuant to Article 9(2) of Directive 2001/20/EC as accepted by the competent authorities.

2   The manufacturer shall regularly review his manufacturing methods in the light of scientific and technical progress and the development of the investigational medicinal product.

If a variation to the marketing authorisation dossier or an amendment to the request referred to in Article 9(2) of Directive 2001/20/EC is necessary, the application for modification shall be submitted to the competent authorities.

Article 6

QUALITY ASSURANCE SYSTEM

The manufacturer shall establish and implement an effective pharmaceutical quality assurance system, involving the active participation of the management and personnel of the different departments.

Article 7

PERSONNEL

1   At each manufacturing site, the manufacturer shall have a sufficient number of competent and appropriately qualified personnel at his disposal to achieve the pharmaceutical quality assurance objective.

2   The duties of the managerial and supervisory staff, including the qualified persons, responsible for implementing and operating good manufacturing practice, shall be defined in job descriptions. Their hierarchical relationships shall be defined in an organisation chart. Organisation charts and job descriptions shall be approved in accordance with the manufacturer's internal procedures.

3   The staff referred to in paragraph 2 shall be given sufficient authority to discharge their responsibility correctly.

4   The personnel shall receive initial and ongoing training, the effectiveness of which shall be verified, covering in particular the theory and application of the concept of quality assurance and good manufacturing practice, and, where appropriate, the particular requirements for the manufacture of investigational medicinal products.

5   Hygiene programmes adapted to the activities to be carried out shall be established and observed. These programmes shall, in particular, include procedures relating to health, hygiene practice and clothing of personnel.

Article 8

PREMISES AND EQUIPMENT

1   Premises and manufacturing equipment shall be located, designed, constructed, adapted and maintained to suit the intended operations.

2   Premises and manufacturing equipment shall be laid out, designed and operated in such a way as to minimise the risk of error and to permit effective cleaning and maintenance in order to avoid contamination, cross-contamination and, in general, any adverse effect on the quality of the product.

3   Premises and equipment to be used for manufacturing operations, which are critical to the quality of the products, shall be subjected to appropriate qualification and validation.

Article 9

DOCUMENTATION

1   The manufacturer shall establish and maintain a documentation system based upon specifications, manufacturing formulae and processing and packaging instructions, procedures and records covering the various manufacturing operations performed. Documents shall be clear, free from error and kept up to date. Pre-established procedures for general manufacturing operations and conditions shall be kept available, together with specific documents for the manufacture of each batch. That set of documents shall enable the history of the manufacture of each batch and the changes introduced during the development of an investigational medicinal product to be traced.

For a medicinal product, the batch documentation shall be retained for at least one year after the expiry date of the batches to which it relates or at least five years after the certification referred to in Article 51(3) of Directive 2001/83/EC, whichever is the longer period.

For an investigational medicinal product, the batch documentation shall be retained for at least five years after the completion or formal discontinuation of the last clinical trial in which the batch was used. The sponsor or marketing authorisation holder, if different, shall be responsible for ensuring that records are retained as required for marketing authorisation in accordance with the Annex I to Directive 2001/83/EC, if required for a subsequent marketing authorisation.

2   When electronic, photographic or other data processing systems are used instead of written documents, the manufacturer shall first validate the systems by showing that the data will be appropriately stored during the anticipated period of storage. Data stored by those systems shall be made readily available in legible form and shall be provided to the competent authorities

at their request. The electronically stored data shall be protected, by methods such as duplication or back-up and transfer on to another storage system, against loss or damage of data, and audit trails shall be maintained.

Article 10

PRODUCTION

1   The different production operations shall be carried out in accordance with pre-established instructions and procedures and in accordance with good manufacturing practice. Adequate and sufficient resources shall be made available for the in-process controls. All process deviations and product defects shall be documented and thoroughly investigated.

2   Appropriate technical or organisational measures shall be taken to avoid cross-contamination and mix-ups. In the case of investigational medicinal products, particular attention shall be paid to the handling of products during and after any blinding operation.

3   For medicinal products, any new manufacture or important modification of a manufacturing process of a medicinal product shall be validated. Critical phases of manufacturing processes shall be regularly re-validated.

4   For investigational medicinal products, the manufacturing process shall be validated in its entirety in so far as is appropriate, taking into account the stage of product development. At least the critical process steps, such as sterilisation, shall be validated. All steps in the design and development of the manufacturing process shall be fully documented.

Article 11

QUALITY CONTROL

1   The manufacturer shall establish and maintain a quality control system placed under the authority of a person who has the requisite qualifications and is independent of production. That person shall have at his disposal, or shall have access to, one or more quality control laboratories appropriately staffed and equipped to carry out the necessary examination and testing of the starting materials and packaging materials and the testing of intermediate and finished products.

2   For medicinal products, including those imported from third countries, contract laboratories may be used if authorised in accordance with Article 12 of this Directive and point (b) of Article 20 of Directive 2001/83/EC.

    For investigational medicinal products, the sponsor shall ensure that the contract laboratory complies with the content of the request referred to in Article 9(2) of Directive 2001/20/EC, as accepted by the competent authority. When the products are imported from third countries, analytical control shall not be mandatory.

3   During the final control of the finished product before its release for sale or distribution or for use in clinical trials, the quality control system shall take into account, in addition to analytical results, essential information such as the production conditions, the results of in-process controls, the examination of the manufacturing documents and the conformity of the product to its specifications, including the final finished pack.

4   Samples of each batch of finished medicinal product shall be retained for at least one year after the expiry date. For an investigational medicinal product, sufficient samples of each batch of bulk formulated product and of key packaging components used for each finished product batch shall be retained for at least two years after completion or formal discontinuation of the last clinical trial in which the batch was used, whichever period is the longer.

Unless a longer period is required under the law of the Member State of manufacture, samples of starting materials, other than solvents, gases or water, used in the manufacturing process shall be retained for at least two years after the release of product. That period may be shortened if the period of stability of the material, as indicated in the relevant specification, is shorter. All those samples shall be maintained at the disposal of the competent authorities. Other conditions may be defined, by agreement with the competent authority, for the sampling and retaining of starting materials and certain products manufactured individually or in small quantities, or when their storage could raise special problems.

Article 12

WORK CONTRACTED OUT

1   Any manufacturing operation or operation linked thereto which is carried out under contract shall be the subject of a written contract.

2   The contract shall clearly define the responsibilities of each party and shall define, in particular, the observance of good manufacturing practice to be followed by the contract acceptor and the manner in which the qualified person responsible for certifying each batch is to discharge his responsibilities.

3   The contract-acceptor shall not subcontract any of the work entrusted to him under the contract without written authorisation from the contract-giver.

4   The contract-acceptor shall comply with the principles and guidelines of good manufacturing practice and shall submit to inspections carried out by

the competent authorities pursuant to Article 111 of Directive 2001/83/EC and Article 15 of Directive 2001/20/EC.

Article 13

COMPLAINTS, PRODUCT RECALL AND EMERGENCY UNBLINDING

1   In the case of medicinal products, the manufacturer shall implement a system for recording and reviewing complaints together with an effective system for recalling, promptly and at any time, medicinal products in the distribution network. Any complaint concerning a defect shall be recorded and investigated by the manufacturer. The manufacturer shall inform the competent authority of any defect that could result in a recall or abnormal restriction on supply and, in so far as is possible, indicate the countries of destination. Any recall shall be made in accordance with the requirements referred to in Article 123 of Directive 2001/83/EC.

2   In the case of investigational medicinal products, the manufacturer shall, in cooperation with the sponsor, implement a system for recording and reviewing complaints together with an effective system for recalling promptly and at any time investigational medicinal products which have already entered the distribution network. The manufacturer shall record and investigate any complaint concerning a defect and shall inform the competent authority of any defect that could result in a recall or abnormal restriction on supply.

   In the case of investigational medicinal products, all trial sites shall be identified and, in so far as is possible, the countries of destination shall be indicated.

   In the case of an investigational medicinal product for which a marketing authorisation has been issued, the manufacturer of the investigational medicinal product shall, in cooperation with the sponsor, inform the marketing authorisation holder of any defect that could be related to the authorised medicinal product.

3   The sponsor shall implement a procedure for the rapid unblinding of blinded products, where this is necessary for a prompt recall as referred to in paragraph 2. The sponsor shall ensure that the procedure discloses the identity of the blinded product only in so far as is necessary.

Article 14

SELF-INSPECTION

The manufacturer shall conduct repeated self-inspections as part of the quality assurance system in order to monitor the implementation and respect of good manufacturing practice and to propose any necessary corrective measures. Records shall be maintained of such self-inspections and any corrective action subsequently taken.

Article 15

LABELLING

In the case of an investigational medicinal product, labelling shall be such as to ensure protection of the subject and traceability, to enable identification of the product and trial, and to facilitate proper use of the investigational medicinal product.

Article 16

REPEAL OF DIRECTIVE 91/356/EEC

Directive 91/356/EEC is repealed. References to the repealed Directive shall be construed as references to this Directive.

Article 17

TRANSPOSITION

1   Member States shall bring into force the laws, regulations and administrative provisions necessary to comply with this Directive by 30 April 2004 at the latest. They shall forthwith communicate to the Commission the text of the provisions and correlation table between those provisions and the provisions of this Directive.

When Member States adopt those provisions, they shall contain a reference to this Directive or be accompanied by such a reference on the occasion of their official publication. The Member States shall determine how such reference is to be made.

2   Member States shall communicate to the Commission the text of the main provisions of national law which they adopt in the field covered by this Directive.

Article 18

ENTRY INTO FORCE

This Directive shall enter into force on the 20th day following that of its publication in the *Official Journal of the European Union*.

Article 19

ADDRESSEES

This Directive is addressed to the Member States.

UK Legislation on Manufacture

Contents

The Medicines for Human Use (Manufacturing, Wholesale Dealing and Miscellaneous Amendments) Regulations 2005 (SI 2005 No. 2789)

Interpretation

1   (1) These Regulations may be cited as the Medicines for Human Use (Manufacturing, Wholesale Dealing and Miscellaneous Amendments) Regulations 2005.

(2) In these Regulations:

"the Act" means the Medicines Act 1968;

"the 1994 Regulations" means the Medicines for Human Use (Marketing Authorisations Etc.) Regulations 1994;

"the Applications Regulations" means the Medicines (Applications for Manufacturer's and Wholesale Dealer's Licences) Regulations 1971;

"the Standard Provisions Regulations" means the Medicines (Standard Provisions for Licences and Certificates) Regulations 1971;

"Commission Directive 2003/94/EC" means Commission Directive 2003/94/EC laying down the principles and guidelines of good manufacturing practice in respect of medicinal products for human use and for investigational medicinal products for human use;

"the Directive" means Directive 2001/83/EC, of the European Parliament and of the Council on the Community code relating to medicinal products for human use, as amended by:

(a) Directive 2002/98/EC of the European Parliament and of the Council of 27 January 2003 setting standards of quality and safety for the collection, testing, processing, storage and distribution of human blood and blood components,

(b) Commission Directive 2003/63/EC amending Directive 2001/83/EC on the Community code relating to medicinal products for human use,

(c) Directive 2004/24/EC of the European Parliament and of the Council amending, as regards traditional herbal medicinal products, Directive 2001/83/EC on the Community code relating to medicinal products for human use and

(d) Directive 2004/27/EC of the European Parliament and of the Council amending Directive 2001/83/EC on the Community code relating to medicinal products for human use;

"EEA State" means a member State, Norway, Iceland or Liechtenstein;

"the guidelines on good distribution practice" means the Guidelines on Good Distribution Practice of Medicinal Products for Human Use (94/C63/03) published by the European Commission pursuant to Article 84 of the Directive;

"the principles and guidelines of good manufacturing practice" means the principles and guidelines of good manufacturing practice set out in Commission Directive 2003/ 94/EC.

Requirement that manufacturer's licence holders comply with certain obligations in relation to the manufacture and assembly of relevant medicinal products

2 (1) In relation to the manufacture and assembly of relevant medicinal products, a manufacturer's licence holder shall:

(a) comply with the principles and guidelines of good manufacturing practice;

(b) comply with the requirements of paragraph (3); and

(c) subject to paragraph (2), use active substances as starting materials only where those active substances have been manufactured or assembled in accordance with the principles and guidelines of good manufacturing practice applicable to starting materials;

(2) A manufacturer's licence holder shall not be required to comply with the requirement of paragraph (1)(c) in relation to the manufacture or assembly of relevant medicinal products pursuant to his manufacturer's licence, insofar as such activity is limited to the manufacture or assembly of exempt relevant medicinal products.

(3) The requirements of this paragraph are that the manufacturer's licence holder shall:

(a) maintain such staff, premises, equipment and facilities as are necessary for such stages of the manufacture and assembly of relevant medicinal products as are undertaken by him in accordance with the requirements of:
  (i) his licence, and
  (ii) the marketing authorizations of the relevant medicinal products in question;

(b) maintain such staff, premises, equipment and facilities for the handling, control, storage and distribution of the relevant medicinal products which he handles, stores and distributes under his licence, as are necessary to maintain the quality of those medicinal products;

(c) ensure that any arrangements he makes with any person for the control, storage and distribution of the relevant medicinal products are adequate to maintain the quality of those products;

(d) not carry out any manufacture or assembly of relevant medicinal products other than:
  (i) the manufacture or assembly of those classes of relevant medicinal product specified in his licence, and
  (ii) at the premises specified in his licence;

(e) not use any premises for the handling, control, storage or distribution of relevant medicinal products other than those specified in his licence as approved by the licensing authority for that purpose, or approved by the licensing authority for that purpose from time to time;

(f) inform the licensing authority before making any material alteration to the premises or facilities used under his licence, or in the operations for which they are used;

(g) inform the licensing authority of any change that he proposes to make to any personnel named in his licence as responsible for quality control of the medicinal products being manufactured or assembled by him, including the person named as the qualified person for the purposes of regulation 4;

(h) for the purpose of enabling the licensing authority to ascertain whether there are any grounds:
  (i) for suspending, revoking or varying any licence granted under Part II of the Act; or
  (ii) suspending or terminating any licence in accordance with the provisions of Part II of the Act, permit, and provide all necessary facilities to enable, any person duly authorised in writing by the licensing authority, on production if required of his credentials, to carry out such inspection or to take such samples or copies, in relation to things belonging to, or any business carried on by, the holder of the licence, as such person would have the right to carry out or take under the Act for the purpose

of verifying any statement contained in an application for a licence;

(i) ensure that any blood or blood component imported into the United Kingdom and used by him as a starting material or raw material in the manufacture of a relevant medicinal product shall meet equivalent standards of quality and safety to those laid down in Commission Directive 2004/33/EC, implementing Directive 2002/98/EC of the European Parliament and of the Council as regards certain technical requirements for blood and blood components; and

(j) shall, where he distributes by way of wholesale dealing, any relevant medicinal product manufactured or assembled pursuant to his licence, comply with the requirements of regulations 8(1)(a) and (b) and (2), and 9 (2) and (3), as if he was the holder of a wholesale dealer's licence.

Requirement that manufacturer's licence holders comply with certain obligations in relation to the import from a third country of relevant medicinal products

3   In relation to the import from a third country of any relevant medicinal product, a manufacturer's licence holder shall:

(a) comply with the principles and guidelines of good manufacturing practice insofar as they are relevant to the import of relevant medicinal products;

(b) comply with the guidelines on good distribution practice;

(c) ensure that any relevant medicinal products (other than exempt relevant medicinal products) imported by him from a third country use active substances as starting materials only where those active substances have been manufactured in accordance with the principles and guidelines of good manufacturing practice applicable to starting materials;

(d) maintain such staff, premises, equipment and facilities for the handling, control, storage and distribution of the relevant medicinal products which he handles, stores and distributes under his licence, as are necessary to maintain the quality of those medicinal products;

(e) ensure that any arrangements he makes with any person for the storage and distribution of the medicinal products are adequate to maintain the quality of those products;

(f) not use any premises for the handling, control, storage or distribution of relevant medicinal products other than those specified in his licence as approved by the licensing authority for that purpose, or approved by the licensing authority for that purpose from time to time;

(g) inform the licensing authority before making any material alteration in the premises or facilities used under his licence, or in the operations for which they are used;

(h) inform the licensing authority of any change that he proposes to make to any personnel named in his licence as responsible for quality control of the medicinal products being imported by him including the person named as the qualified person for the purposes of regulation 4;

(i) for the purpose of enabling the licensing authority to ascertain whether there are any grounds:

  (i) for suspending, revoking or varying any licence granted under Part II of the Act; or

  (ii) suspending or terminating any licence in accordance with the provisions of Part II of the Act, permit, and provide all necessary facilities to enable, any person duly authorised in writing by the licensing authority, on production if required of his credentials, to carry out such inspection or to take such samples or copies, in relation to things belonging to, or any business carried on by, the holder of the licence, as such person would have the right to carry out or take under the Act for the purpose of verifying any statement contained in an application for a licence; and

(j) where he distributes by way of wholesale dealing, any relevant medicinal product manufactured or assembled pursuant to his licence, comply with the requirements of regulations 8(1)(a) and (b) and (2), and 9 (2) and (3), as if he was the holder of a wholesale dealer's licence.

Requirements as to qualified persons

4   (1) Subject to paragraphs (7) and (8), where a manufacturer's licence relates to the manufacture, assembly or importation of relevant medicinal products, a manufacturer's licence holder shall ensure that he has at all times at his disposal the services of at least one qualified person who is responsible for carrying out, in relation to those products, the duties specified in Article 51 of the Directive in respect of relevant medicinal products manufactured, assembled or imported by him.

(2) If a licence holder satisfies the requirements as to qualifications and experience specified in the definition of "qualified person" in regulation 1(2), he may act as the qualified person in accordance with paragraph (1) for the purposes of that licence.

(3) For the purposes of this paragraph, but without prejudice to paragraph (4) below, the licence holder may regard a person as satisfying

the provisions of Article 49 or 50 of the Directive as respects formal qualifications if he produces evidence that:

(a) he is a member of:
   (i)   the Institute of Biology,
   (ii) the Pharmaceutical Society,
   (iii) the Royal Society of Chemistry, or
   (iv) such other body as may appear to the licensing authority to be an appropriate body for the purpose of this paragraph; and
(b) he is regarded by the body of which he is a member as so satisfying those provisions.

(4) The licence holder:
   (a) shall notify the licensing authority of the name and address and degrees, diplomas or qualifications and experience of the person who will carry out the functions of qualified person;
   (b) shall notify the licensing authority of any change to the qualified person; and
   (c) shall not permit any person to act as qualified person other than the person named in his licence as qualified person or, subject to paragraph (5), any other such person whose name is notified to the licensing authority.

(5) Where, after giving the licence holder and the person acting as a qualified person the opportunity of making representations to them (orally or in writing), the licensing authority is of the opinion that:
   (a) the person so acting does not satisfy:
      (i) the provisions of Articles 49 and 50 of the Directive as respects qualifications and experience, or
      (ii) the requirements as to qualifications and experience specified in paragraph (b) of the definition of "qualified person" in regulation 1(2); or
   (b) he is failing to carry out the duties referred to in paragraph (1) adequately or at all, and has notified the licence holder accordingly in writing, the licence holder shall not permit that person to act as a qualified person.

(6) Subject to paragraph (7), the licence holder shall at all times provide and maintain such staff, premises, equipment and facilities as will enable the qualified person who is at his disposal pursuant to paragraph (1), to carry out the duties referred to in that subsection.

(7) A licence holder shall not be required to meet the requirements of this regulation in relation to any activity carried out pursuant to his licence which consists of the manufacture, assembly or import from a third country of relevant medicinal products pursuant to a manufacturer's licence insofar as such activity is limited to the manufacture, assembly or importation of:

    (a) exempt relevant medicinal products; or

    (b) products which may be placed on the market in any EEA State without a marketing authorization by virtue of legislation adopted by that State under Article 5(2) of the Directive.

(8) Where the conditions specified in paragraph 2 of Article 51 of the Directive are satisfied, a qualified person shall not be required to meet the requirements of point (b) of the first subparagraph of paragraph 1 of Article 51 of the Directive in respect of the import of any relevant medicinal product from a third country.

Offence relating to the sale and supply of starting materials for use in the manufacture of relevant medicinal products

5   (1) Any person who, in the course of a business carried on by him, sells or supplies any active substance in circumstances where the active substance:

    (a) has not been manufactured in accordance with the principles of good manufacturing practice applicable to starting materials; and

    (b) is intended to be used by the person to whom it is sold or supplied in the manufacture of a relevant medicinal product other than an exempt relevant medicinal product, shall be guilty of an offence.

(2) It shall be a defence to an offence under paragraph (1) for the person who sells or supplies the relevant medicinal product in question to show that he could not, by reasonable diligence have discovered that it was not manufactured in accordance with the principles of good manufacturing practice applicable to starting materials.

(3) A person guilty of an offence under paragraph (1) shall be liable:

    (a) on summary conviction to a fine not exceeding the statutory maximum or to imprisonment for a term not exceeding three months or to both; or

    (b) on conviction on indictment to a fine or to imprisonment for a term not exceeding two years or to both.

Additional standard provisions for manufacturer's licences which relate to vaccines, toxins and sera

7   (1) In addition to the standard provisions for manufacturer's licences set out in Schedules 1 and 2, there shall be the following additional standard provisions for manufacturer's licences, insofar as those licences relate to relevant medicinal products which are vaccines for human use:

(a) for all vaccines, including smallpox and BCG vaccines, those pro-visions set out in Part 1 of Schedule 3;

(b) for smallpox vaccine, those provisions set out in Part 2 of Schedule 3; and

(c) for BCG vaccine, those provisions set out in Part 3 of Schedule 3.

(2) In addition to the standard provisions for manufacturer's licences set out in Schedules 1 and 2, there shall be the following additional standard provisions for manufacturer's licences relating to relevant medicinal products which are toxins and sera for human use:

(a) for toxins, those provisions set out in Part 4 of Schedule 3; and

(b) for sera, those provisions set out in Part 5 of Schedule 3.

Schedule 1 of the Regulations

Standard provisions which may be incorporated in a manufacturer's licence relating to the manufacture and assembly of relevant medicinal products

1 The manufacturer's licence holder shall place the quality control system referred to in Article 11(1) of Commission Directive 2003/94/EC under the authority of the person notified to the licensing authority in accordance with paragraph 7(2) of Schedule 1 to the Applications Regulations as being responsible for quality control.

2 The manufacturer's licence holder may use a contract laboratory pursuant to Article 11(2) of Commission Directive 2003/94/EC if operated by a person approved by the licensing authority.

3 The manufacturer's licence holder shall provide such information as may be requested by the licensing authority:

(a) about the products currently being manufactured or assembled under his authorisation; and

(b) about the operations being carried out in relation to such manufacture or assembly.

4 The manufacturer's licence holder shall inform the licensing authority of any change that he proposes to make to any personnel named in his licence as respectively:

(a) responsible for supervising the production operations;

(b) in charge of the animals from which are derived any substances used in the production of the medicinal products being manufactured or assembled; or

(c) responsible for the culture of any living tissues used in the manufacture of the medicinal products being manufactured or assembled.

5　The manufacturer's licence holder shall:

(a) keep readily available for inspection by a person authorised by the licensing authority the batch documentation referred to in Article 9(1) of Commission Directive 2003/94/EC; and
(b) permit the person authorised to take copies or make extracts from such documentation.

6　The manufacturer's licence holder shall keep readily available for examination by a person authorised by the licensing authority, the samples of each batch of finished relevant medicinal product referred to in Article 11(4) of Commission Directive 2003/94/EC.

7　Where the manufacturer's licence holder has been informed by the licensing authority that any batch of any relevant medicinal product to which his licence relates has been found not to conform as regards strength, quality or purity with:

(a) the specification of the relevant product; or
(b) the provisions of these Regulations, the Act or any other Regulations under the Act that are applicable to the relevant medicinal product, he shall, if so directed, withhold such batch from distribution, so far as may be reasonably practicable, for such a period not exceeding six weeks as may be specified by the licensing authority.

8　The manufacturer's licence holder shall ensure that any tests for determining conformity with the standards and specifications applying to any particular product used in the manufacture of a relevant medicinal product shall, except so far as the conditions of the product specification for that product otherwise provide, be applied to samples taken from the medicinal product after all manufacturing processes have been completed, or at such earlier stage in the manufacture as may be approved by the licensing authority.

9　Where the manufacturer's licence relates to the assembly of any relevant medicinal product or class of product, and the licence holder supplies that relevant medicinal product at such a stage of assembly that does not fully comply with the provisions of the product specification that relate to labelling, the licence holder shall communicate the particulars of those provisions to the person to whom that product has been so supplied.

10   Where:

(a) the manufacturer's licence relates to the assembly of a relevant medicinal product;

(b) that medicinal product is not manufactured by the licence holder; and

(c) particulars as to the name and address of the manufacturer of, or of the person who imports, that relevant medicinal product have been given by the licence holder to the licensing authority, the licence holder shall forthwith notify the licensing authority in writing of any changes in such particulars.

11   The licence holder shall keep readily available for examination by a person authorised by the licensing authority durable records of the details of manufacture of any intermediate products held by him which are for use in the manufacture of biological medicinal products for human use, and these records shall:

(a) be in such form as to ensure that the licence holder has a comprehensive record of all matters that are relevant to an evaluation of the safety, quality and efficacy of any finished biological medicinal product for human use which he manufactures using those intermediate products; and

(b) not be destroyed without the consent of the licensing authority until the records of the details of manufacture of any finished medicinal products which were or may be manufactured using those intermediate products may be destroyed in accordance with the requirements of these Regulations.

12   Where:

(a) animals are used in the production of any medicinal products; and

(b) relevant marketing authorizations contain provisions relating to them,

the manufacturer's licence holder shall arrange for those animals to be housed in premises of such a nature, and be managed in such a manner as to facilitate compliance with such provisions.

13   The licence holder shall take all reasonable precautions and exercise all due diligence to ensure that any information he provides to the licensing authority which is relevant to an evaluation of the safety, quality or efficacy of:

(a) any medicinal product for human use which he manufactures or assembles; or

(b) any starting materials or intermediate products that he holds which are for use in the manufacture of relevant medicinal products, is not false or misleading in any material particular.

Schedule 2 of the Regulations

Standard provisions which may be incorporated in a manufacturer's licence relating to the import of relevant medicinal products from a third country

1   The manufacturer's licence holder shall place the quality control system referred to in Article 11(1) of Commission Directive 2003/94/EC under the authority of the person notified to the licensing authority in accordance with paragraph 7(2) of Schedule 1 to the Applications Regulations as being responsible for quality control.

2   The manufacturer's licence holder may use a contract laboratory pursuant to Article 11(2) of Commission Directive 2003/94/EC if operated by a person approved by the licensing authority.

3   The manufacturer's licence holder shall provide such information as may be requested by the licensing authority concerning the type and quantity of any medicinal products which he imports.

4   The manufacturer's licence holder shall:

   (a) keep readily available for inspection by a person authorised by the licensing authority the batch documentation referred to in Article 9(1) of Commission Directive 2003/94/EC; and
   (b) permit the person authorised to take copies or make extracts from such documentation.

5   Where the manufacturer's licence holder has been informed by the licensing authority that any batch of any medicinal product to which his licence relates has been found not to conform as regards strength, quality or purity with:

   (a) the specification of the relevant product; or
   (b) the provisions of these Regulations, the Act or any regulations under the Act that are applicable to the investigational medicinal product, he shall, if so directed, withhold such batch from distribution, so far as may be reasonably practicable, for such a period not exceeding six weeks as may be specified by the licensing authority.

6   The manufacturer's licence holder shall ensure that any tests for determining conformity with the standards and specifications applying to any particular product used in the manufacture of a relevant medicinal product shall, except so far as the conditions of the product specification for that product otherwise provide, be applied to samples taken from the medicinal product after all manufacturing processes have been completed, or at

such earlier stage in the manufacture as may be approved by the licensing authority.

7   (1)   Where and insofar as the licence relates to relevant medicinal products to which paragraph 1 of Schedule 1 to the 1994 regulations applies, the licence holder shall only import such products from a third country:

      (a) in response to an order which satisfies the requirements of paragraph 1 of Schedule 1 to the 1994 Regulations; and

      (b) where the conditions set out in sub-paragraphs (2) to (9) are complied with.

  (2)   No later than 28 days prior to each importation of an exempt imported product, the licence holder shall give written notice to the licensing authority stating his intention to import that medicinal product and stating the following particulars:

      (a) the name of the medicinal product, being the brand name or the common name, or the scientific name, and any name, if different, under which the medicinal product is to be sold or supplied in the United Kingdom;

      (b) any trademark or the name of the manufacturer of the medicinal product;

      (c) in respect of each active constituent of the medicinal product, any international non-proprietary name or the British approved name or the monograph name or, where that constituent does not have an international non-proprietary name, a British approved name or a monograph name, the accepted scientific name or any other name descriptive of the true nature of that constituent;

      (d) the quantity of medicinal product which is to be imported which shall not exceed the quantity specified in sub-paragraph (6); and

      (e) the name and address of the manufacturer or assembler of that medicinal product in the form in which it is to be imported and, if the person who will supply that medicinal product for importation is not the manufacturer or assembler, the name and address of such supplier.

  (3)   Subject to sub-paragraph (4), the licence holder shall not import the exempt imported product if, before the end of 28 days from the date on which the licensing authority sends or gives the licence holder an acknowledgement in writing by the licensing authority that they have received the notice referred to in sub-paragraph (2) above, the licensing authority have notified him in writing that the product should not be imported.

  (4)   The licence holder may import the exempt imported product referred to in the notice where he has been notified in writing by the

licensing authority, before the end of the 28-day period referred to in sub-paragraph (3), that the exempt imported product may be imported.

(5) Where the licence holder sells or supplies exempt imported products, he shall, in addition to any other records which he is required by the provisions of his licence to make, make and maintain written records relating to:

(a) the batch number of the batch of the product from which the sale or supply was made; and

(b) details of any adverse reaction to the product so sold or supplied of which he becomes aware.

(6) The licence holder shall import no more on any one occasion than such amount as is sufficient for 25 single administrations, or for 25 courses of treatment where the amount imported is sufficient for a maximum of three months' treatment, and on any such occasion shall not import more than the quantity notified to the licensing authority under sub-paragraph (2)(d).

(7) The licence holder shall inform the licensing authority forthwith of any matter coming to his attention which might reasonably cause the licensing authority to believe that the medicinal product can no longer be regarded either as a product which can safely be administered to human beings or as a product which is of satisfactory quality for such administration.

(8) The licence holder shall not issue any advertisement, catalogue, price list or circular relating to the exempt relevant medicinal product or make any representations in respect of that product.

(9) The licence holder shall cease importing or supplying an exempt imported product if he has received a notice in writing from the licensing authority directing that, as from a date specified in that notice, a particular product or class of products shall no longer be imported or supplied.

(10) In this paragraph:

"British approved name" means the name which appears in the current edition of the list prepared by the appropriate body in accordance with Section 100 of the Act and published by the Ministers on the recommendation of the Commission and "current" in this definition means current at the time the notice is sent to the licensing authority;

"common name" means the international non-proprietary name or, if one does not exist, the usual common name;

"international non-proprietary name" means a name which has been selected by the World Health Organization as a recommended international non-proprietary name and in respect of which the

Director-General of the World Health Organization has given notice to that effect in the World Health Organization Chronicle; and

"monograph name" means the name or approved synonym which appears at the head of a monograph in the current edition of the British Pharmacopoeia, the British Pharmaceutical Codex, the European Pharmacopoeia or a foreign or international compendium of standards and "current" in this definition means current at the time the notice is sent to the licensing authority.

8   The licence holder shall take all reasonable precautions and exercise all due diligence to ensure that any information he provides to the licensing authority which is relevant to an evaluation of the safety, quality or efficacy of any medicinal product for human use which he imports from a third country, handles, stores or distributes is not false or misleading in a material particular.

Schedule 3 of the Regulations

Standard provisions which may be incorporated in a manufacturer's licence which relates to vaccines

1   (1) The licence holder shall provide separate premises or separate parts of premises referred to in this Part as "the designated premises," for the activities specified in the following sub-paragraphs, namely:

(a) the production and the testing involved in the production of cell cultures for use in the production of vaccine;

(b) the production and the testing involved in the production of vaccine prepared from viruses; and

(c) the production and the testing involved in the production of vaccine prepared from micro-organisms or detoxified microbial toxins, and shall ensure that only persons necessary to each of the above mentioned activities shall have access to the designated premises provided for that activity.

2   The licence holder shall ensure that any procedure which, in the course of any of the activities specified in the preceding paragraph involves or might involve:

(a) the presence of transmissible agents; or

(b) the use of cell cultures, animal tissues or micro-organisms, other than those from which the vaccine is produced, shall not be carried out in the designated premises referred to in paragraph 1.

3   The licence holder shall ensure that no person who has been in contact with transmissible agents or experimental animals (other than those connected with the vaccine being produced in the designated premises referred to in paragraph 1) shall enter the designated premises on the same day that such contact has occurred.

4   Before an animal is used in the production of a vaccine, the licence holder shall take all reasonable steps to ensure that it is free from disease, and to that end shall keep the animal in quarantine and under observation for such period as the licensing authority may specify.

5   The licence holder shall ensure:

(a) that animals used in the production of vaccine are isolated and shall provide separate premises (not being the designated premises referred to in paragraph 1) for this purpose; and
(b) that only persons engaged in the production and testing of vaccines or in the maintenance of animals or premises shall have access to the separate premises in which the animals are isolated.

6   The licence holder shall provide a separate room in the premises referred to in paragraph 5 which is capable of being washed and disinfected and which is to be used for the purpose of:

(a) the inoculation of animals; and
(b) the collection of material to be used in the preparation of vaccine.

7   Without prejudice to any other requirements to keep records, where vaccines contain or might contain micro-organisms or microbial toxins, the licence holder shall keep a durable record, readily available for inspection by a person authorised by the licensing authority, of the origin, properties and characteristics of the cell cultures used in the production of those vaccines and shall ensure that that record is not destroyed for a period of five years from the date when the relevant production occurred.

8   Nothing in this Schedule shall operate so as to restrict the right of access to any premises of any person who is duly authorised by the enforcement authority to enter those premises in accordance with section 111 of the Act.

Standard provisions which may be incorporated in a manufacturer's licence which relates to smallpox vaccines

1   The licence holder shall ensure that animals used in the production of smallpox vaccine:

(a) shall only be inoculated on a part of the skin that has been depilated and cleansed and which cannot be soiled by urine or faeces, and

(b) are kept under observation for 28 days after the collection of the vaccinal material.

2 Should any animal during the 28 day period referred to in paragraph 1 be found to be suffering from any infection other than vaccinia or show serious or persistent signs of ill health, vaccinal material obtained from that animal shall not be used in the production of smallpox vaccine.

3 Where it is necessary for an animal which has been inoculated for use in the production of smallpox vaccine to be killed, the licence holder shall ensure that:

(a) the vaccinal material is collected immediately after the animal has been killed;

(b) if the licensing authority so directs, a post-mortem examination of the carcass of the animal is made by a person with experience of the diseases of the particular animal which has been killed;

(c) a durable record of the examination is made and retained for a period of five years from the date when the animal was killed, and kept readily available for inspection by a person authorised by the licensing authority; and

(d) where the examination indicates that the animal was suffering from diseases other than vaccinia, no vaccinal material obtained from that animal is used in the production of smallpox vaccine.

Standard provisions which may be incorporated in a manufacturer's licence which relates to BCG vaccines

1 The licence holder shall provide separate premises or separate parts of premises for the production of BCG vaccine, and shall ensure that only persons necessary to the production and testing of that vaccine shall have access to those separate premises or separate parts of premises.

2 The licence holder shall ensure that any procedure which involves or might involve:

(a) the presence of transmissible agents other than BCG, or

(b) the use of microbial cultures other than BCG, shall not be carried out in the separate premises or separate parts of premises referred to in paragraph 1 of this Schedule.

3   The licence holder shall ensure that all media, glassware and other apparatus issued in the production of BCG vaccine shall be kept and prepared for use in the separate premises or separate parts of premises referred to in paragraph 1 of this Part of this Schedule.

4   The licence holder shall not permit animals to be in the separate premises or separate parts of premises referred to in paragraph 1 of this Part of this Schedule and where it is necessary to use animals for testing BCG vaccine, the tests shall not be carried out in those separate premises or separate parts of premises.

5   (1) The licence holder shall arrange for all persons engaged in the production of BCG vaccine to be examined clinically by a doctor and where appropriate, radiologically and bacteriologically, at least every twelve months and whenever such a person shows signs of ill health.

     (2) The licence holder shall ensure (as far as paragraph (c) below is concerned, in so far as is reasonably practicable), that persons falling within the following descriptions shall not engage in the production of BCG vaccine, that is to say:

       (a) persons examined as aforesaid who are found to be suffering from active or potentially active tuberculosis lesions,

       (b) persons who show a negative reaction when tested with tuberculin, or

       (c) persons who are in close contact with a person who is suffering from any active form of tuberculosis.

     (3) If on examination in accordance with subparagraph (1), a person engaged in the production of BCG vaccine is found to be suffering from active or potentially active tuberculosis lesions, then, after that person has been removed from the separate premises or separate parts of premises referred to in paragraph (1), the licence holder shall:

       (a) make arrangements for those separate premises or separate parts of premises and all equipment used in the production of BCG vaccine to be treated in such a manner as to remove the risk of contamination of the vaccine; and

       (b) cease to use any unsealed cultures of BCG and all current preparations of BCG vaccine which may have become contaminated with other *Mycobacterium tuberculosis* organisms.

6   The licence holder shall ensure that no person who has been in contact with transmissible agents other than BCG vaccine shall enter the separate premises or separate parts of premises referred to in paragraph 1 on the same day that such contact has been made.

Standard provisions which may be incorporated in a manufacturer's licence which relates to toxins

1   The licence holder shall provide separate premises or separate parts of premises for the production and the testing involved in the production of toxins and shall ensure that only persons necessary to the production and testing of toxins (or related toxoids) shall have access to the separate premises or separate parts of those premises.

2   Nothing in paragraph 1 shall operate so as to restrict the right of access to any premises of any person who is duly authorised by the enforcement authority to enter those premises in accordance with Section 111 of the Act.

3   The licence holder shall ensure that any procedure which in the course of the production and testing referred to in the previous paragraph involves or might involve the presence of micro-organisms, plants or animals other than those from which the toxins are to be produced, shall not be carried out in the separate premises or separate parts of premises referred to in paragraph 1.

Standard provisions which may be incorporated in a manufacturer's licence which relates to sera

1   The licence holder shall ensure that blood used in the production of any serum shall only be collected from living animals in separate premises which:

(a) are used for no other purpose,
(b) have impervious walls and floors, and
(c) are capable of being washed and chemically disinfected.

2   The licence holder shall ensure that an adequate system of manure removal is in operation in the separate premises referred to in paragraph 1.

3   Before an animal is used in the production of any serum, the licence holder shall take all reasonable steps to ensure that it is free from disease and to this end shall keep the animal in quarantine and under observation for such period as the licensing authority may direct.

4   The licence holder shall notify the licensing authority if any animal which has been used in the production of any serum is found to be suffering from an infection other than an infection produced by living organisms against which it is being immunised or shows serious or persistent signs of ill-health not attributable to the process of immunisation and shall withhold

any serum obtained from that animal from sale, supply or exportation until he has obtained the consent of the licensing authority in writing to its release.

5   The licence holder shall notify the licensing authority if any post-mortem examination on any animal indicates that any other animals used in the production of any serum are or are likely to be unhealthy, and the licence holder shall not use those animals for the production of any serum until either he has obtained the consent of the licensing authority in writing or has complied with any requirements the licensing authority may consider necessary in the interest of safety.

6   The licence holder shall ensure that laboratories in which any serum is processed are separate from premises in which animals are housed.

7   The licence holder shall provide such number of sterilizers as are necessary for the sterilization of all glassware and other apparatus used in the production of sera.

8   Without prejudice to any other requirements to keep records, the licence holder shall keep the following durable records relating to the production of sera readily available for inspection by a person authorised by the licensing authority, and shall ensure that those records are not destroyed for a period of five years from the date when the relevant production occurred:

(a) as to the cultures used:
    (i)   the source from which the culture was obtained,
    (ii) the nature of the material from which the culture was isolated,
    (iii) the date of the isolation, and
    (iv) evidence of the identity and specificity of the culture;
(b) as to the procedure used in the immunizing of animals:
    (i)   the method of preparing the culture or antigen used for immunization,
    (ii) the dosage and methods employed in administering the culture or antigen, and
    (iii) the time in the course of immunization at which blood is withdrawn for preparation of the serum; and
(c) the results of any tests which may have been applied to the serum to determine its content of specific antibodies or its specific therapeutic potency.

9   Nothing in this Part shall operate so as to restrict the right of access to any premises of any person who is duly authorised by the enforcement authority to enter those premises in accordance with section 111 of the Act.

Prescribed Conditions for Manufacturer's Undertakings for Imported Products (SI 1977 No. 1038)

Extract from: The Medicines (Manufacturer's Undertakings for Imported Products) Regulations 1977 (SI 1977 No. 1038) as amended by SI 1992 No. 2845 and SI 2005/2745.

Editor's note This extract from the Regulations is presented for the reader's convenience. For any definitive information reference must be made to the original Regulations.

An additional Regulation (Regulation 1A) is inserted by SI 2005 No. 2745 to exclude veterinary medicinal products; and Regulation 4 is inserted by SI 1992 No. 2845 to exclude from the scope of the Regulations applications for products coming from another Member State of the EU.

Schedule

Prescribed conditions for manufacturer's undertakings

1 The manufacturer shall provide and maintain such staff, premises, and plant as are necessary for the carrying out in accordance with the relevant product licences of such stages of the manufacture and assembly of the medicinal products to which the relevant product licences relate as are undertaken by him.

2 The manufacturer shall provide and maintain such staff, premises, equipment and facilities for the handling, storage and distribution of the medicinal products to which the relevant product licences relate which he handles, stores or distributes as are necessary to avoid deterioration of the medicinal products.

2A In relation to medicinal products for human use, the manufacturer shall provide and maintain a designated quality control department having authority in relation to quality control and being independent of all other departments.

3 The manufacturer shall conduct all manufacture and assembly operations in such a way as to ensure that the medicinal products to which the relevant product licences relate conform with the standards of strength, quality and purity applicable to them under the relevant product licences.

3A   In relation to medicinal products for human use, the manufacturer shall maintain an effective pharmaceutical quality assurance system involving the active participation of the management and personnel of the different services involved.

4   Where animals are used in the production of any medicinal product and the relevant product licences contain provisions relating to them the manufacturer shall arrange for the animals to be housed in premises of such a nature and to be managed in such a way as will facilitate compliance with such provisions.

5   The manufacturer shall make such adequate and suitable arrangements as are necessary for carrying out in accordance with the relevant product licences any tests of the strength, quality or purity of the medicinal products to which the licences relate.

6   The manufacturer shall inform the holder of the relevant product licences of any material alteration in the premises or plant used in connection with the manufacture or assembly of the medicinal products to which the relevant product licences relate or in the operations for which such premises or plant are so used and of any change, since the granting of the relevant product licences in respect of any person:

(a) responsible for supervising the production operations, or
(b) responsible for quality control of the medicinal products to which the relevant product licences relate, or
(c) in charge of the animals from which are derived any substance used in the production of the medicinal products to which the relevant product licences relate, or
(d) responsible for the culture of any living tissues used in the manufacture of the medicinal products to which the relevant product licences relate.

7   The manufacturer shall keep readily available for inspection by a person authorised by the licensing authority durable records of the details of manufacture and assembly of each batch of every medicinal product to which each relevant product licence relates and of the tests carried out thereon in such a form that the records will be easily identifiable from the number of the batch as shown on each container in which the medicinal product is exported from the country where it has been manufactured or assembled; the manufacturer shall permit the person authorised to take copies of or make extracts from such records. Such records shall not be destroyed:

(a) in relation to a medicinal product for human use, for a period of five years from the date of release of the relevant batch, or for a period of one year after the expiry date of the relevant batch, whichever expires later, (**b**) in any other case, for a period of five years from the date when the manufacture or assembly of the relevant batch of the medicinal product occurred.

7A   In relation to medicinal products for human use to which a product licence relates, the manufacturer shall keep readily available for examination by a person authorised by the licensing authority, samples of:

(**a**) each batch of finished products for at least a period of one year after their expiry date; and

(**b**) starting materials (other than solvents, gases or water) for at least a period of two years after release of the medicinal product of which the relevant starting materials formed part;

except where the manufacturer is authorised by the licensing authority to destroy such samples earlier.

7B   (**1**) The manufacturer shall implement a system for recording and reviewing complaints in relation to medicinal products for human use to which a product licence relates together with an effective system for recalling promptly and at any time the medicinal products in the distribution network.

(**2**) The manufacturer shall record and investigate all complaints described in sub-paragraph (1) of this paragraph and shall immediately inform the licensing authority of any defect which could result in a recall from sale, supply or exportation or in an abnormal restriction on such sale, supply or exportation.

8   The manufacturer shall inform the holder of the relevant product licence of any material change since the date upon which such licence was granted in respect of:

(**a**) the facilities and equipment available at each of the premises of the manufacturer for carrying out any stage of the manufacture or assembly of the medicinal products to which the relevant product licences relate, or

(**b**) the facilities and equipment available in each of the premises of the manufacturer for the storage of the medicinal products to which the relevant product licences relate on, and distribution of the products from or between, such premises, or

(**c**) any manufacturing operations, not being operations in relation to the medicinal products to which the relevant product licences relate, which are carried on by the manufacturer on or near any of the premises on which such medicinal products are manufactured or assembled and the substances or articles in respect of which such operations are carried on, or

(d) the arrangements for the identification and storage of materials and ingredients before and during manufacture of the medicinal products to which the relevant product licences relate and the arrangements for the storage of the medicinal products after they have been manufactured or assembled, or

(e) the arrangements for ensuring a satisfactory turnover of stocks of medicinal products to which the relevant product licences relate, or

(f) the arrangements for maintaining production records and records of analytical and other testing procedures applied in the course of manufacture or assembly of the medicinal products to which the relevant product licences relate, or

(g) the arrangements for keeping reference samples of materials used in the manufacture of any medicinal products to which the relevant product licences relate and reference samples of such medicinal products.

GUIDANCE ON WHOLESALE DISTRIBUTION PRACTICE

6

EU Guidance on Wholesale Distribution Practice

Contents

GUIDELINES ON GOOD DISTRIBUTION PRACTICE OF MEDICINAL PRODUCTS FOR HUMAN USE (94/C 63/03)

Introduction

These guidelines have been prepared in accordance with Article 10 of Council Directive 92/25/EEC of 31 March 1992 on the wholesale distribution of medicinal products for human use[1]. They do not cover commercial relationships between parties involved in distribution of medicinal products nor questions of safety at work.

Principle

The Community pharmaceutical industry operates at a high level of quality assurance, achieving its pharmaceutical quality objectives by observing

---

[1] OJ No L 113, 30.4, 1992, p. 1.

Good Manufacturing Practice to manufacture medicinal products which must then be authorised for marketing. This policy ensures that products released for distribution are of the appropriate quality.

This level of quality should be maintained throughout the distribution network so that authorised medicinal products are distributed to retail pharmacists and other persons entitled to sell medicinal products to the general public without any alteration of their properties. The concept of quality management in the pharmaceutical industry is described in Chapter I of the Community Guide to Good Manufacturing Practice for medicinal products and should be considered when relevant for the distribution of medicinal products. The general concepts of quality management and quality systems are described in the CEN standards (series 29 000).

In addition, to maintain the quality of the products and the quality of the service offered by wholesalers, Directive 92/25/EEC provides that wholesalers must comply with the principles and guidelines of good distribution practice published by the Commission of the European Communities.

The quality system operated by distributors (wholesalers) of medicinal products should ensure that medicinal products that they distribute are authorised in accordance with Community legislation, that storage conditions are observed at all times, including during transportation, that contamination from or of other products is avoided, that an adequate turnover of the stored medicinal products takes place and that products are stored in appropriately safe and secure areas. In addition to this, the quality system should ensure that the right products are delivered to the right addressee within a satisfactory time period. A tracing system should enable any faulty product to be found and there should be an effective recall procedure.

Personnel

1   A management representative should be appointed in each distribution point, who should have defined authority and responsibility for ensuring that a quality system is implemented and maintained. He should fulfil his responsibilities personally. This person should be appropriately qualified: although a degree in pharmacy is desirable, the qualification requirements may be established by the Member State on whose territory the wholesaler is located.

2   Key personnel involved in the warehousing of medicinal products should have the appropriate ability and experience to guarantee that the products or materials are properly stored and handled.

3   Personnel should be trained in relation to the duties assigned to them and the training sessions recorded.

Documentation

4   All documentation should be made available on request of competent authorities.

Orders

5   Orders from wholesalers should be addressed only to persons authorised to supply medicinal products as wholesalers in accordance with Article 3 of Directive 92/25/EEC or holders of a manufacturing or importing authorisation granted in accordance with Article 16 of Directive 75/319/EEC.[2]

Procedures

6   Written procedures should describe the different operations which may affect the quality of the products or of the distribution activity: receipt and checking of deliveries, storage, cleaning and maintenance of the premises (including pest control), recording of the storage conditions, security of stocks on site and of consignments in transit, withdrawal from saleable stock, records, including records of clients orders, returned products, recall plans, etc. These procedures should be approved, signed and dated by the person responsible for the quality system.

Records

7   Records should be made at the time each operation is taken and in such a way that all significant activities or events are traceable. Records should be clear and readily available. They should be retained for a period of five years at least.

8   Records should be kept of each purchase and sale, showing the date of purchase or supply, name of the medicinal product and quantity received or supplied and name and address of the supplier or consignee. For transactions between manufacturers and wholesalers and between wholesalers (i.e. to the exclusion of deliveries to persons entitled to supply medicinal products to the public), records should ensure the traceability of the origin and destination of products, for example by use of batch numbers, so that all the suppliers of, or those supplied with, a medicinal product can be identified.

---

[2] OJ No L 147, 9.6, 1975, p. 13.

Premises and equipment

9   Premises and equipment should be suitable and adequate to ensure proper conservation and distribution of medicinal products. Monitoring devices should be calibrated.

Receipt

10   Receiving bays should protect deliveries from bad weather during unloading. The reception area should be separate from the storage area. Deliveries should be examined at receipt in order to check that containers are not damaged and that the consignment corresponds to the order.

11   Medicinal products subject to specific storage measures (e.g. narcotics, products requiring a specific storage temperature) should be immediately identified and stored in accordance with written instructions and with relevant legislative provisions.

Storage

12   Medicinal products should normally be stored apart from other goods and under the conditions specified by the manufacturer in order to avoid any deterioration by light, moisture or temperature. Temperature should be monitored and recorded periodically. Records of temperature should be reviewed regularly.

13   When specific temperature storage conditions are required, storage areas should be equipped with temperature recorders or other devices that will indicate when the specific temperature range has not been maintained. Control should be adequate to maintain all parts of the relevant storage area within the specified temperature range.

14   The storage facilities should be clean and free from litter, dust and pests. Adequate precautions should be taken against spillage or breakage, attack by micro-organisms and cross-contamination.

15   There should be a system to ensure stock rotation ("first in first out") with regular and frequent checks that the system is operating correctly. Products beyond their expiry date or shelf life should be separated from usable stock and neither sold nor supplied.

16   Medicinal products with broken seals, damaged packaging, or suspected of possible contamination should be withdrawn from saleable stock, and if not immediately destroyed, they should be kept in a clearly separated area so that they cannot be sold in error or contaminate other goods.

Deliveries to customers

17   Deliveries should be made only to other authorised wholesalers or to persons authorised to supply medicinal products to the public in the Member State concerned.

18   For all supplies to a person authorised or entitled to supply medicinal products to the public, a document must be enclosed, making it possible to ascertain the date, the name and pharmaceutical form of the medicinal product, the quantity supplied, the name and address of the supplier and addressee.

19   In case of emergency, wholesalers should be in a position to supply immediately the medicinal products that they regularly supply to the persons entitled to supply the products to the public.

20   Medicinal products should be transported in such a way that:

   (a) their identification is not lost;
   (b) they do not contaminate, and are not contaminated by, other products or materials;
   (c) adequate precautions are taken against spillage, breakage or theft;
   (d) they are secure and not subjected to unacceptable degrees of heat, cold, light, moisture or other adverse influence, nor to attack by micro-organisms or pests.

21   Medicinal products requiring controlled temperature storage should also be transported by appropriately specialised means.

Returns

Returns of non-defective medicinal products

22   Non-defective medicinal products which have been returned should be kept apart from saleable stock to prevent redistribution until a decision has been reached regarding their disposal.

23   Products which have left the care of the wholesaler, should only be returned to saleable stock if:

   (a) the goods are in their original unopened containers and in good condition;
   (b) it is known that the goods have been stored and handled under proper conditions;
   (c) the remaining shelf life period is acceptable;
   (d) they have been examined and assessed by a person authorised to do so. This assessment should take into account the nature of the product,

any special storage conditions it requires, and the time elapsed since it was issued. Special attention should be given to products requiring special storage conditions. As necessary, advice should be sought from the holder of the marketing authorisation or the Qualified Person of the manufacturer of the product.

24 Records of returns should be kept. The responsible person should formally release goods to be returned to stock. Products returned to saleable stock should be placed such that the "first in first out" system operates effectively.

Emergency plan and recalls

25 An emergency plan for urgent recalls and a non-urgent recall procedure should be described in writing. A person should be designated as responsible for execution and co-ordination of recalls.

26 Any recall operation should be recorded at the time it is carried out and records should be made available to the competent authorities of the Member States on whose territory the products were distributed.

27 In order to ensure the efficacy of the emergency plan, the system of recording of deliveries should enable all destinees of a medicinal product to be immediately identified and contacted. In case of recall, wholesalers may decide to inform all their customers of the recall or only those having received the batch to be recalled.

28 The same system should apply without any difference to deliveries in the Member States having granted the authorisation for wholesaling and in other Member States.

29 In case of batch recall, all customers (other wholesalers, retail or hospital pharmacists and persons entitled to sell medicinal products to the public) to whom the batch was distributed should be informed with the appropriate degree of urgency. This includes customers in other Member States than the Member State having granted the wholesaling authorisation.

30 The recall message approved by the holder of the marketing authorisation, and, when appropriate, by the competent authorities, should indicate whether the recall should be carried out also at retail level. The message should request that the recalled products be removed immediately from the saleable stock and stored separately in a secure area until they are sent back according to the instructions of the holder of the marketing authorisation.

Counterfeit medicinal products

31 Counterfeit medicinal products found in the distribution network should be kept apart from other medicinal products to avoid any confusion. They

should be clearly labelled as not for sale and competent authorities and the holder of marketing authorisation of the original product should be informed immediately.

Special provisions concerning products classified as not for sale

32   Any return, rejection, and recall operation and receipt of counterfeit products should be recorded at the time it is carried out and records should be made available to the competent authorities. In each case, a formal decision should be taken on the disposal of these products and the decision should be documented and recorded. The person responsible for the quality system of the wholesaler and, where relevant, the holder of the marketing authorisation should be involved in the decision making process.

Self inspections

33   Self-inspections should be conducted (and recorded) in order to monitor the implementation of and compliance with this guideline.

Provision of information to Member States in relation to wholesale activities

34   Wholesalers wishing to distribute or distributing medicinal products in Member State(s) other than the Member State in which the authorisation was granted should make available on request to the competent authorities of the other Member State(s) any information in relation to the authorisation granted in the Member State of origin, namely the nature of the wholesaling activity, the address of sites of storage and distribution point(s) and, if appropriate, the area covered. Where appropriate, the competent authorities of this (these) other Member State(s) will inform the wholesaler of any public service obligation imposed on wholesalers operating on their territory.

7

UK Guidance on Wholesale Distribution Practice

Contents

Wholesale Dealer's Obligations

The holder of a wholesale dealer's licence must comply with certain obligations in relation to the wholesale distribution of relevant medicinal products. These obligations are set out in Regulations 8–11 of The Medicines for Human Use (Manufacturing, Wholesale Dealing and Miscellaneous Amendments) Regulations 2005 [SI 2005/2789]. They require that the licence holder shall:

(a) comply with the guidelines on Good Distribution Practice (GDP);[1]
(b) ensure, within the limits of his responsibility as a distributor of relevant medicinal products, the appropriate and continued supply of such

---

[1] Guidelines on Good Distribution Practice (GDP) of medicinal products for human use (94/C63/03) and Rules and Guidance for Pharmaceutical Manufacturers and Distributors.

relevant medicinal products to pharmacies and persons who may lawfully sell such products by retail or who may lawfully supply them in circumstances corresponding to retail sale;

(c) provide and maintain such staff, premises, equipment and facilities for the handling, storage and distribution of the relevant medicinal products which he handles, in accordance with his licence as are necessary to maintain the quality of, and ensure proper distribution of the medicinal products (see Control and Monitoring of Storage and Transportation Temperatures);

(d) inform the licensing authority of any proposed structural alteration to, or discontinued use of, premises to which the licence relates or premises which have been approved by the licensing authority;

(e) inform the licensing authority of the name and address and degrees, diplomas or qualifications and experience of the person who will carry out the functions of responsible person;

(f) inform the licensing authority of any change to the responsible person.

The holder of a wholesale dealer's licence shall not sell or offer for sale or supply any relevant medicinal product unless:

(a) there is a marketing authorisation for the time being in force in respect of that product; and

(b) the sale or offer for sale is in accordance with the provisions of that authorisation.

The restrictions on the holder of a wholesale dealer's licence shall not apply to:

(a) the sale or offer for sale of any exempt relevant medicinal product; and

(b) the export to an EEA State, or supply for the purposes of such export, of a relevant medicinal product which may be placed on the market in that State without a marketing authorisation by virtue of legislation adopted by that State under Article 5(2) of Directive 2001/83/EC, as amended.

The holder of a wholesale dealer's licence shall:

(a) keep such documents relating to the sale of medicinal products to which his licence relates as will facilitate the withdrawal or recall from sale of relevant medicinal products in accordance with paragraph (b);

(b) have in place an emergency plan which will ensure effective implementation of the recall from the market of any relevant medicinal products where such recall is:

(i) ordered by the licensing authority or by the competent authority of any other EEA State; or

(ii) carried out in co-operation with the manufacturer of, or the holder of the marketing authorisation for, the product in question;

(c) keep such records, which may be in the form of purchase and sales invoices, or on a computer or in any other form, which give, as a minimum, where any relevant medicinal products are received or dispatched, the following information:

(i)   the date of receipt or, as the case may be, dispatch,

(ii) the name of the relevant medicinal product,

(iii) the quantity received or, as the case may be, dispatched, and

(iv) the name and address of, as may be applicable in each case, the person from whom the products are received or to whom they are sold or supplied.

Where the holder of a wholesale dealer's licence imports from another EEA State any relevant medicinal product in respect of which he is not either the marketing authorisation holder in respect of that product; or acting on behalf of the marketing authorisation holder in importing that product. He shall notify the marketing authorisation holder and the licensing authority of his intention to import it.

The licence holder, for the purpose of enabling the licensing authority to ascertain whether there are any grounds:

(a) for suspending, revoking or varying any licence granted under Part II of the Act; or

(b) suspending or terminating any licence in accordance with the provisions of Part II of the Act, shall permit, and provide all necessary facilities to enable, any person duly authorised in writing by the licensing authority, on production if required of his credentials, to carry out such inspection or to take such samples or copies, in relation to things belonging to, or any business carried on by, the holder of the licence, as such person would have the right to carry out or take under the Act for the purpose of verifying any statement contained in an application for a licence.

The holder of a wholesale dealer's licence shall obtain supplies of relevant medicinal products only from:

(a) a manufacturer's licence holder or wholesale dealer's licence holder in respect of such products; or

(b) a person who holds an authorisation granted by another EEA State authorizing the manufacture of such products or their distribution by way of wholesale dealing.

The holder of a wholesale dealer's licence shall distribute relevant medicinal products by way of wholesale dealing only to:

(a) a holder of a wholesale dealer's licence relating to those products;

IV

(**b**) a holder of an authorisation granted by the competent authority of another EEA State authorising the supply of those products by way of wholesale dealing;

(**c**) any person who may lawfully sell those products by retail or who may lawfully supply them in circumstances corresponding to retail sale; or

(**d**) any person who may lawfully administer those products.

Where any relevant medicinal product is supplied to any person who may lawfully sell those products by retail or who may lawfully supply them in circumstances corresponding to retail sale, the licence holder shall enclose with the product a document which makes it possible to ascertain:

(**a**) the date on which the supply took place;

(**b**) the name and pharmaceutical form of the product supplied;

(**c**) the quantity of product supplied; and

(**d**) the names and addresses of the person or persons from whom the products were supplied to the licence holder.

The licence holder shall:

(**a**) keep a record of the information supplied where any relevant medicinal product is supplied to any person who may lawfully sell those products by retail or who may lawfully supply them in circumstances corresponding to retail sale for a minimum period of five years after the date on which it is supplied; and

(**b**) ensure, during that period, that that record is available to the licensing authority for inspection.

Where a wholesale dealer's licence relates to relevant medicinal products, the wholesale dealer's licence holder shall at all times have at his disposal the services of a responsible person who, in the opinion of the licensing authority:

(**a**) has knowledge of the activities to be carried out and of the procedures to be performed under the licence which is adequate for performing the functions of responsible person; and

(**b**) has experience in those procedures and activities which is adequate for those purposes.

The functions of the responsible person shall be to ensure, in relation to relevant medicinal products, that the conditions under which the licence has been granted have been, and are being, complied with and the quality of relevant medicinal products which are being handled by the wholesale dealer's licence holder are being maintained in accordance with the requirements of the marketing authorisations applicable to those products.

The standard provisions for wholesale dealer's licences, that is, those provisions which may be included in all licences unless the licence specifically provides otherwise, insofar as those licences relate to relevant medicinal products, shall be those provisions set out in Schedule 4 of The Medicines for Human Use (Manufacturing, Wholesale Dealing and Miscellaneous Amendments) Regulations 2005 [SI 2005/2789].

The licence holder shall not use any premises for the purpose of the handling, storage or distribution of relevant medicinal products other than those specified in his licence or notified to the licensing authority by him and approved by the licensing authority.

The licence holder shall provide such information as may be requested by the licensing authority concerning the type and quantity of any relevant medicinal products which he handles, stores or distributes.

Where and insofar as the licence relates to relevant medicinal products to which paragraph 1 of Schedule 1 to "the 1994 Regulations" apply which do not have a UK or EMA authorisation and are commonly known as "specials" (refer to Guidance Note 14), the licence holder shall only import such products from another EEA State:

(i)   in response to an order which satisfies the requirements of paragraph 1 of Schedule 1 to "the 1994 Regulations"; and
(ii) where the following conditions are complied with:

(1) No later than 28 days prior to each importation of an exempt imported product, the licence holder shall give written notice to the licensing authority stating his intention to import that medicinal product and stating the following particulars:

(a) the name of the medicinal product, being the brand name or the common name, or the scientific name, and any name, if different, under which the medicinal product is to be sold or supplied in the United Kingdom,

(b) any trademark or name of the manufacturer of the medicinal product;

(c) in respect of each active constituent of the medicinal product, any international non-proprietary name or the British approved name or the monograph name or, where that constituent does not have an international non-proprietary name, a British approved name or a monograph name, the accepted scientific name or any other name descriptive of the true nature of that constituent;

(d) the quantity of medicinal product which is to be imported which shall not exceed the quantity specified in subparagraph (5); and

(f) the name and address of the manufacturer or assembler of that medicinal product in the form in which it is to be imported and, if the person who will supply that medicinal product for importation is not the manufacturer or assembler, the name and address of such supplier.

(2) Subject to subparagraph (3), the licence holder shall not import the exempt imported product if, before the end of 28 days from the date on which the licensing authority sends or gives the licence holder an acknowledgement in writing by the licensing authority that they have received the notice referred to in subparagraph (1) above, the licensing authority have notified him in writing that the product should not be imported.

(3) The licence holder may import the exempt imported product referred to in the notice where he has been notified in writing by the licensing authority, before the end of the 28 day period referred to in subparagraph (2), that the exempt imported product may be imported.

(4) Where the licence holder sells or supplies exempt imported products, he shall, in addition to any other records which he is required by the provisions of his licence to make, make and maintain written records relating to:

(i) the batch number of the batch of the product from which the sale or supply was made; and

(ii) details of any adverse reaction to the product so sold or supplied of which he becomes aware.

(5) The licence holder shall import no more on any one occasion than such amount as is sufficient for 25 single administrations, or for 25 courses of treatment where the amount imported is sufficient for a maximum of three months' treatment, and on any such occasion shall not import more than the quantity notified to the licensing authority under subparagraph (1)(d).

(6) The licence holder shall inform the licensing authority forthwith of any matter coming to his attention which might reasonably cause the licensing authority to believe that the medicinal product can no longer be regarded either as a product which can safely be administered to human beings or as a product which is of satisfactory quality for such administration.

(7) The licence holder shall not issue any advertisement, catalogue, price list or circular relating to the exempt relevant medicinal product or make any representations in respect of that product.

(8) The licence holder shall cease importing or supplying an exempt imported product if he has received a notice in writing from the licensing authority directing that, as from a date specified in that notice, a particular product or class of products shall no longer be imported or supplied.

The licence holder shall take all reasonable precautions and exercise all due diligence to ensure that any information he provides to the licensing authority which is relevant to an evaluation of the safety, quality or efficacy of any medicinal product for human use which he handles, stores or distributes is not false or misleading in a material particular.

Appointment and Duties of the Responsible Person

Title VII of the Directive on the Community code relating to medicinal products for human use (Directive 2001/83/EC) obliges holders of a distribution authorisation to have a "qualified person designated as responsible". Regulation 10(1) of the Medicines for Human Use (Manufacturing, Wholesale dealing & Miscellaneous Amendments) Regulations 2005 state the requirement for a Responsible Person (RP) within the UK. The RP is responsible for safeguarding product users against potential hazards arising from poor distribution practices as a result, for example, of purchasing suspect products, poor storage or failure to establish the bona fides of purchasers.

The RP should ensure that the conditions of the wholesale dealer's licence (WL) are met and that the guidelines on Good Distribution Practice (GDP) are complied with. If the RP is not adequately carrying out his duties, the licensing authority may consider the suspension of the licence, withdrawal of acceptance of the RP on that licence and his acceptability on any other licence.

The RP does not have to be an employee of the licence holder but he must be at his disposal. Where the RP is not an employee there should be a written contract which specifies his responsibilities, duties, authority and so on. In the case of small companies the licensing authority may accept the licence holder as the nominated RP. In larger companies, however, this is not desirable.

There is no statutory requirement for the RP to be a pharmacist, although this is desirable. However, he should have access to pharmaceutical knowledge and advice when it is required, and have personal knowledge of:

IV

(a) The relevant provisions of the Medicines Act 1968 as amended and the Medicines for Human Use (Marketing Authorisations, Etc.) Regulations 1994 (SI 1994/3144) as amended.
(b) Directive 2001/83/EC as amended on the wholesale distribution of medicinal products for human use.
(c) Guidelines on GDP of medicinal products for human use (94/C 63/03).
(d) The conditions of the WL for which he is nominated.
(e) The products traded under the licence and the conditions necessary for their safe storage and distribution.
(f) The categories of persons to whom products may be distributed.

Where the RP is not a pharmacist or eligible to act as a Qualified Person (QP) (as defined in Directive 2001/83/EC as amended), he should have at least one year's practical experience in both or either of the following areas:

(a) Handling, storage and distribution of medicinal products.
(b) Transactions in or selling or procuring medicinal products. In addition, the RP should have at least one year's managerial experience in controlling and directing the wholesale distribution of medicinal products on a scale, and of a kind, appropriate to the licence for which he is nominated.

To carry out his responsibilities the RP should:

(a) Have a clear reporting line to either the licence holder or the Managing Director.
(b) Have access to all areas, sites, stores and records which relate to the licensable activities being carried out.
(c) Regularly review and monitor all such areas, sites, etc. or have delegated arrangements whereby he receives written reports that such actions have been carried out on his behalf. Where arrangements are delegated, the RP remains responsible and he should personally carry out the delegated functions at least once a year.
(d) Focus on the management of licensable activities, the accuracy and quality of records, compliance with established standard operating procedures, the quality of handling and storage equipment and facilities, and the standards achieved.
(e) Keep appropriate records relating to the discharge of his responsibilities.

Where the licence covers a number of sites, the RP may have a nominated deputy with appropriate reporting and delegating arrangements. However, the RP should assure himself and the licensing authority that the necessary controls and checks are in place.

For his part, the licence holder should ensure that there is a written standard operating procedure for receiving advice and comment from the RP and recording the consequent action taken.

Should it prove impossible to resolve a disagreement between the licence holder and the RP, the licensing authority should be consulted. Whilst a joint referral is clearly to be preferred, either party may approach the licensing authority independently. If an RP finds that he is in difficulty over his statutory responsibilities and the activities being carried out under the licence he should, in strict confidence, consult the licensing authority.

Control and Monitoring of Storage and Transportation Temperatures

Editor's note Legislation and good practices oblige pharmaceutical manufacturers and distributors to exercise control over the distribution chain to ensure that the quality of medicines is maintained. Critical in this regard is control of the environmental conditions under which medicines are stored and transported. The MHRA's recommendations concerning the control and monitoring of storage and transportation temperatures were published in The Pharmaceutical Journal in July 2001.[2] A summary of these is given below.

Introduction

1   EU requirements and guidelines on Good Distribution Practice (GDP) require distributors to "ensure that storage conditions are observed at all times, including during transportation". The requirements are applicable not only to medicines that need to be stored at low temperatures (known as cold chain products) but also to medicines that should be stored below 25°C or 30°C (known as temperate chain products). In addition, an increasing number of products require storage and transportation at sub-zero temperatures and the application of appropriate controls to these is equally important. What follows gives guidance on how compliance with relevant standards of good practice may be achieved.

Cold storage

2   Many medicinal products require storage at controlled low temperature. Some of these such as vaccines, insulins, blood products and some products of biotechnology can be denatured by freezing and thus must be maintained within a narrow temperature range above freezing point.

3   The temperature in small refrigerators used to store medicines should be measured continuously and the maximum and minimum temperatures recorded daily. Sufficient space should be maintained to permit adequate air circulation. If the refrigerator is filled to capacity the effect on temperature distribution should be investigated. Refrigerators used for vaccines and other sensitive products should be capable of maintaining the temperature between 2°C and 8°C with the minimum of intervention. Temperature

---

[2] Taylor J. Recommendations on the control and monitoring of storage and transportation temperatures of medicinal products. *Pharm J* 2001; 267: 128–131.

monitoring of these should be by electronic max/min thermometer, with an accuracy of $\pm 0.5°C$, which should be readable from outside the unit. Refrigerators should not be sited in an environment where extremes of temperature (i.e. $< 10°C$ or $> 32°C$) will affect their performance.

4   Large commercial refrigerators and walk-in cold rooms should be monitored with an electronic temperature-recording device that measures load temperature in one or more locations, depending on the size of the unit. Portable data-loggers that can be downloaded onto a computer may be used instead of a fixed device. Records should be checked daily. Internal air temperature distribution should be mapped on installation in the empty and full state and annually thereafter under conditions of normal use. Products should not be stored in areas shown by temperature mapping to present a risk (e.g. in the airflow from the refrigeration unit). Condensate from chillers should not be collected inside the unit.

5   Temperature alarms should be fitted to large and walk-in units and those smaller units used to store products at risk from freezing.

Controlled room temperature storage

6   The simplest monitoring would be with a max/min thermometer placed at a strategic location and read, recorded and reset at least weekly, more frequently during periods of exceptionally hot or cold weather. With the exception of very small stores, temperatures should be recorded at low and high levels. Continuous temperature recording is recommended for large warehouses. Self-contained storage areas within warehouses, (e.g. CD store, flammables store) should be included in temperature monitoring programmes.

7   All warehouses should be temperature mapped to determine the temperature distribution under extremes of external temperature. Mapping should be repeated every two to three years and after any significant modification to the premises, stock layout, or heating system. Medicines should not be stored in areas shown by temperature mapping or other consideration to be unsuitable, e.g. at high level in poorly insulated stores, or next to heaters.

Transportation

COLD-CHAIN GOODS

8   The route and time of transportation, the local seasonal temperatures and the nature of the load should all be considered when arranging cold-chain distribution. For small volumes of cold-chain goods, insulated containers

may be used; in which case it is vital that products damaged by freezing are prevented from coming into direct contact with ice packs at sub-zero temperatures.

9   Larger volumes of cold-chain goods should be shipped in refrigerated transport, particularly if transit times may be prolonged. Temperatures within loads of products at risk from freezing should be strictly controlled and monitored with recording probes or individual temperature monitoring devices, giving consideration to the temperature gradient within the load. The temperature records for each consignment should be reviewed and there should be a procedure for implementing corrective action in the case of adverse events.

10   Distributors should ensure that consignments of cold-chain goods are clearly labelled with the required storage/transport conditions. Receivers should satisfy themselves that the goods have been transported under appropriate conditions and should place them in appropriate storage facilities as soon as possible after receipt.

OTHER GOODS

11   Consideration should be given to the possible extremes of temperature inside uninsulated, unventilated delivery vehicles and precautions should be taken to protect all products from heat challenge. This includes representatives' samples kept in car boots and goods distributed using postal services.

SYSTEMS CHECKS AND CALIBRATION

12   Any systems whose performance is critical to preserving the product should be tested and demonstrated to achieve what is intended. Measuring and recording devices that are used in critical areas (e.g. temperature monitoring of storage and transport facilities for cold-chain goods at risk from freezing) should be calibrated at least annually against a traceable reference device. Records should include pre- and post-calibration readings and details of any adjustments made or corrections to be applied. Alarms should be checked for correct functioning at the designated set temperatures.

Counterfeits/Ensuring Bona Fides

The supply of counterfeit medicines is a growing problem worldwide and one which the MHRA is taking very seriously. Counterfeit medicines represent a threat to the legitimate UK supply chain and to patient safety. They are fraudulent and may be deliberately mislabelled with respect to identity, composition and/or source. Counterfeiting can apply to both innovator and generic products, prescription and self-medication, as well as to traditional herbal remedies. Counterfeit medicines may include products with the correct ingredients but fake packaging, with the wrong ingredients, without active ingredients or with insufficient active ingredients, and may even contain harmful or poisonous substances.

The supply and distribution of medicines is tightly controlled within the European Community. All licensed wholesalers must comply with the Community's agreed standards of GDP and there exist strict licensing and regulatory requirements in UK domestic legislation to safeguard patients against potential hazards arising from poor distribution practices: for example, purchasing suspect or counterfeit products, failing to establish the "bona fides" of suppliers and purchasers, inadequate record keeping, and so on.

Of principal importance to wholesale dealers is paragraph 31 of the EU Guide to GDP, which states:

"Counterfeit medicinal products found in the distribution network should be kept apart from other medicinal products to avoid any confusion. They should be clearly labelled as not for sale and competent authorities and the holder of marketing authorisation of the original product should be informed immediately."

Manufacturers and wholesale dealers should inform the Competent Authority of any defect that could result in a recall or abnormal restriction on the supply of a product. They must also have effective recall procedures in place.

Wholesale dealers in particular should maintain a high level of vigilance against the procurement or supply of potentially counterfeit product. Such product may be offered for sale below the established market price so rigorous checks should be made on the bona fides of the supplier and the origin of the product. It is known that some wholesalers are themselves developing good practice strategies – such as conducting rigorous physical inspections of packs when grey market purchases are made – and this is encouraged. Any suspicious activity should be reported to the MHRA's Intelligence Unit.

The Competent Authority will take regulatory action where breaches of legislation are identified; this may take the form of adverse licensing action e.g. make a variation to an existing licence, suspension or revocation of a licence and/or the instigation of criminal proceedings.

Diverted Medicines

Diversion is the term used for the fraudulent activity where medicines destined for non-EU markets re-enter the EU and are placed back on to the European market at a higher price.

The diversion of medicines involves medicinal products being offered at preferential prices and exported to specific markets (normally developing countries) outside the EU. Diversion occurs when unscrupulous traders, on receipt of the medicines, re-export the pharmaceutical products back to the EU – meaning that patients for whom these preferentially-priced medicines were intended are denied access to them. Such products appearing on the EU market are then known as "diverted" from their intended market. This represents not only a corrupt diversion for profit but such activity also poses the risk of inappropriate or unlicensed use, and the quality of the product may also be compromised.

As with counterfeit products, wholesale dealers in particular should maintain a high level of vigilance against the procurement or supply of potentially diverted product. Such product may be offered for sale below the established market value, so appropriate checks should be made on the bona fides of the supplier and the origin of the product.

The Licensing Authority will take regulatory action where breaches of legislation are identified; this may take the form of adverse licensing action e.g. make a variation to an existing licence, suspension or revocation of a licence and/or the instigation of criminal proceedings.

Parallel Distribution

Parallel distribution embodies two fundamental principles of the European Community's founding Treaty (of Rome): the free movement of goods and Community-wide exhaustion of intellectual property rights. It is also referred to as parallel trade and also, less correctly (since the EEA[3] is a single market with no internal borders), as parallel importing.

Parallel distribution exists in the absence of price harmonisation of pharmaceutical products within the European Union, i.e. when there are significant price differences between countries; this is the case in the European Union, where prices of medicines are not governed by free competition laws, but are generally fixed by the government.

It involves the transfer of genuine, original branded products, authorised in accordance with Community legislation, marketed in one Member State of the EEA at a lower price (the source country) to another EEA member state (the country of destination) by a parallel distributor, and placed on the market in competition with a therapeutically identical product already marketed there at a higher price by or under licence from the owner of the brand.

---

[3] The member states of the European Union plus Iceland, Norway and Liechtenstein.

The pharmaceutical products which are distributed in this way are identical in all respects to the branded version marketed by the originator in the country into which it is imported. They are not copies; they do not vary in any respect from the original; and they are manufactured normally by the originator or by the licensee to the approved product specification. All such products require a Product Licence for Parallel Import (PLPI) which is a "piggy-back" authorisation granted by the competent regulatory authority (the MHRA in the UK), after extensive checks to ensure that the imported drug is therapeutically the same as the domestic version.

Parallel distributors operating in the UK are subject to a system of licensing and inspection, which ensures that licensed medicinal products conform to internationally agreed standards, and that those medicines are stored and distributed in compliance with the required regulatory standards. Distributors are required to hold a Wholesale Dealer's Licence, in accordance with Article 77 of Directive 2001/83/EC, as amended. The only exception is if a manufacturing authorisation includes provision for wholesale dealing. In accordance with the wholesaling authorisation, parallel distributors are obliged to follow GDP guidelines in accordance with Article 84 of the Directive, employ a Responsible Person and are subject to periodic inspection by the competent (licensing) authority.

In addition, parallel distributors in the country of destination (the receiving country) involved in repackaging or relabelling of product must employ at least one Qualified Person (QP), who has received the relevant education and training (in accordance with Article 48 of the Directive), with responsibility to ensure that a quality system is implemented and maintained. A Manufacturing (assembly) Authorisation is also required. Regular GMP inspections are undertaken at parallel assemblers and distributors (performing relabelling/repacking activities) by the Competent Authority in the Member State concerned to ensure that GMP is adhered to.

Parallel distributors are required to have effective recall procedures in place. The MHRA has systems in place to receive and investigate reports of packaging and labelling problems with medicines, including parallel traded products.

Relabelling/repackaging

The goods should remain in their original packaging as long as possible. However, once the received product is approved for processing, relabelling may be undertaken in accordance with the national simplified marketing authorisation of the parallel-distributed product, under conditions of GMP, i.e. exactly the same procedures as those followed by all pharmaceutical manufacturers.

This either involves replacement of the original outer carton with a brand new one or over-stickering the original outer carton, with both providing the approved label text in the language of the country of destination. In all cases, the existing package leaflet is removed and replaced by a new one originated by the parallel distributor in accordance with the simplified marketing authorisation in the language of the country of destination. In addition to the requirements of the PLPI marketing authorization it may be necessary, as part of any repackaging specifications, for the applicant to address any trademark concerns that might arise. This may involve technical and commercial discussions between the trademark holder and the PLPI applicant.

Both the original cartons – if these are replaced – and the original leaflets must be destroyed. No handling of the actual product (e.g. open units of tablets or capsules) within its immediate packaging (e.g. blister or foil packs) should take place during replacement of the original carton and it is important to maintain the audit trail back to the origin.

As with any other pharmaceutical manufacturer, parallel distributor operators involved in relabelling and/or repackaging should be given regular training in GMP. Batch documentation should be retained for each batch.

Maintenance of the integrity of the supply chain

Parallel distributors should only purchase medicinal products with marketing authorisations from authorised wholesalers or manufacturers in other EEA countries. The supplying wholesaler should make available before sale a copy of its wholesale authorisation and provide assurance that the supplies were obtained from the original manufacturer and/or an authorised wholesaler within the EEA.

Parallel distributors should also only sell or supply medicinal products with marketing authorisations to authorised wholesalers, registered pharmacies or other persons entitled to sell medicinal products to the general public. A copy of the authorisation should be requested if there is any doubt.

Continued Supply

Under Article 23a of Directive 2001/83/EC, as inserted by Article 1(22) of Directive 2004/27/EC, the marketing authorisation holder is required to notify the Competent Authority (MHRA in the UK) of the date of actual marketing of the medicinal product, taking account of the various presentations authorised, and to notify the Competent Authority if the product ceases to be placed on the market either temporarily or permanently. Except in exceptional circumstances, the notification must be made no less than two months before the interruption.

Any authorisation which within three years of granting is not placed on the market will cease to be valid. In respect of generic medicinal products, the three year period will start on the grant of the authorisation, or at the end of the period of market exclusivity or patent protection of the reference product, whichever is the later date. If a product is placed on the market after authorisation, but subsequently ceases to be available on the market in the UK for a period of three consecutive years, it will also cease to be valid. In these circumstances the MHRA will, however, when it is aware of the imminent expiry of the three year period, notify the marketing authorisation holder in advance that their marketing authorisation will cease to be valid. In exceptional circumstances, and on public health grounds, the MHRA may grant an exemption from the invalidation of the marketing authorisation after three years. Whether there are exceptional circumstances and public health grounds for an exemption will be assessed on a case by case basis. When assessing such cases, MHRA will, in particular, consider the implications for patients and public health more generally of an marketing authorisation no longer being valid.

The MHRA has received requests for advice on implications for maintaining the harmonisation of an authorisation across Member States if a presentation of a product is withdrawn from the market of the Reference Member State (RMS) and remains unavailable on that market for three years. Discussions on applying the sunset clause provision in such circumstances continue at EU level. In the meantime the MHRA will address the implications of this issue on a case by case basis.

Those provisions are implemented in the UK by Regulation 7 of, and Schedule 3 to, the Medicines for Human Use (Marketing Authorisations Etc.) Regulations 1994, as amended; in particular, paragraph 6(cc) and 6B of Schedule 3 each provide that breach of the relevant notification obligation by a UK marketing authorisation holder constitutes a criminal offence. Failure to notify a cessation or interruption, or failure to notify within the time limit is, however, not an offence if the marketing authorisation holder took all reasonable precautions and exercised all due diligence to avoid such a failure.

In accordance with the MHRA's interpretation of the expression "placing on the market" when used elsewhere in the Directive, the MHRA's view is that a product is "placed on the market" at the first transaction by which the product enters the distribution chain in the UK. The marketing authorisation holder must, therefore, notify the MHRA when a product with a new marketing authorisation is first placed into the distribution chain, rather than the first date it becomes available to individual patients. The MHRA requests that you notify us of this first "placing on the market" within one calendar month. In order to ensure that a marketing authorisation continues to be valid, the marketing authorisation holder must ensure that at least one packaging presentation (e.g. bottle or blister pack) of the product, which can include own label supplies, authorised under that marketing authorisation is present on the market.

The marketing authorisation holder must report all cessations/ interruptions to the MHRA. However, the MHRA does not need to be notified of the following:

(a) normal seasonal changes in manufacturing and/or distribution schedules (such as cold and flu remedies);
(b) short-term temporary interruptions in placing on the market that will not affect normal availability to distributors.

If you are in doubt about whether or not you need to notify an interruption in supply, you should err on the side of caution and report it to the MHRA in the normal way. You must notify the MHRA if any of the presentations authorised under a single marketing authorisation cease to be placed on the market either temporarily or permanently, but, as stated above, the absence of availability of one or more presentations – as long as one presentation of the product authorised under the single marketing authorisation remains on the market – will not invalidate the marketing authorisation. Problems relating to manufacturing or assembly should also be discussed with the appropriate GMP Inspector and issues of availability of medicines relating to suspected or confirmed product defects should be directly notified to, and discussed with, the Defective Medicines Reporting Centre (Tel: 020 7084 2574).

The Department of Health (DH) also has an interest in the availability of products for supply to the NHS, and together with the Association of the British Pharmaceutical Industry (ABPI) and the British Generics Manufacturers Association (BGMA), has developed best practice guidelines for notifying medicine shortages. These guidelines, together with DH/ABPI guidelines "Ensuring Best Practice in the Notification of Product Discontinuations" complement the statutory requirements under the European legislation and may be found (in PDF format) on the DH website (www.dh.gov.uk). Marketing authorisation holders should, therefore, continue to notify the Department of Health about interruptions and cessations of marketing in accordance with these guidelines.

In this context, your attention is also drawn to Article 81 of Directive 2001/83/EC as substituted by Article 1(57) of Directive 2004/27/EC, under which the marketing authorisation holder and the distributors of a medicinal product actually placed on the market shall, within the limits of their responsibilities, ensure appropriate and continued supplies of that medicinal product to pharmacies and persons authorised to supply

IV

medicinal products so that the needs of patients in the Member State in question are covered. Failure by a marketing authorisation holder to comply with this obligation is a criminal offence, unless the marketing authorisation holder took all reasonable precautions and exercised all due diligence to avoid such a failure.

Product Recall/Withdrawal

The Medicines Act imposes certain obligations on licence holders with regard to withdrawal and recall from sale. The aim of the Defective Medicines Report Centre (DMRC) within the MHRA is to minimise the hazard to patients arising from the distribution of defective (human) medicinal products by providing an emergency assessment and communications system between the suppliers (manufacturers and distributors), the regulatory authorities and the end user. The DMRC achieves this by receiving reports of suspected defective (human) medicinal products; monitoring and, as far as is necessary, directing and advising actions by the relevant licence holder(s) and communicating the details of this action with the appropriate urgency and distribution to users of the products. The communication normally used is a "Drug Alert".

A defective medicinal product is one whose quality does not conform to the requirements of its marketing authorisation, specification or for some other reason of quality is potentially hazardous. A defective product may be suspected because of a visible defect or contamination or as a result of tests performed on it, or because it has caused untoward reactions in a patient or for other reasons involving poor manufacturing or distribution practice.

An adverse drug reaction means a response to a medicinal product which is noxious and unintended and which occurs at doses normally used in man for the prophylaxis, diagnosis or therapy of disease or for the restoration, correction or modification of physiological function.

Counterfeits are considered as defective products.

Immediately a hazard is identified from any source, it will be necessary to evaluate the level of danger, and the category of recall, if required. Where the reported defect is a confirmed defect, the DMRC will then take one of the following courses of action and obtain a report from the manufacturer on the nature of the defect, their handling of the defect and action to be taken to prevent its recurrence.

Issue a "recall"

Under normal circumstances a recall is always required where a defect is confirmed unless the defect is shown to be of a trivial nature and/or there are unlikely to be significant amounts of the affected product remaining in the market.

It is the licence holder's responsibility to recall products from customers, in a manner agreed with the DMRC. The company should provide copies of draft recall letters for agreement with the DMRC. If the company (licence holder) does not agree to a recall voluntarily, the MHRA, as Licensing Authority, may be obliged to take compulsory action.

Issue a "Drug Alert"

Recall and withdrawal of product from the market is normally the responsibility of the licence holder. However, where a product has been distributed widely and/or there is a serious risk to health from the defect, the MHRA can opt to issue a Drug Alert letter. The Drug Alert cascade mechanism ensures rapid communication of safety information; it is not a substitute for, but complimentary to, any action taken by the licence holder. The text of the Alert should be agreed between the MHRA and the company concerned.

In some cases, where a product has been supplied to a small number of known customers, the MHRA may decide that notification will be adequate and a Drug Alert is not needed.

The DMRC may also request companies to insert notification in the professional press in certain cases.

Management of the recall

The company should directly contact wholesalers, hospitals, retail pharmacies and overseas distributors supplied. The DMRC is likely to take the lead in notifying Regional Contacts for NHS Trusts and Provider Units and Health Authorities, special and Government hospitals and overseas regulatory authorities.

The DMRC will liaise with the company and discuss arrangements for the recall, requesting the dates that supply started and ceased and a copy of any letters sent out by that company concerning the recall. Again, it is desirable that the text of the notices sent via the company and by the DMRC should be mutually agreed.

IV

Follow-up action

The DMRC will monitor the conduct and success of the recall by the manufacturer or distributor. As follow-up action, it may be necessary to consider any or all of the following:

- arrange a visit to the licence holder/manufacturer/distributor;
- arrange a visit to the point of discovery of the defect;
- refer to the Inspectorate to arrange an inspection;

- seek special surveillance of adverse reaction reports;
- refer the matter for adverse licensing and/or enforcement action.

Reporting a suspected defect

Suspected defects can be reported by telephone, fax, e-mail or letter or using our online form:

Address:
DMRC, Room 17-157, Market Towers, 1 Nine Elms Lane, London SW8 5NQ, UK.
Telephone: +44 (0)20 7084 2574 (weekdays 0900–1700)
Telephone: +44 (0)20 7210 3000 (other times)
Fax: +44 (0)20 7084 2676
E-mail: info@mhra.gsi.gov.uk
Online form: www.mhra.gov.uk

LEGISLATION ON WHOLESALE DISTRIBUTION

8

EU Legislation on Wholesale Distribution

Contents

DIRECTIVE 2001/83/EC, AS AMENDED, TITLE VII, WHOLESALE DISTRIBUTION

Directive 2001/83/EC of the European Parliament and of the Council of 6 November 2001 on the Community code relating to medicinal products for human use as amended by Directive 2004/27/EC.

Editor's note	Title VII of this directive is reproduced below. Reference should be made to the full Directive for the preamble, definitions and the general and final provisions.

Title VII: Wholesale Distribution of Medicinal Products

Article 76

1   Without prejudice to Article 6, Member States shall take all appropriate action to ensure that only medicinal products in respect of which a marketing authorization has been granted in accordance with Community law are distributed on their territory.

2   In the case of wholesale distribution and storage, medicinal products shall be covered by a marketing authorisation granted pursuant to Regulation (EC) No. 726/2004 or by the competent authorities of a Member State in accordance with this Directive.

3   Any distributor, not being the marketing authorisation holder, who imports a product from another Member State, shall notify the marketing authorisation holder and the competent authority in the Member State to which the product will be imported of his intention to import it. In the case of products which have not been granted an authorisation pursuant to Regulation (EC) No. 726/2004, the notification to the competent authority shall be without prejudice to additional procedures provided for in the legislation of that Member State.

Article 77

1   Member States shall take all appropriate measures to ensure that the wholesale distribution of medicinal products is subject to the possession of an authorization to engage in activity as a wholesaler in medicinal products, stating the place for which it is valid.

2   Where persons authorized or entitled to supply medicinal products to the public may also, under national law, engage in wholesale business, such persons shall be subject to the authorization provided for in paragraph 1.

3   Possession of a manufacturing authorization shall include authorization to distribute by wholesale the medicinal products covered by that authorization. Possession of an authorization to engage in activity as a wholesaler in medicinal products shall not give dispensation from the obligation to possess a manufacturing authorization and to comply with the conditions set out in that respect, even where the manufacturing or import business is secondary.

4   At the request of the Commission or any Member State, Member States shall supply all appropriate information concerning the individual authorizations which they have granted under paragraph 1.

5   Checks on the persons authorized to engage in the activity of wholesaler in medicinal products and the inspection of their premises shall be carried

out under the responsibility of the Member State which granted the authorization.

6   The Member State which granted the authorization referred to in paragraph 1 shall suspend or revoke that authorization if the conditions of authorization cease to be met. It shall forthwith inform the other Member States and the Commission thereof.

7   Should a Member State consider that, in respect of a person holding an authorization granted by another Member State under the terms of paragraph 1, the conditions of authorization are not, or are no longer met, it shall forthwith inform the Commission and the other Member State involved. The latter shall take the measures necessary and shall inform the Commission and the first Member State of the decisions taken and the reasons for those decisions.

Article 78

Member States shall ensure that the time taken for the procedure for examining the application for the distribution authorization does not exceed 90 days from the day on which the competent authority of the Member State concerned receives the application.

The competent authority may, if need be, require the applicant to supply all necessary information concerning the conditions of authorization. Where the authority exercises this option, the period laid down in the first paragraph shall be suspended until the requisite additional data have been supplied.

Article 79

In order to obtain the distribution authorization, applicants must fulfil the following minimum requirements:

(a) they must have suitable and adequate premises, installations and equipment, so as to ensure proper conservation and distribution of the medicinal products;

(b) they must have staff, and in particular, a qualified person designated as responsible, meeting the conditions provided for by the legislation of the Member State concerned;

(c) they must undertake to fulfil the obligations incumbent on them under the terms of Article 80.

Article 80

Holders of the distribution authorization must fulfil the following minimum requirements:

(a) they must make the premises, installations and equipment referred to in Article 79(a) accessible at all times to the persons responsible for inspecting them;

(b) they must obtain their supplies of medicinal products only from persons who are themselves in possession of the distribution authorization or who are exempt from obtaining such authorization under the terms of Article 77(3);

(c) they must supply medicinal products only to persons who are themselves in possession of the distribution authorization or who are authorized or entitled to supply medicinal products to the public in the Member State concerned;

(d) they must have an emergency plan which ensures effective implementation of any recall from the market ordered by the competent authorities or carried out in cooperation with the manufacturer or marketing authorization holder for the medicinal product concerned;

(e) they must keep records either in the form of purchase/sales invoices, or on computer, or in any other form, giving for any transaction in medicinal products received or dispatched at least the following information:
- date,
- name of the medicinal product,
- quantity received or supplied,
- name and address of the supplier or consignee, as appropriate;

(f) they must keep the records referred to under (e) available to the competent authorities, for inspection purposes, for a period of five years;

(g) they must comply with the principles and guidelines of good distribution practice for medicinal products as laid down in Article 84.

Article 81

With regard to the supply of medicinal products to pharmacists and persons authorised or entitled to supply medicinal products to the public, Member States shall not impose upon the holder of a distribution authorisation which has been granted by another Member State any obligation, in particular public service obligations, more stringent than those they impose on persons whom they have themselves authorised to engage in equivalent activities.

The holder of a marketing authorisation for a medicinal product and the distributors of the said medicinal product actually placed on the market in a Member State shall, within the limits of their responsibilities, ensure appropriate and continued supplies of that medicinal product to pharmacies and persons authorised to supply medicinal products so that the needs of patients in the Member State in question are covered.

The arrangements for implementing this Article should, moreover, be justified on grounds of public health protection and be proportionate in relation to the objective of such protection, in compliance with the Treaty rules, particularly those concerning the free movement of goods and competition.

Article 82

For all supplies of medicinal products to a person authorized or entitled to supply medicinal products to the public in the Member State concerned, the authorized wholesaler must enclose a document that makes it possible to ascertain:

- the date;
- the name and pharmaceutical form of the medicinal product;
- the quantity supplied;
- the name and address of the supplier and consignor.

Member States shall take all appropriate measures to ensure that persons authorized or entitled to supply medicinal products to the public are able to provide information that makes it possible to trace the distribution path of every medicinal product.

Article 83

The provisions of this Title shall not prevent the application of more stringent requirements laid down by Member States in respect of the wholesale distribution of:

- narcotic or psychotropic substances within their territory;
- medicinal products derived from blood;
- immunological medicinal products;
- radiopharmaceuticals.

Article 84

The Commission shall publish guidelines on good distribution practice. To this end, it shall consult the Committee for Medicinal Products for Human Use and the Pharmaceutical Committee established by Council Decision 75/320/EEC.

Article 85

This Title shall apply to homeopathic medicinal products.

UK Legislation on Wholesale Distribution

Contents

The Medicines for Human Use (Manufacturing, Wholesale Dealing and Miscellaneous Amendments) Regulations 2005 (SI 2005 No. 2789)

Editor's note	These extracts from the Regulations and Standard Provisions of The Medicines for Human Use (Manufacturing, Wholesale Dealing and Miscellaneous Amendments) Regulations 2005 [SI 2005 No. 2789] are presented for the reader's convenience. Reproduction is with the permission of HMSO and the Queen's Printer for Scotland. For any definitive information reference must be made to the original Regulations. The numbering and content within this section corresponds with the regulations set out in the published Statutory Instrument (SI 2005 No. 2789).

Interpretation

1   (1) These Regulations may be cited as The Medicines for Human Use (Manufacturing, Wholesale Dealing and Miscellaneous Amendments) Regulations 2005.

(2) In these Regulations:

"the Act" means the Medicines Act 1968;

"the 1994 Regulations" means the Medicines for Human Use (Marketing Authorisations Etc.) Regulations 1994;

"the Applications Regulations" means the Medicines (Applications for Manufacturer's and Wholesale Dealer's Licences) Regulations 1971;

"the Standard Provisions Regulations" means the Medicines (Standard Provisions for Licences and Certificates) Regulations 1971;

"the Directive" means Directive 2001/83/EC, of the European Parliament and of the Council on the Community code relating to medicinal products for human use, as amended by:

(a) Directive 2002/98/EC of the European Parliament and of the Council of 27 January 2003 setting standards of quality and safety for the collection, testing, processing, storage and distribution of human blood and blood components,

(b) Commission Directive 2003/63/EC amending Directive 2001/83/EC on the Community code relating to medicinal products for human use,

(c) Directive 2004/24/EC of the European Parliament and of the Council amending, as regards traditional herbal medicinal products, Directive 2001/83/EC on the Community code relating to medicinal products for human use, and

(d) Directive 2004/27/EC of the European Parliament and of the Council amending Directive 2001/83/EC on the Community code relating to medicinal products for human use;

"EEA State" means a Member State, Norway, Iceland or Liechtenstein;

"exempt relevant medicinal product" means a relevant medicinal product to which paragraph 1 of Schedule 1 to the 1994 Regulations or any equivalent legislation in any EEA State other than the United Kingdom applies;

"the guidelines on good distribution practice" means the Guidelines on Good Distribution Practice of Medicinal Products for Human Use (94/C63/03) published by the European Commission pursuant to Article 84 of the Directive;

"relevant medicinal product" means a medicinal product for human use to which the provisions of the Directive apply;

(3) Expression used in these Regulations which are used in any provision of the Act have the meaning which they bear in the Act.

Requirement that holders of wholesale dealer's licences comply with certain obligations

8 (1) The holder of a wholesale dealer's licence, insofar as that licence relates to relevant medicinal products, shall:

(a) comply with the guidelines on good distribution practice;

(b) ensure, within the limits of his responsibility as a distributor of relevant medicinal products, the appropriate and continued supply of such relevant medicinal products to pharmacies and persons who may lawfully sell such products by retail or who may lawfully supply them in circumstances corresponding to retail sale so that the needs of patients in the United Kingdom are covered;

(c) provide and maintain such staff, premises, equipment and facilities for the handling, storage and distribution of the relevant medicinal products which he handles, stores or distributes under his licence as are necessary to maintain the quality of, and ensure proper distribution of, the medicinal products which he handles, stores or distributes pursuant to his licence;

(d) inform the licensing authority of any proposed structural alteration to, or discontinuance of use of, premises to which the licence relates or premises which have been approved from time to time by the licensing authority.

(2) Subject to paragraph (3), the holder of a wholesale dealer's licence shall not sell or offer for sale or supply any relevant medicinal product unless:

(a) there is a marketing authorization for the time being in force in respect of that product; and

(b) the sale or offer for sale is in conformity with the provisions of that authorisation.

(3) The restriction in paragraph (2) shall not apply to:

(a) the sale or offer for sale of any exempt relevant medicinal product; and

(b) the export to an EEA State, or supply for the purposes of such export, of a relevant medicinal product which may be placed on the market in that State without a marketing authorization by virtue of legislation adopted by that State under Article 5(2) of the Directive.

(4) The holder of a wholesale dealer's licence shall:

(a) keep such documents relating to the sale of medicinal products to which his licence relates as will facilitate the withdrawal or recall from sale of relevant medicinal products in accordance with paragraph (b);

(b) have in place an emergency plan which will ensure effective implementation of the recall from the market of any relevant medicinal products where such recall is:

(i) ordered by the licensing authority or by the competent authority of any other EEA State; or

(ii) carried out in co-operation with the manufacturer of, or the holder of the marketing authorization for, the product in question;

(c) keep such records, which may be in the form of purchase and sales invoices, or on a computer or in any other form, which give, as a minimum, where any relevant medicinal products are received or dispatched, the following information:

(i) the date of receipt or, as the case may be, dispatch,

(ii) the name of the relevant medicinal product,

(iii) the quantity of relevant medicinal product received or, as the case may be, dispatched, and

(iv) the name and address of, as may be applicable in each case, the person from whom the products are received or to whom they are sold or supplied.

(5) Where the holder of a wholesale dealer's licence imports from another EEA State any relevant medicinal product in respect of which he is not either:

(a) the marketing authorization holder in respect of that product; or

(b) acting on behalf of the marketing authorization holder in importing that product, he shall notify the marketing authorization holder and the licensing authority of his intention to import it.

(6) The licence holder, for the purpose of enabling the licensing authority to ascertain whether there are any grounds:

(a) for suspending, revoking or varying any licence granted under Part II of the Act; or

(b) suspending or terminating any licence in accordance with the provisions of Part II of the Act, shall permit, and provide all necessary facilities to enable, any person duly authorised in writing by the licensing authority, on production if required of his credentials, to carry out such inspection or to take such samples or copies, in relation to things belonging to, or any business carried on by, the holder of the licence, as such person would have the right to carry out or take under the Act for the purpose of verifying any statement contained in an application for a licence.

Requirement that wholesale dealers deal only with specified persons

9 (1) The holder of a wholesale dealer's licence shall obtain supplies of relevant medicinal products only from either:

(a) a manufacturer's licence holder or wholesale dealer's licence holder in respect of such products; or

(b) a person who holds an authorisation granted by another EEA State authorizing the manufacture of such products or their distribution by way of wholesale dealing.

(2) The holder of a wholesale dealer's licence shall distribute relevant medicinal products by way of wholesale dealing only to:

(a) a holder of a wholesale dealer's licence relating to those products;

(b) a holder of an authorization granted by the competent authority of another EEA State authorising the supply of those products by way of wholesale dealing;

(c) any person who may lawfully sell those products by retail or who may lawfully supply them in circumstances corresponding to retail sale; or

(d) any person who may lawfully administer those products.

(3) Where any relevant medicinal product is supplied to any person pursuant to paragraph (2)(c), the licence holder shall enclose with the product a document which makes it possible to ascertain:

(a) the date on which the supply took place;

(b) the name and pharmaceutical form of the product supplied;

(c) the quantity of product supplied; and

(d) the names and addresses of the person or persons from whom the products were supplied to the licence holder.

(4) The licence holder shall:

(a) keep a record of the information supplied pursuant to paragraph (3) for a minimum period of five years after the date on which it is supplied; and

(b) ensure, during that period, that that record is available to the licensing authority for inspection.

Requirement as to responsible persons

10 (1) Where a wholesale dealer's licence relates to relevant medicinal products, the wholesale dealer's licence holder shall at all times have at his disposal the services of a person (referred to in this regulation as "a responsible person") who, in the opinion of the licensing authority:

(a) has knowledge of the activities to be carried out and of the procedures to be performed under the licence which is adequate for performing the functions of responsible person; and

(b) has experience in those procedures and activities which is adequate for those purposes.

(2) The functions of the responsible person shall be to ensure, in relation to relevant medicinal products, that:

(a) the conditions under which the licence has been granted have been, and are being, complied with; and

(b) the quality of relevant medicinal products which are being handled by the wholesale dealer's licence holder are being maintained in accordance with the requirements of the marketing authorizations applicable to those products.

(3) The licence holder shall:
  (a) notify the licensing authority of the name and address and degrees, diplomas or qualifications and experience of the person who will carry out the functions of responsible person;
  (b) notify the licensing authority of any change to the responsible person; and
  (c) not permit any person to act as responsible person other than the person named in his licence as responsible person or, subject to paragraph (4) any other such person whose name is notified to the licensing authority.
(4) Where, after giving the licence holder and the person acting as a responsible person the opportunity of making representations to them (orally or in writing), the licensing authority are of the opinion that:
  (a) the person so acting does not satisfy the provisions of paragraph (1) as respects qualifications and experience, or
  (b) he is failing to carry out the duties referred to in paragraph (2) adequately or at all, and have notified the licence holder accordingly in writing, the licence holder shall not permit that person to act as a responsible person.

Standard provisions for wholesale dealer's licences

11   The standard provisions, for the purposes of Part II of the Act, for wholesale dealer's licences, insofar as those licences relate to relevant medicinal products, shall be those provisions set out in Schedule 4 to these Regulations.

Schedule 4 Standard Provisions Which May be Incorporated in a Wholesale Dealer's Licence

1   The licence holder shall not use any premises for the purpose of the handling, storage or distribution of relevant medicinal products other than those specified in his licence or notified to the licensing authority by him from time to time and approved by the licensing authority.

2   The licence holder shall provide such information as may be requested by the licensing authority concerning the type and quantity of any medicinal products which he handles, stores or distributes.

3   (1)   Where and insofar as the licence relates to relevant medicinal products to which paragraph 1 of Schedule 1 to the 1994 Regulations apply, the licence holder shall only import such products from another EEA State:
        (a) in response to an order which satisfies the requirements of paragraph 1 of Schedule 1 to the 1994 Regulations; and

       (b) where the conditions set out in sub-paragraphs (2) to (9) are complied with.

(2) No later than 28 days prior to each importation of an exempt imported product, the licence holder shall give written notice to the licensing authority stating his intention to import that medicinal product and stating the following particulars:

       (a) the name of the medicinal product, being the brand name or the common name, or the scientific name, and any name, if different, under which the medicinal product is to be sold or supplied in the United Kingdom;

       (b) any trademark or name of the manufacturer of the medicinal product;

       (c) in respect of each active constituent of the medicinal product, any international non-proprietary name or the British approved name or the monograph name or, where that constituent does not have an international non-proprietary name, a British approved name or a monograph name, the accepted scientific name or any other name descriptive of the true nature of that constituent;

       (d) the quantity of medicinal product which is to be imported which shall not exceed the quantity specified in sub-paragraph (6); and

       (e) the name and address of the manufacturer or assembler of that medicinal product in the form in which it is to be imported and, if the person who will supply that medicinal product for importation is not the manufacturer or assembler, the name and address of such supplier.

(3) Subject to sub-paragraph (4), the licence holder shall not import the exempt imported product if, before the end of 28 days from the date on which the licensing authority sends or gives the licence holder an acknowledgement in writing by the licensing authority that they have received the notice referred to in sub-paragraph (2) above, the licensing authority have notified him in writing that the product should not be imported.

(4) The licence holder may import the exempt imported product referred to in the notice where he has been notified in writing by the licensing authority, before the end of the 28-day period referred to in sub-paragraph (3), that the exempt imported product may be imported.

(5) Where the licence holder sells or supplies exempt imported products, he shall, in addition to any other records which he is required by the provisions of his licence to make, make and maintain written records relating to:

       (a) the batch number of the batch of the product from which the sale or supply was made; and

       (b) details of any adverse reaction to the product so sold or supplied of which he becomes aware.

(6)   The licence holder shall import no more on any one occasion than such amount as is sufficient for 25 single administrations, or for 25 courses of treatment where the amount imported is sufficient for a maximum of three months' treatment, and on any such occasion shall not import more than the quantity notified to the licensing authority under sub-paragraph (2)(d).

(7)   The licence holder shall inform the licensing authority forthwith of any matter coming to his attention which might reasonably cause the licensing authority to believe that the medicinal product can no longer be regarded either as a product which can safely be administered to human beings or as a product which is of satisfactory quality for such administration.

(8)   The licence holder shall not issue any advertisement, catalogue, price list or circular relating to the exempt relevant medicinal product or make any representations in respect of that product.

(9)   The licence holder shall cease importing or supplying an exempt imported product if he has received a notice in writing from the licensing authority directing that, as from a date specified in that notice, a particular product or class of products shall no longer be imported or supplied.

(10) In this paragraph:
- "British approved name" means the name which appears in the current edition of the list prepared by the appropriate body in accordance with Section 100 of the Act and published by the Ministers on the recommendation of the Commission and "current" in this definition means current at the time the notice is sent to the licensing authority;
- "common name" means the international non-proprietary name or, if one does not exist, the usual common name;
- "international non-proprietary name" means a name which has been selected by the World Health Organization as a recommended international non-proprietary name and in respect of which the Director-General of the World Health Organization has given notice to that effect in the World Health Organization Chronicle; and
- "monograph name" means the name or approved synonym which appears at the head of a monograph in the current edition of the British Pharmacopoeia, the British Pharmaceutical Codex, the European Pharmacopoeia or a foreign or international compendium of standards and "current" in this definition means current at the time the notice is sent to the licensing authority.

4   The licence holder shall take all reasonable precautions and exercise all due diligence to ensure that any information he provides to the licensing authority which is relevant to an evaluation of the safety, quality or efficacy of any medicinal product for human use which he handles, stores or distributes is not false or misleading in a material particular.

GLOSSARY OF LEGISLATION

Glossary of Legislation

Contents

European Legislation

Council Directive 2001/83/EC on the Community code relating to medicinal products for human use as amended by Directive 2004/27/EC and Directive 2004/24/EC and Directive 2002/98/EC

This legislation regulates the licensing, manufacture of and wholesale dealing in medicinal products within the European Community.

Council Directive 2003/94/EC laying down the principles and guidelines of good manufacturing practice in respect of medicinal products for human use and investigational medicinal products

This Directive lays down the principles and guidelines of good manufacturing practice in respect of medicinal products for human use whose manufacture requires an authorisation.

Primary (UK) Legislation

Medicines Act 1968 as amended

This Act regulates, in part, the manufacture, distribution and importation of medicinal products.

Secondary Legislation (UK Statutory Instruments)

The Medicines for Human Use (Manufacturing, Wholesale Dealing and Miscellaneous Amendments) Regulations 2005 (SI 2005 No. 2789)

Replaces, as respects medicinal products to which the relevant EU legislation applies ("relevant medicinal products"), the existing regulations which implement the Directive 2001/83/EC, as amended. Sets out the obligations with which holders of manufacturer's and wholesale dealer's licenses must comply in respect of those licences.

The Medicines (Applications for Manufacturer's and Wholesale Dealer's Licences) Regulations 1971 (SI 1971 No. 974), as amended

These Regulations relates to applications for the grant of manufacturer's and wholesale dealer's licences other than licences of right. They prescribe the form and manner in which such applications are to be made, and specify the information that shall accompany each application.

Medicines (Manufacturer's Undertakings for Imported Products) Regulations 1977 (SI 1977 No. 1038), as amended

These Regulations relate to prescribed conditions for manufacturer's undertakings for imported products.

Medicines for Human Use (Marketing Authorisations Etc.) Regulations 1994 (SI 1994 No. 3144), as amended

Provide the functions for the Competent Authority of a member State under the relevant Community provisions Directive 2001/83/EC as amended by 2004/27/EC are, except as otherwise provided, to be performed in the UK by the Licensing Authority. They also provide that no medicinal product for human use which is subject to the relevant Community provisions may be placed on the market or distributed in the UK other than in accordance with a current marketing authorisation granted by the Licensing Authority or the European Commission.

The Medicines (Products for Human Use – Fees) Regulations 1995 (SI 1995 No. 1116), as amended

These Regulations make provision for the fees payable under the Medicines Act 1971 in respect of marketing authorizations, licences and certificates relating to medicinal products for human use.

The Medicines for Human Use (Clinical Trials) Regulations 2004 (SI 2004 No. 1031) as amended

These Regulations implement Directive 2001/20/EC on the approximation of laws, regulations and administrative provisions of the Member States relating to the implementation of good clinical practice in the conduct of clinical trials on medicinal products for human use.

The Unlicensed Medicinal Products for Human Use (Transmissible Sponigform Encephalopathies) (Safety) Regulations 2003 (SI 2003 No. 1680)

Regulates the importation and marketing of unlicensed medicinal products for human use in order to minimise the risk of the transmission of Transmissible Spongiform Encephalopathies via those products.

Prescription Only Medicines (Human Use) Order 1997 (as amended) (SI 1997 No. 1830), as amended

This order specifies the descriptions and classes of prescription only medicines.

INDEX

Index

F

Q

S